The American
Two-Year College

EXPLORATION SERIES IN EDUCATION

Under the Advisory Editorship of

JOHN GUY FOWLKES

The American
Two-Year College

TYRUS HILLWAY
Colorado State College

HARPER & BROTHERS, PUBLISHERS, NEW YORK

To the Memory of

WALDO E. CLARKE

Junior College Founder

Library of Congress catalog card number: 57–10572

Contents

Editor's Introduction

"WE NEED more junior colleges and soon. They should serve a district large enough to finance an effective program. Otherwise we'll have a two-year college at every crossroad." [1] This statement by the president of the National Congress of Parents and Teachers, which includes in its membership a goodly sample of professional educators along with its thousands of lay members, reflects a philosophical conviction concerning the fundamental necessity for expanding our two-year colleges. At the same time it presents an equally sober warning concerning the possibility of unwise though well-intended action toward the establishment of junior colleges. In short, Mrs. Brown forthrightly states the clearly established case for junior colleges but offers the admonition that the establishment of such institutions must reflect wisdom in terms of size of population and areas to be served, and also must consider the financial resources from which the support of such colleges can be enjoyed; therefore not only the operating efficiency but the quality and kind of educational program will be adequate and appropriate in keeping with value per dollar expended.

The approximate number of junior colleges in the United States for selected years is as follows:

1922	200
1950	600
1956–1957	650

Enrollments in junior colleges for the corresponding years were as follows:

[1] Mrs. Rollin Brown, *Nation's Schools*, March, 1957, p. 70.

1922	16,000
1950	500,000
1956–1957	800,000

It is interesting to note that the enrollment in high schools in the United States in 1900 was approximately the same as the enrollment in junior colleges in 1950—about 500,000. Here is graphic evidence that this country believes in and desires educated citizens. Toward the fulfillment of this belief and desire, it seems clear that in the immediate years ahead many junior colleges which are so seriously needed will be founded.

This volume is a happy and valuable combination of the treatment of the place of the junior college in our contemporary society and a down-to-earth guide for the organization, financing and operation of this essential educational unit.

Along with his formal education and the many experiences which qualify the author to write this work are the actual accomplishments of having served as a leader in the establishment and administration of an excellent junior college. It is hoped that this book will serve students in universities and colleges who want to familiarize themselves with the junior college, and also those who are responsible for the establishment and operation of these important educational institutions.

JOHN GUY FOWLKES

July, 1957

Preface

THIS book has grown out of the author's long experience in two-year college work. It has taken shape gradually from the time when he first became a student of the junior college movement under Walter Crosby Eells at the University of California in the thirties. Since then he has been a junior college teacher, dean, and president. He has helped write junior college legislation. He served for a considerable time on two important committees which inspected and appraised the junior colleges of the New England area. In recent years he has been active in the training of junior and community college teachers and administrators.

There is need for a comprehensive and yet simply written book on the two-year college in America. During the past quarter-century two standard works on the junior college have appeared. One of these, *The Junior College*, by Walter Crosby Eells, has long been out of print. The other, Jesse P. Bogue's *The Community College*, treats admirably the main issues in this field of education but requires of the reader a fairly intimate knowledge of the subject. The present book has been prepared not only for those who already have a speaking acquaintance with junior and community colleges, but also for those who know nothing or little about them.

The modern American community college, developing out of the junior college movement of the last 50 or 75 years, probably constitutes the most significant contribution which our nation has made to the entire history of education. In today's world, the community college seems to offer a promising solution to the problem of providing equal and adequate collegiate opportunities to all qualified citizens. For these reasons every teacher and administrator in the schools and colleges of the United States ought to know at least the rudimentary facts about the two-year college. The general public as well should be informed about this uniquely American institution of learning.

This book attempts to supply a comprehensive and understandable picture of the American two-year college in compact, readable form. It is intended partly to serve as a textbook for introductory courses dealing with junior and community colleges. It seeks to answer the basic essential questions relating to this type of institution. Among these questions are the following: What is the nature of the two-year college? How did it start, and how fast has it grown? What are its functions, present status, and areas of service? What varieties of the two-year college exist in this country at present, and what kinds will be needed in the future? What are the major unsolved problems of the junior college movement, and how do these affect the prospects for the future growth of educational opportunity in our nation? What should be the place of the two-year college in our educational system?

In preparing this book for the reader, the author owes an inestimable debt of gratitude to those educational pioneers who helped in establishing the junior and community college, to the scholars who studied and appraised its work, and to those practical workers in the field who have recorded their experiences as teachers and administrators of the two-year college. Every student of the junior college movement must lean heavily upon the early studies made by Leonard V. Koos and Walter Crosby Eells. In recent years B. Lamar Johnson and S. V. Martorana, among others, have contributed significantly to our knowledge of the subject. In addition, a broad understanding of junior and community college possibilities has become common property of all American citizens through the report of the President's Commission on Higher Education, a basic work for anyone interested in a knowledge of the two-year college.

Wherever possible, specific debts to friends and colleagues in the junior college field have been acknowledged in footnotes. The sources of information for a book of this kind are, of course, numerous. Besides the works listed in the bibliography, data have been used which were made available by the American Association of Junior Colleges, several hundred articles in scholarly periodicals, junior college committees and study groups, institutional catalogues, and direct comments of junior college staffs. To all these generous (and in part anonymous) helpers the author is deeply grateful. All have a part in this book. For the generalizations and opinions expressed here, however, the author must accept full responsibility. It should be understood that his point of view cannot avoid being colored somewhat by long, first-hand experience with all the many practical problems which are entailed in the successful organization and operation of the two-year college.

TYRUS HILLWAY

August, 1957

I

The Nature of the Two-Year College

BILL and Mary Smith are brother and sister now attending high school in Centerville, U.S.A. Centerville is a town in the agricultural Middle West with a population of about 25,000. It has excellent public schools but no college. The nearest institution of higher learning in its immediate neighborhood is a teachers college in a town 40 miles away.

Neither Bill nor Mary plans to enter teaching. In fact, Bill hopes to operate a chicken farm, and Mary would like to become a secretary. Each would be interested in a few terms of college work, not only to train for a vocation but also to secure more general knowledge. The Smith family, however, is not wealthy; even by saving their earnings from part-time and summer jobs, Bill and Mary probably will be unable to afford the cost of tuition, transportation, and room and board in a good college away from home.

Bill and Mary, though fictionalized in this example, are typical of several thousands of young Americans who this year and next will be graduating from our public high schools. Will they have the privilege of entering college?

Lack of money is denying great numbers of our young citizens the opportunity to secure a college education. This conclusion, reached by a national committee of 30 outstanding civic leaders and

1

educators who conducted a survey of higher education in the United States immediately following World War II, poses a major challenge to the American dream of equal educational opportunities for all our citizens.

How shall this challenge be met? The committee, commonly known as the President's Commission on Higher Education, proposed in its report (1947) a number of possible answers. According to the Commission, the time has come to make education through the fourteenth grade universally available throughout the country, just as free high-school education is now available. The time has come to provide monetary assistance to competent but needy students in the tenth grade through the fourteenth grade who might otherwise discontinue their education. The time has come for a great expansion of our adult education programs and for placing these under the supervision of our colleges and universities. In short, the time has come to make education at every level accessible to all Americans who can benefit from it, regardless of age, race, creed, sex, national origin, or economic status.

Here is a problem of tremendous magnitude and significance for American education and for the American people. Can it be solved? The President's Commission on Higher Education thinks it can, and proposes as one part of the solution the establishment of hundreds of new two-year collegiate institutions throughout the country. These would be known as community colleges. Many such institutions already exist, but more are needed. Through them, the Commission contends, the principal barriers to educational opportunity may well be broken down.

THE COMMISSION'S REPORT

A formal and complete report of the Commission's epoch-making study appeared in December, 1947. It should be read carefully not only by every educator but by every thinking citizen. Undertaken as "an examination of the functions of higher education in our democracy and of the means by which they can best be performed," the study analyzed the needs of American students and suggested various improvements in our educational system aimed at more adequately meeting these needs. The six parts of the report are the following: Volume I, Establishing the Boards; Volume II, Equalizing and Expanding Individual Opportunity; Volume III, Organizing Higher Education; Volume IV, Staffing Higher Education; Volume V, Financing Higher Education; and Volume VI, Resource Data.

Almost immediately after publication of the report, a considerable number of collegiate institutions in the United States, many of which previously had called themselves "junior colleges," quickly adopted the new title, "community college." Why they did so may perhaps best be understood by considering the following recommendation which the Commission presented in Volume III of its report:

Only a few decades ago, high school education in this country was for the few. Now most of our young people take at least some high school work, and more than half of them graduate from the high school.

Until recently college education was for the *very* few. Now a fifth of our young people continue their education beyond the high school.

Many young people want less than a full four-year college course. The two-year college—that is, the thirteenth and fourteenth years of our educational system—is about as widely needed today as the four-year high school was a few decades ago. Such a college must fit into the community life as the high school has done.

Hence the President's Commission suggests the name "community college" to be applied to the institution designed to serve chiefly local community education needs. It may have various forms of organization and may have curricula of various lengths. Its dominant feature is its intimate relation to the life of the community it serves.[1]

This forceful recommendation of the Commission attracted instant attention among the two-year colleges of the United States, many of which had been established for the purpose of serving purely local educational needs. The name "community college" at once became

[1] *Higher Education for American Democracy*, Harper & Brothers, 1948, III, 5.

accepted and popular. It was adopted by many of the publicly supported two-year institutions, and even a number of those privately
controlled began to use it.

WHAT IS A COMMUNITY COLLEGE?

While the report of the President's Commission on Higher Education popularized the name and gave widespread currency to the
idea, the community college itself was not new in 1947. It had been
taking shape, in fact, over a period of several decades. Numerous
institutions of this kind had been established in the twenties and
thirties and were functioning successfully in several parts of the
nation. In some states, however, public apathy and even outright
opposition had hindered its development. Not until a serious over-
crowding of our higher educational facilities was brought about by
the sudden and unexpected influx of World War II veterans into our
colleges and universities during the academic year 1946–1947, did
Americans recognize with greater clarity the urgent need for community colleges.

After the war, educators began to feel that the time was ripe for
the spread of the community college idea into all the states. In
several states, committees were formed for the purpose of investigat-
ing in detail the educational needs and existing facilities and of
making recommendations for future development. Significantly, in
almost every case these committees urged the establishment of
more community colleges offering two-year programs.

Among the many important writers on education who, at about
this time, were strongly suggesting the expansion of public education beyond the twelfth grade, none raised a more powerful voice
than did James Bryant Conant, then president of Harvard University. In one of the most widely read of all modern books on education, Conant wrote:

Those institutions which are now coming to be called "community colleges" offer the best hope of meeting the postwar surge for vast expansion

of education beyond the high school. They likewise can serve most effectively as centers for adult education. Their curricula should combine general education and vocational training, and they should be defined as terminal two-year colleges. . . .

The movement to establish more two-year free colleges locally has been gaining ground in the last few years. For these colleges to fulfill the desired function, however, will require genuine public support, not merely the educators' blessing. But before such support is forthcoming, there will have to be a rather complete change in public opinion. By and large, people think of colleges as four-year colleges or universities. The new status of a local two-year institution will require careful and repeated explanation in many states. Above all, the new institutions will have to be made as attractive as possible. . . .

Those of us who believe the two-year community colleges are a significant step forward in the march toward our goal of equalizing educational opportunity have high hopes that they will prosper in every state.[2]

In writing the statement quoted above, President Conant undoubtedly was expressing a point of view shared by many of our foremost educational thinkers.

From the statements of the President's Commission and of Conant, it should be fairly easy to formulate a general description of what is meant when we use the term "community college." We may attempt a working definition by first listing the three important characteristics which are specified above:

1. In the first place, the community college is an institution of learning whose program is related closely to the life of the community it serves. This is to say that what it offers in the way of curriculum and additional sponsored activities must be determined not so much by mere academic tradition as by the real needs of the local student body. This assumes, of course, that all or nearly all the students who are served by the community college live within commuting distance of the campus—near enough, in fact, to continue living at home while attending college.

2. In the second place, the institution typically is a college that offers two years of collegiate work rather than four years. In some

[2] James Bryant Conant, *Education in a Divided World,* Harvard University Press, 1948, pp. 200–201.

cases this arrangement is accomplished by extending the program of the public high school into the thirteenth and fourteenth grades. In other cases a completely separate institution offering post-high-school work may be organized as part of the school system. There are further variations in the pattern as well. For example, a four-year college or university may separate its freshman and sophomore years of work into a separate academic unit serving local students who have no interest in the four-year baccalaureate degree.

Programs in the community college need not be two years in length, but they are ordinarily shorter than the traditional four years. In theory, at least, the college that seeks to serve its community fully must arrange programs of every conceivable length— some one year, some two years, some three years, and so on. The prevailing pattern at present, however, and the one which appears most useful and natural for this type of institution, is the two-year program.

3. In the third place, the program of the typical community college is geared very closely to the *vocational* needs of students. This does not excuse the institution from its responsibility to provide those general courses of collegiate level which are found customarily in the freshman and sophomore years of the four-year college or university. On the other hand, the community-serving college must offer not simply a university-parallel program but several practical kinds of training which will prepare students for definite vocations in the community. In view of the steadily increasing need for more highly trained personnel in our industries, retail stores, and other lines of the nation's business (for example, accountants, junior executives, draftsmen, foremen, junior engineers, and the like), this constitutes an extremely valuable and particularly practical service on the part of the community college to its constituency.

We may summarize this description of the community college, then, by saying that *it is an institution of higher learning aimed at serving the educational needs of a particular community,* that *it is prevailingly a two-year college,* and that *it offers in its curriculum various programs which prepare students to enter definite vocations.*

WHAT IS A JUNIOR COLLEGE?

Some educators use the terms "community college" and "junior college" interchangeably. Nevertheless, there are clear differences between the terms. While, generally speaking, both community colleges and junior colleges are two-year collegiate institutions, there are many junior colleges which do not function as community-serving institutions. Both community colleges and junior colleges constitute portions of the same educational movement. As a matter of fact, the modern community college may be thought of as an outgrowth of the junior college movement which began 50 to 75 years ago.

Two-year colleges vary greatly in their purposes, organization, and programs. Many of them simply duplicate the first two years of the standard four-year college course. Others offer vocational subjects only. Some enroll only local students, while others maintain extensive dormitories and enroll students from all over the world. This almost infinite variation has created much difficulty for those who have attempted in the past to supply an accurate definition for the junior college. Walter Crosby Eells, one of the leaders in junior college work and for years executive secretary of the American Association of Junior Colleges, used to remark jokingly that the only sure method of determining whether a given institution could be classified as a junior college was to have it identify itself as one!

It is possible, nevertheless, to formulate a satisfactory description. It is possible also to show a difference between the junior college in general and that special kind of junior college known as the community college.

In 1922, representatives of American two-year colleges meeting in a national convention adopted a resolution officially defining the junior college as "an institution offering two years of instruction of strictly collegiate grade." Three years later this definition was revised and expanded to read as follows:

The Junior College is an institution offering two years of instruction of strictly collegiate grade. The curriculum may include those courses usually offered in the first two years of the four year college; in which case these courses must be identical, in scope and thoroughness, with corresponding courses of the standard four year college.

The junior college may, and is likely to, develop a different type of curriculum suited to the larger and ever changing civic, social, religious, and vocational needs of the entire community in which the college is located. It is understood that in this case also the work offered shall be on a level appropriate for high school graduates.[3]

It will be seen from the statement just quoted that, as early as 1925, when the term "community college" had not yet come into vogue, service to the community was already recognized as a distinctive characteristic of some two-year colleges.

"Junior college" may be regarded as the generic term to identify an institution of higher learning which offers two years of education beyond the high school. "Community college" is the name applied to an institution which is primarily concerned with providing educational services on the collegiate level to a particular community. The community college draws a student body almost exclusively from among the graduates of the local high schools, while the typical junior college may draw from a wide area. The community college most frequently is under public control and is a part of the local school system, whereas the junior college not primarily interested in community service may be privately or church controlled.

As an example, Colby Junior College, New London, New Hampshire, a highly respected junior college under private control, provides two years of collegiate education for young women who come to its campus from several states and from foreign countries. Although it serves its own small community in many interesting ways, such activities are only incidental to its main purpose. It could not by any stretch of the imagination be considered a community college. Actually, its curriculum compares favorably in variety and extent with that of many a community-serving institution in a larger center of population. Yet its program is aimed not at serving the

---

[3] From the report of the Committee on Standards of the American Association of Junior Colleges, adopted February 21, 1925.

special needs of the village of New London but at serving young women from all parts of the United States and from abroad.

JUNIOR TO WHAT?

Ever since the term "junior college" was first used over half a century ago, there have been frequent and numerous objections to it, especially from teachers and administrators within the junior college movement itself. The name, they insist, has done mischief to the institutions and to the entire movement. It has instilled erroneous notions in the public mind. Too many persons have confused the "junior college" with the "junior high school" and have inferred the same sort of relationship between the junior college and the four-year college as exists between the junior high school and the high school. The junior college, they point out, is not really *junior* to anything.

In view of the common misunderstandings which may still be found in many sections of the country, it will perhaps be helpful to enumerate some of the things which the junior college is *not*. For example, it is not a "finishing school," as we ordinarily understand that expression. That is to say, it is not the old-fashioned female seminary, so popular in accounts of the nineteenth century, in which, if we are to believe the legends, young ladies were prepared for their entrance into proper society. It is not a preparatory school, in which the students receive tutoring for admission to the freshman year of the standard college. It is not "half a college," offering merely the less difficult portions of a collegiate curriculum, so that its graduates go into the world knowing half of Shakespeare, half of the science of chemistry, and so forth. It is not a refuge for the lazier and less capable students who cannot secure admission to "regular" colleges.

The junior college is, instead, a particular kind of collegiate institution, and one quite capable of standing on its own feet and justifying its existence.

Dissatisfaction with the early designation "junior college" undoubtedly constituted the main reason why so many institutions eagerly accepted the recommendation of the President's Commission to call themselves community colleges. The new title avoids many of the misleading implications of the old.

WHY DO STUDENTS CHOOSE THE TWO-YEAR COLLEGE?

While students themselves give a vast variety of replies when asked why they chose to attend a two-year college (junior or community college), most school administrators believe that a significant factor in attracting them to this type of institution is the matter of convenience. It is commonly recognized that colleges of every kind enroll more students from the area immediately surrounding the campus than from anywhere else. Koos discovered as long ago as 1921 that, in 39 four-year colleges which he studied, 27 percent of the students came from the local community and 41 percent from within a radius of 25 miles.[4] With much larger numbers now in college, the tendency of students to attend local institutions is no doubt even more prevalent today. Communities in which institutions of higher education are located nearly always have a larger proportion of their young people going to college than do those in which there are no colleges. In Minnesota a commission appointed to study the facilities and needs of higher education in that state recently reported the following situation: "One-fourth of our young people who live within 10 miles of a college are attending college the first year after they graduate from high school. But among the youth who live more than 25 miles from a college the ratio is one in seven."[5]

It may be seen, then, that convenience plays a large part in determining whether students will enter college. If educational opportunities are to be extended and equalized, there should be a college within commuting distance (ordinarily within 20 or 25 miles) of

[4] Leonard V. Koos, "The Residential Distribution of College Students and Its Meaning for the Junior-College Problem," *School and Society*, XIII (May 7, 1921), 557–562.

[5] *Tomorrow's Resources*, a report of the Minnesota Commission on Higher Education, 1949, p. 7.

every student. In sparsely settled areas this arrangement would obviously prove impossible, but in many sections of our nation such a distribution of educational facilities does not seem at all out of the question.

Closely related to the matter of convenience is that of cost. The necessary expense of room and board on the campus prevents many a capable student from entering college or from continuing once he has entered. In a typical private college of high academic standing, the cost of tuition alone will be in the neighborhood of $600, and the annual expense of room and board in a dormitory will amount to $1,000 or more (usually somewhat higher in the women's colleges). If the student can live at home while attending classes in a local institution, he may save several hundred dollars. In those towns and cities which operate publicly supported colleges, of course, the cost for the student is reduced still further. Thus, for the student of limited means, the doors to educational opportunity are opened wider. The unexectedly vast numbers of war veterans who entered college under Public Law 346 gave, in the opinion of many educational authorities, a good indication of the demand for collegiate education which emerges in the United States when the economic barriers have been removed.

A third reason for attending the two-year college is the availability of training programs which are not generally offered in the standard four-year college. By and large, the four-year college tends to favor traditional programs in the liberal arts or in those courses which provide groundwork for later professional study. For the preparation of capable secretaries, accountants, junior engineers, medical assistants, and the like, four years of college would seem an unnecessarily long period. Because they do not fit the predetermined pattern of the standard college, shorter programs of this type are not likely to be available there. It is the two-year college that has assumed responsibility for providing education of this kind. While offering many courses paralleling those of the freshman and sophomore years in the university, the junior or community college usually lays considerable emphasis upon a large variety of two-year programs which give immediate and fully adequate preparation for useful jobs.

Convenience of location, financial savings, and the availability of desirable two-year vocational programs probably constitute the most powerful forces impelling students to enter the junior and community colleges of America.

Other advantages have been claimed. One of these is the presumed economic benefit of keeping young people out of the labor market for two additional years. While this reduces the competition for jobs, it also gives youth an opportunity to secure better training for more responsible and remunerative positions. Another factor is the preference of many young people for the shorter curriculum. Some students consider four years of college too long a period for preparation. They are eager for economic independence or for marriage, and the two-year course of study fits their time schedule admirably. Still another argument is the relative immaturity of many college freshmen. While some persons upon graduation from high school are mature enough to adjust themselves to a complete separation from the home, a large number find the transition an exceedingly difficult one. Delaying the separation for one or two years may sometimes mean the difference between success and failure in college work. Exactly how many of our students can do better by remaining at home for a time after finishing the twelfth grade it would not be easy to say, but there seems to be no question about the psychological advantage of this arrangement for a considerable number of adolescents. Finally, the social and extracurricular programs of the two-year college do seem to stimulate social development and maturity. As a freshman or sophomore in a four-year college or university, the student has only limited possibilities of becoming a leader in clubs, dramatics, publications, and similar activities. He must wait until his junior or senior year, as a rule, before he is elected president of a club. In the two-year college he very quickly rises to a position of leadership—or at least receives the opportunity to do so. Some educators believe that this situation increases the self-confidence of a student and thereby hastens his maturity. It may account for the very marked success which two-year college graduates have enjoyed when transferring as juniors to the four-year college.

CAN THE TWO-YEAR COLLEGE OFFER ACADEMIC DEGREES?

Americans have long displayed a high degree of respect for the academic degree. Graduates of collegiate institutions appear almost uniformly to want something as evidence of their achievement besides a mere certificate or diploma. For this reason, an increasing number of junior and community colleges now confer a degree or title. This is usually called an associate degree (Associate in Arts, Associate in Science, and others of a similar nature).

A few educators have proposed that the bachelor's degree be conferred at the end of two years of college. As a matter of fact, the idea that all junior colleges should award the baccalaureate degree was presented seriously at the first meeting of the American Association of Junior Colleges in 1920. Furthermore, President Conant has quite recently written: "I believe that the two-year community colleges should be authorized to grant a bachelor's degree. This is the badge of respectability for most Americans; indeed, the letters have almost mystical significance in the United States. To give the same degree as the four-year college (the A.B. or B.S.) would merely be confusing to all concerned. But a two-year degree of bachelor of general studies (B.G.S.) might well represent the final degree for a majority of college students." [6] It will be recalled that the University of Chicago for several years followed the practice of granting a bachelor's degree at the end of the second year of study.

In spite of such proposals and experiments, however, it is fairly safe to predict that the baccalaureate degree will continue, as at present, to represent four years of collegiate education and that junior and community colleges as a group will cling to the associate degree.

[6] Conant, *op. cit.*, p. 201.

Several American universities now offer the Associate in Arts degree (or title) for students who do not wish to go beyond the second year. A glance backward into educational history reveals that the University of Chicago instituted, in 1899, a degree called Associate in the University. According to Eells, this designation was very probably suggested by an even earlier use of the degree of Associate in some of the British universities.[7] Harvard University once experimented with an associate degree for nonresident students but abandoned the plan. In recent years the University of Houston, the University of Minnesota, Illinois Wesleyan University, the University of Louisville, and several other institutions have granted an Associate in Arts. Not all, of course, recognize it as a degree; some refer to it as a title or diploma. Following World War II, Princeton University began giving the Associate in Arts to veterans who enrolled for only two years.

It seems evident that the associate degree will become increasingly popular, both in the two-year college and in the lower division of the university. While the Associate in Arts and the Associate in Science (also known as the Associate *of* Arts, etc.) are most common, one may also find such degrees or titles as Associate in Education, Associate in Engineering, Associate in Fine Arts, Associate in Music, and numerous others.

HOW FAST HAS THE TWO-YEAR COLLEGE GROWN?

The two-year college has frequently been called the fastest growing institution of learning in the whole history of American education. The facts of its growth are, indeed, rather impressive.

Colvert has reported that, at the beginning of the twentieth century, there were only eight known junior colleges with a combined enrollment of fewer than a hundred students.[8] By mid-century the

[7] For a discussion of the subject, see Walter Crosby Eells, *Associate's Degree and Graduation Practices in Junior Colleges,* American Association of Junior Colleges, 1942.

[8] C. C. Colvert, "A Half-Century of Junior Colleges," *Junior College Journal,* XVII (February, 1947), 244–247.

number of such institutions in the continental United States had risen to 621, and the combined enrollment to 557,663 students. The tabulation by states given below indicates the distribution of two-

Distribution of Junior and Community Colleges by States, 1955

State	Institutions			Enrollment		
	Total	Public	Private	Total	Public	Private
Alabama	10	1	9	1,693	245	1,448
Arizona	2	2	0	3,800	3,800	0
Arkansas	4	3	1	2,542	1,894	648
California	71	66	5	318,960	318,443	517
Colorado	8	7	1	7,786	7,423	363
Connecticut	7	0	7	9,693	0	9,693
Delaware	1	0	1	222	0	222
Dist. of Columbia	7	0	7	2,927	0	2,927
Florida	10	5	5	5,969	3,822	2,147
Georgia	18	9	9	14,407	12,804	1,603
Idaho	2	2	0	2,396	2,396	0
Illinois	23	13	10	33,627	30,548	3,079
Indiana	8	5	3	8,750	8,484	266
Iowa	23	16	7	11,915	9,957	1,958
Kansas	22	14	8	7,478	6,069	1,409
Kentucky	13	2	11	3,424	715	2,709
Louisiana	1	1	0	259	259	0
Maine	4	0	4	601	0	601
Maryland	11	7	4	2,959	2,492	467
Massachusetts	18	2	16	6,837	373	6,464
Michigan	16	14	2	21,579	21,329	250
Minnesota	11	9	2	8,769	8,456	313
Mississippi	23	15	8	9,934	8,540	1,394
Missouri	19	8	11	10,816	6,712	4,104
Montana	3	3	0	1,032	1,032	0
Nebraska	5	4	1	2,172	2,013	159
Nevada	1	1	0	370	370	0
New Hampshire	1	0	1	461	0	461
New Jersey	10	2	8	3,151	911	2,240
New Mexico	0	0	0	0	0	0
New York	31	16	15	26,173	24,350	1,823
North Carolina	22	5	17	8,389	2,498	5,891
North Dakota	4	4	0	1,761	1,761	0
Ohio	7	1	6	6,493	328	6,165
Oklahoma	16	13	3	5,984	5,634	350
Oregon	4	2	2	2,772	1,362	1,410
Pennsylvania	25	12	13	17,629	15,240	2,389
Rhode Island	1	0	1	608	0	608

Distribution of Junior and Community Colleges by States, 1955

State	Institutions			Enrollment		
	Total	Public	Private	Total	Public	Private
South Carolina	8	0	8	1,649	0	1,649
South Dakota	3	0	3	467	0	467
Tennessee	10	1	9	2,952	725	2,227
Texas	45	34	11	61,103	58,544	2,559
Utah	4	4	0	7,388	7,388	0
Vermont	2	0	2	516	0	516
Virginia	16	3	13	9,521	7,029	2,492
Washington	11	10	1	20,494	20,433	61
West Virginia	4	1	3	1,753	546	1,207
Wisconsin	12	10	2	7,750	7,628	122
Wyoming	4	4	0	3,571	3,571	0
Totals (U.S.)	581	331	250	691,502	616,124	75,378

year colleges and their enrollment as recorded by the American Association of Junior Colleges in 1956. Separate figures for the public and private institutions have been given.

From the tabulation it will be seen that four states lead the others by a comfortable margin both as to the number of two-year institutions and as to total enrollment. These are California, with 71 institutions and 318,960 students; Texas, with 45 institutions and 61,103 students; New York, with 31 institutions and 26,173 students; and Illinois, with 23 institutions and 33,627 students. Iowa, although ranking high in the number of institutions, has a comparatively small number of students enrolled. Three of the states which rank in the highest group (California, Texas, and Illinois) have been consistent leaders in the development of the public junior or community college.

Figure 1 shows the present general distribution of two-year colleges throughout the United States.

GROWTH SINCE 1900

The growth in the number of junior and community colleges remained steady but gradual until just after World War I, when there was a sharp rise in the number of new institutions established

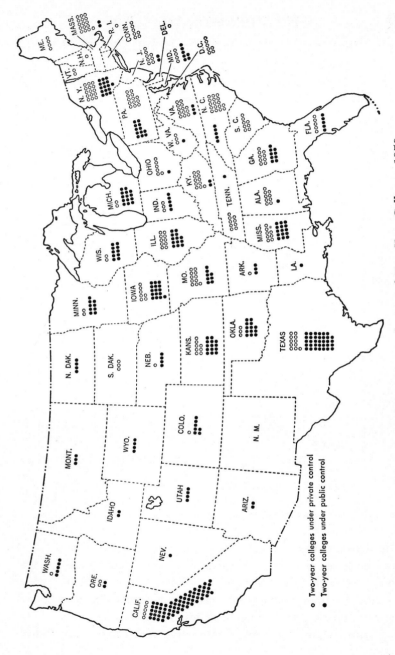

FIGURE 1. Geographical Distribution of Two-Year Colleges, 1956.

o Two-year colleges under private control
• Two-year colleges under public control

(or at least in those recognized as junior colleges). There was no falling off in this rapid rate of growth until about 1948, when some of the institutions became four-year colleges and others closed for lack of sufficient financial backing. Closings, incidentally, occurred largely among the privately controlled junior colleges. The number of public institutions appears to be rising even today.

Figure 2 shows the approximate curve which has been followed in the growth of junior and community colleges (by number of in-

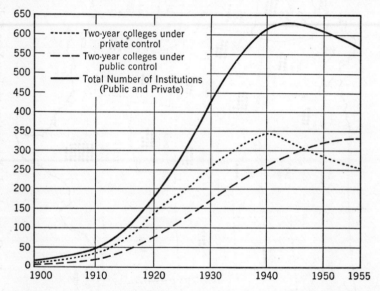

FIGURE 2. The Growth of Two-Year Colleges, 1900–1955, by Number of Institutions. Only the junior and community colleges of the 48 states and the District of Columbia have been included.

stitutions) in the continental United States from 1900 to 1955. It will be noted that, while the privately sponsored institutions first increased in number somewhat more rapidly than did the public institutions, those under public auspices have had a steady rise and now exceed the private junior colleges in number.

Figure 3 shows the approximate curve which has been followed by the increasing enrollment in the two-year colleges. It will be noted that the number of students rose rather sharply in the thirties and forties. Most of this increase was in the public two-year colleges, perhaps because of lower or free tuition rates. Since about 1920 the publicly supported institutions have decisively outstripped those under private control in the enrollment of students.

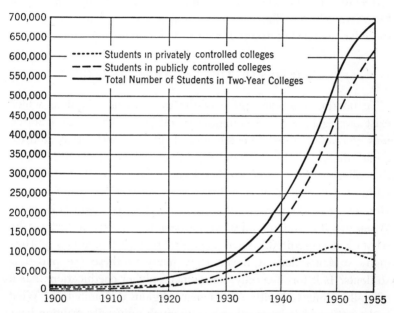

FIGURE 3.   The Growth of Two-Year Colleges, 1900–1955, by Number of Students Enrolled. Only the students of two-year colleges in the 48 states and the District of Columbia have been included.

About 1930 the average student body in the private junior college numbered roughly 115 students, while that in the publicly controlled two-year institution was over 240 students. Within 25 years these averages had noticeably increased, so that in 1955 the respective average enrollments in private and public junior and community colleges had become 301 and 1,861. Both types, then, have shown remarkable growth both in number and in size.

No community colleges, in the present sense of the term, existed in the United States before 1925, and very few before 1945. While several junior colleges were organized before 1900, the movement was hardly well established even by the turn of the century. Most of the two-year colleges in operation today can trace their histories in the junior college movement back only as far as the 1920's, if that far. Thus it can be seen that the entire movement is, by and large, a twentieth-century affair, though we shall discuss later its roots in the educational theories and events of the preceding century.

VARIETIES OF THE TWO-YEAR COLLEGE

To obtain some conception of the tremendous variations which exist among junior and community colleges of the United States, pick at random 15 or 20 catalogues of different institutions and examine them, keeping in mind the following questions: What does the college call itself? Where is it located, and in what kind of community? Is it privately or publicly controlled? How is it financed? How many academic years of work—and which years—does it cover? When was it founded, and what has been its subsequent history? By whom is it accredited? When did it first receive accreditation? How many students does it have? How many of these are part-time students? Is it for men only, for women only, or coeducational? Is it officially connected with a particular religious denomination? What is the nature of its curriculum? How much university training have members of its faculty, and how much previous teaching experience? What special features and programs does it claim? Perhaps nothing can give one a quicker and more startling picture of the vast variations in the junior college movement than such a survey of catalogues.

It will be seen that among these institutions may be found *nearly every kind of program on the collegiate level which has proved useful to American students.* Confusing as this variety may be, it suggests a richness of opportunity unsurpassed in any country of the world.

Junior and community colleges may logically be classified into several types, though such classification is likely to be rather arbitrary at best. One might justifiably classify them by size (from those with as few as 15 students to others with as many as 30,000), by type of control (public, proprietary, denominational, private nonprofit, etc.), by unit of control (state, county, local district, board of trustees, private ownership, or church), by the nature of the curriculum (liberal arts, commercial, agricultural, technological, etc.), by race or sex admitted (Negro colleges, men's colleges, women's colleges, coeducational institutions, and the like), by the number of years covered in the program, or by some other characteristic indicating the clear differences among two-year colleges.

A logical and useful system of classification is employed below to show the reader the various common types of the two-year college found in the United States today. Each classification is described briefly, and at least one example is cited for each. Most junior and community colleges can be listed under one of these five headings: (1) private nonprofit junior colleges, including the church-related institutions; (2) public community colleges; (3) private nonprofit community colleges; (4) technical institutes; and (5) university branches or separately organized lower divisions. In addition to these five we may include a (6) miscellaneous classification, which will account for institutions not otherwise classified, such as those under proprietary (profit-making) control.

PRIVATE NONPROFIT JUNIOR COLLEGES

In general, the private nonprofit junior college may be described as an institution which offers two years of collegiate instruction (sometimes with two or more years of high school work as well) and which draws a student body not merely from its own community but from all parts of the United States and abroad. It does not regard itself as primarily a community-serving institution. Many two-year colleges of this type are church-related, and a considerable number are endowed. The curriculum is likely to follow closely the pattern of the freshman and sophomore years in the traditional four-year college. Enrollment may be limited to one sex or the other, though some of these institutions are coeducational. While the majority of private nonprofit junior colleges are to be found east of the Mississippi River, especially in New England and the South, many have been established in the western states as well.

Examples of this type are Stephens College in Missouri (for women), Bradford Junior College in Massachusetts (for women), Colorado Woman's College in Colorado (for women), and Nichols Junior College in Massachusetts (for men). The last two named are briefly described below.

Colorado Woman's College.   Organized in Denver in 1888 as an educational institution for women, Colorado Woman's College, under Baptist auspices, first began offering instruction in 1909, after a rather long period of preparation and financial uncertainty. It became a junior college in 1920. Privately controlled but with church connections, it operates as a nonprofit organization under a self-perpetuating board of managers.

Various two-year programs of study are offered, including liberal arts, business education, home economics, art, and music. Some of the programs prepare students for definite careers: secretary, journalist, dress designer, interior decorator, and music teacher. Other programs give the foundation for later specialization at professional schools—for example, pre-law, pre-nursing, pre-library science, pre-teaching, pre-dietetics, and the like.

The cost of room, board, and tuition at Colorado Woman's College for the academic year 1956–1957 was $1,500. Students not living in dormitories (residents of Denver) paid $450 in tuition and fees. Normal enrollment is approximately 400.

Nichols Junior College.   Situated in a rural section of southern Massachusetts, Nichols Junior College offers to men a two-year program exclusively in business administration. Founded as a private academy in 1815, it gradually saw its original function superseded by the public high school, and its existence as an academy came to an end. In 1931 the trustees decided that use of the buildings, then idle, might be continued if the school were reorganized as a junior college. Its charter was amended by the state legislature during the following year, and in 1938 it received the privilege of conferring degrees. Except for an interim period of three years during World War II, the college has operated with marked academic and financial success since the establishment of the two-year program. A single course of study is offered, leading to the degree of Associate in Business Administration. A training unit of the United States Army Quartermaster Corps maintained on the campus has been a special feature of the program.

Board, room, and tuition (with activities fee) at Nichols for the academic year 1956–1957 amounted to $1,550. Day students not living on the campus paid a tuition fee of $550. Normal enrollment is in the neighborhood of 275.

PRIVATE COMMUNITY COLLEGES

While the community college has generally been thought of as an extension of the public school system, in several states there are independent community-serving collegiate institutions which operate without the support of public funds. They may thus be classified as community colleges in function, though they are not actually part of the local school system nor under direct municipal authority.

Such institutions usually derive their financial support from private gifts and endowments, from coöperative arrangements with nearby business and industrial firms for whom training programs are conducted or other educational services provided, and from tuition charges. Except for methods of financing their work, these colleges, because their curriculums are adapted to the special needs of their local constituencies, offer exactly the same sort of service as do the publicly supported and controlled community colleges. Though their total number is relatively small, several of these independent community-serving institutions may be found in the Ohio Valley, in New England, and elsewhere. They are not commonly located in parts of the country in which public willingness to support higher education through taxation has been especially strong.

One example of this type of two-year college is the New Haven Junior College in Connecticut.

New Haven Junior College. First established in 1920 at the YMCA, New Haven, Connecticut, as a branch of Northeastern University, the New Haven Junior College (officially known as the New Haven YMCA Junior College) became an independent educational institution six years later. For a long time it remained chiefly interested in supplying part-time technical courses during the evening for young men working in the New Haven factories.

By a fortunate arrangement, it was moved from the YMCA to the campus of Yale University, which donated, as a public service, the use of classroom facilities during the late afternoon and evening. Starting about 1930, the practice of offering merely a variety of unrelated courses was gradually replaced by planned programs of study extending over periods of two or more years. The right of conferring the Associate in Science degree was granted by the state legislature in 1935. From 1938 on, the institution has made its community service increasingly effective by establishing close working relationships with business and industrial firms of the area which are interested in securing special types of training for their employees. After 1949 a coöperative plan of education (alternating periods of work and class attendance) was initiated. This plan relates the student's class work directly to his occupation and gives him the opportunity of continuing in college while earning a living.

This coeducational two-year college functions as an entirely independent institution within the physical framework of Yale University. Tuition for the academic year 1956–1957 was $115 for a full evening schedule of three courses, or $425 for an afternoon and evening program taken as full-time college work. No dormitories are maintained. Enrollment within recent years has been 1,000 and more, with the majority of students enrolled in part-time courses. One surprising feature is the many very advanced subjects offered to students who are already college graduates but who desire special types of technical training. It is interesting and also unusual to note that at least one other privately controlled institution in the same city, Quinnipiac College, performs the functions of a community college.

Public Community Colleges

Since the modern community college with public tax support has already been discussed in some detail, it is necessary only to mention that this kind of two-year institution ordinarily exists as an extension of the public school system. Control may be vested in a local high school district, in a special junior college district that serves a number of high school districts, in a county, or in a state. Often the superintendent of the district is the titular head of the institution, although actual administrative control may rest with a dean or similar official. The distinguishing characteristic of the institution, of course, lies in the adaptation of its curriculum to the particular educational needs of the district which it serves. Two examples of this, the most familiar type of community college, are given below.

San Bernardino Valley College.   A good example of the publicly controlled and financed community college, San Bernardino Valley College operates under the supervision of the California state department of education in a union junior college district. This unit was created in 1926 out of 14 local districts by vote of the people in the San Bernardino Valley. The college benefits from state funds as well as from local taxation. It is, of course, coeducational.

As is true in all the Califorina public junior colleges, there are no tuition or laboratory charges. The students admitted consist chiefly of graduates of the local high schools, though outsiders are not necessarily barred. The two-year curriculum contains a rich variety of subjects, including liberal arts, pre-law, pre-medicine, prepharmacy, pre-teaching, art, business administration, accounting, secretarial science, merchandising, engineering, electrical technology, drafting, automotive technology, diesel technology, architectural technology, radio and television, broadcasting technology, refrigeration technology, airplane flight operations, nursing, and others. The college conducts both a day program and an extensive evening program. Full-time enrollment in 1955 was just under 2,000 students; part-time, about 10,000 students.

Trinidad State Junior College. Like most junior colleges in Colorado, Trinidad State Junior College is in a county district. The first classes opened in 1926, a year after the institution's official founding, in classrooms of the city high school. At that time only one year of collegiate work was offered, but a second year was added in 1932. In the fall of 1935, the college moved into the vacated building of the former Tillotson Academy. These facilities proved inadequate after five more years, and new buildings were built and occupied in 1941. Meanwhile, under county control, the college gradually had separated itself from the high school. A completely separate administration and faculty had been achieved by 1939.

The present coeducational course of study includes programs in agriculture, automobile mechanics, building trades, business administration, secretarial science, distributive education (retail sales), engineering, gunsmithing, handicrafts, homemaking, liberal arts, pre-teaching, pre-law, pre-medicine, pre-pharmacy, radio and electronics, and many more. An evening division with similar and related courses also forms a part of the organization. Tuition charges amount to approximately $30 per academic year, plus a number of special fees. Nonresidents of the county may attend at a cost of $90 per year in tuition charges. Enrollment is 300 to 400 in the regular day program and over 1,900 in adult evening classes.

TECHNICAL INSTITUTES

Technical institutes are two-year colleges which offer no instruction in the liberal arts but confine their efforts to training for definite careers. Ordinarily these careers may be classified as the semi-professions, for which one, two, or three years of post-high-school study provide adequate preparation. For the most part, such institutions are intended for the student who does not plan to pursue his collegiate education further than the freshman and sophomore years. As a matter of criticism, perhaps one of the weaknesses of the technical institute lies in the difficulty of transferring credit later to a standard four-year college or university if the student proves capable of and interested in continuing his education. The so-called "terminal" program in effect closes the door to further educational opportunity. Typical examples of this type of two-year college are found in the state-supported technical institutes of New York State.

New York State Agricultural and Technical Institutes. The state of New York operates a number of technical institutes which use the same general name. They may be distinguished from one another by location. One, the institute at Canton, New York, was first established as a school of agriculture in 1907. Home economics courses were added the following year. Considered originally a technical high school, the Canton school gradually raised the academic level of its offerings, and since 1937 its major efforts have been directed at instruction in various kinds of industrial technology. It supplies a number of curriculums in business training as well. The present name, New York State Agricultural and Technical Institute, was officially adopted in 1941.

This is a two-year, coeducational institution, state supported and controlled, with both boarding and day students. The stated purpose has long been that of offering post-high-school technical courses which prepare students to enter directly into positions in agriculture, business, industry, home economics, and related fields. A tuition fee of $300 per academic year is assessed against nonresidents of New York State, but residents pay no tuition.

The program of study includes general agriculture, agricultural business, animal husbandry, dairy technology, farm machinery sales and service, poultry husbandry, chemical technology, electrical technology, air conditioning, mechanical technology, food services administration, hospital dietetics, clothing and textiles, small business management, executive office assistantship, and food management for boys. Enrollment is limited to about 400 students.

In connection with the technical institutes, it is interesting to note that the state of Connecticut, which operates a group of technical schools very similar to those of New York State, refuses to consider them a part of the nation-wide junior college movement. Thus the technical institutes of Connecticut are not included in any statistical survey of the two-year colleges of the United States.

UNIVERSITY BRANCHES OR DIVISIONS

A junior college may be organized separately as the lower division (freshman and sophomore years) of a university or as an off-campus branch of the university offering only the first two years of academic work. Several such junior colleges exist, among them the Penn State Centers and the General College of Boston University.

Penn State Centers. The Pennsylvania State University operates two-year branches in Altoona, Erie, DuBois, Harrisburg, Hazleton, Ogontz, and Pottsville, Pennsylvania, which are known as Penn State Centers. Programs of one and two years' duration are offered, and either day or evening classes may be taken. The curriculum includes, besides the liberal arts, programs in agriculture, chemistry and physics, education, engineering, home economics, and mineral industries.

The Penn State Centers are located in buildings made available by the respective communities which they serve. Tuition is $360 for the regular academic year, or $15 per credit hour. All the Centers were established between 1934 and 1950 as the result of requests from the local communities for educational facilities on the junior college level. Graduates of the Centers have the privilege of transferring with full credit as juniors to the main campus of the Pennsylvania State University.

Similar systems of branch colleges exist in Wisconsin and other states; but in few of them is the arrangement as carefully and thoroughly worked out as it is in Pennsylvania.

Boston University. An excellent example of the separate organization of a university lower division is provided by the College of General Education at Boston University. All freshmen are eligible to enroll in this college, which provides instruction of a general and integrated rather than of a specialized character. While the program was instituted in part for the benefit of local students interested in only two years of college, it also provides an adequate foundation for students desiring to enter one of the university's professional schools as juniors. Technically, those planning to study for two years only are enrolled in the Junior College Division, which confers an Associate in Arts degree. Many students, however, transfer at the end of the sophomore year to other colleges of the university, such as the College of Business Administration, the School of Education, or the School of Public Relations and Communications.

The effect of this arrangement is two-fold: (1) it makes possible a completely integrated program (that is, with all its parts inter-related) during the student's freshman and sophomore years of college; and (2) it offers collegiate education to students who do not intend to pursue their studies beyond the second year. Such a variation in the traditional university pattern seems especially desirable for an institution of higher learning located, as is Boston University, in a large center of population.[9] The College of General Education, it should be noted, offers no strictly vocational courses for the two-year student, as do most community colleges. The program is, of course, coeducational. The enrollment has been around 950 full-time students in recent years. The cost of tuition is $600 per academic year (1956–1957).

It may be worth pointing out that Boston University is a privately controlled institution (with Methodist affiliation) which has undertaken to meet local community needs through its Junior College Division.

MISCELLANEOUS TYPES

In addition to those junior and community colleges which are classified under the five headings listed above, there exist several miscellaneous types. Among these are the two-year military colleges, the two-year theological institutes (training for the priesthood or ministry), and the four-year junior college, which is discussed at some length in a later chapter. The latter institution offers two years

[9] See Tyrus Hillway, "The American University of the Future," *School and Society*, LXIX (June 11, 1949), 417–418.

of high school and two years of college—that is, the eleventh through the fourteenth grades.

JUNIOR COLLEGES ABROAD

Although we are concerned in this book almost entirely with the two-year college as it has developed in the United States, it may be well to remind ourselves that such institutions have been established in other countries as well. The directories of the American Association of Junior Colleges list the following foreign junior colleges: Canada, five; Cuba, one; Greece, one; Lebanon, one; and the Republic of the Philippines, one. Territories and protectorates of the United States in which junior colleges have been established include: Alaska, three; the Canal Zone, one; Hawaii, one; and Puerto Rico, one. Eells in 1951 recorded the founding of 181 junior colleges in Japan during the postwar occupation of that nation by American forces.[10]

The two-year college as we know it in twentieth-century America is not, however, characteristic of any other country. It is a distinctly local product of our own educational system. Those established abroad have come largely as the result of American influence. In Japan, for instance, Walter Eells, one of the leading exponents of the junior college idea, served for several years after the war as educational adviser to General Douglas MacArthur and was extremely active in assisting the rehabilitation and reorganization of the Japanese educational system.

MID-CENTURY TRENDS

Studying the catalogues of all junior and community colleges listed in the annual directory of the American Association of Junior Colleges, McLain found in 1953 a number of significant changes

[10] Walter Crosby Eells, "Junior College Development in Japan," *Junior College Journal*, XXII (September, 1951), 3–11.

which have taken place in these institutions in the 30 or more years from 1920 to the time of his investigation.[11]

With respect to curriculum, there seems to have been a decided shift from the liberal arts and other traditional courses to an emphasis upon two-year vocational courses. Purely academic subjects (nonvocational) have dropped since 1920 from 69 percent to 45.2 percent of the total curriculum in public two-year colleges and from 75 percent to 58.1 percent in private two-year colleges. Among vocational courses of study, business programs are the most numerous in both public and private institutions. Engineering courses are especially popular among the public junior colleges. Agricultural programs are found in over 38 percent of the public two-year colleges but in very few of those under private control. Furthermore, approximately one-half of the total enrollment in two-year colleges throughout the country is now in adult evening classes, which tend as a rule to be nonacademic in character. On the other hand, McLain detected a tendency to include more courses of a general and cultural nature in the vocational programs. According to his calculations, among the publicly controlled junior colleges 94.8 percent offer university-parallel programs (for students expecting to transfer), 91.5 percent offer vocational programs, 72.3 percent offer general courses of a terminal nature (for students not planning to transfer), and 67.7 percent have adult programs. Among the privately controlled junior colleges, 88.9 percent give university-parallel courses; 64.2 percent, vocational courses; 56.5 percent, general terminal programs; and 33.4 percent, courses in religious training.

McLain also found much more attention being paid to professional counseling for students in the modern two-year college. Approximately 90 percent of the large junior colleges now employ directors of guidance, and one-fourth to one-half of the smaller two-year institutions have such officers on the staff.

[11] Charles W. McLain, "The Present Status of the Junior College in the United States," unpublished doctoral field study, Colorado State College of Education, 1953.

He also reported higher interest and respect for the associate degree (now awarded by over 60 percent of the junior colleges, especially those with the larger enrollments) and a decidedly upward trend in the academic preparation of the faculty and administrators.

All these facts may be interpreted as indications of increasing adaptability of the two-year colleges to the needs of American students. At the same time the junior and community colleges, as they have become better understood among educators and the general public, have achieved respectability and educational stature. In the next chapter it will be seen how the two-year college movement came of age.

II

The Development of the Two-Year College

ALTHOUGH the junior college movement is essentially a phenomenon of the twentieth century, its roots go back well into the middle of the nineteenth century. At least three major currents in American education have joined forces to create the modern two-year junior and community colleges. These currents have been: (1) the nineteenth-century efforts to reform American university education; (2) the extraordinary growth in the United States of the various types of adult and vocational education as our economy became increasingly industrialized; and (3) the continuing democratic tendency toward the extension and equalization of educational opportunity for all Americans.

UNIVERSITY REFORM

During the latter half of the nineteenth century, American education fell under the very strong influence of the German school system. Germany's achievements in science and technology had made it the leading industrial nation of Europe, for which its educational system received much of the credit. The United States was one of many nations which admired and emulated German leadership. Not only were the kindergarten and the normal school introduced here from Germany during the nineteenth century, but the modern graduate school and the technical institute were also patterned after their German counterparts.

It is well known that in Germany a student enters the university not at the end of the twelfth grade, as in the United States, but after completion of work in a *Gymnasium,* or at the end of the fourteenth grade. The university, freed of responsibility for the relatively immature years of college which would correspond to our freshman and sophomore years, takes the student immediately into advanced work in his field of specialization. This makes the German university primarily an institution for professional training and research.

The idea of our own universities' concentrating on the advanced and specialized studies of the upper two years and beyond, in the German pattern, has long been attractive to American educators. As early as 1851, Henry P. Tappan, who the following year was to become president of the University of Michigan, published a revolutionary book entitled *University Education.* In it he forcefully urged the institutions of higher learning in the United States to become what he called "pure Universities" and to reorganize their programs in the German fashion. In his inaugural address, a year after publication of his book, he again advised the reform of American higher education through the process of relegating the lower division courses to the high schools and admitting to the universities only students who had completed the fourteenth grade or its equivalent.

Seventeen years later, in 1869, William Watts Folwell reiterated this proposal in his own inaugural address at the University of Minnesota. Let the high schools and academies, he said, assume responsibility for the education of boys to about the age of 20. The students would then be mature enough to undertake the serious and advanced studies of the university—"to enter upon the work of a man," as he phrased it.

Neither Tappan nor Folwell proposed the establishment of junior colleges. Nor had they the least notion of instituting terminal courses for those not interested in entering university programs. They were concerned solely with reforming and strengthening the American university and its offerings. To them it was of little moment what happened to the freshman and sophomore years of the collegiate curriculum, so long as the university could be freed of them. On the other hand, a ready solution to that problem seemed quite naturally to lie in the extension of the high school program. Tappan and Folwell apparently considered it logical for the American secondary school to become like the German *Gymnasium* in order to make it possible for the American college to become like the German university.

While few actual attempts were made at changing the traditional pattern of collegiate education imported from England in the seventeenth century, the new theory of a more advanced university kept gathering headway during the second half of the nineteenth century. Besides Tappan and Folwell, a considerable number of important educational leaders favored the German system. Their pleas and arguments, however, had few tangible results. Even today many educators are talking about the desirability of admitting students to the university at the level of the junior year and of limiting the work of this institution, the capstone of our educational system, entirely to advanced and professional studies. Steps in this direction actually have been taken at the Johns Hopkins University (the first major graduate school in this country), at Clark University, at the University of Chicago, at Stanford University, and elsewhere during the past 50 years. Yet, after a century of debate, the traditional English pattern of the four-year undergraduate program still persists. One potent argument advanced against any change has been that a university of the German type would be unable to maintain a satisfactory football team!

THE HIGH SCHOOL AND THE GYMNASIUM

In spite of the insistence of many educators upon the wisdom of extending the work of the secondary school through the fourteenth grade, most communities prefer a high school which ends at the twelfth grade. If additional years of study are offered, the courses are given in a program entirely separate from that of the high school. It seems at present wholly unlikely that our secondary schools will adopt the pattern of continental European schools. This is probably just as well. Although the *Gymnasium* undoubtedly teaches its subjects more thoroughly and extensively, the American high school offers a broader curriculum and has proved itself admirably capable of meeting the principal needs of American students.

European educational systems generally have been established upon the design of setting up frequent barriers to advancement. All but the most promising European students are shunted early into terminal vocational schools; only those of distinctly superior ability manage to reach the universities. The European theory, resulting probably from intense competition for economic security and social position, has been that the less fit must be eliminated from education at certain stages. The American theory, on the other hand, has been that every student should be allowed to advance educationally as far as he justifiably can. During recent years the clamor to adopt the European point of view and consequently set up more terminal institutions (that is, schools in which education terminates, in which the door to further advancement is closed) has continued. To many educators it appears to be a danger which must be faced and conquered by the two-year college.

Many American high schools began in the late nineteenth century to extend their offerings beyond the twelfth grade. The high school of Greeley, Colorado, for example, added an extra year of work (the thirteenth grade) in the 1880's. A few years later, in the 1890's, the University of Michigan admitted into the sophomore class a number of students who had completed five years of study in the Michigan high schools. Nearly all such early experiments eventually were abandoned. In a few cases, however (Joliet, Illinois, is one example), the plan to extend the work of the secondary school resulted finally in the establishment of separate junior colleges.

FATHER OF THE JUNIOR COLLEGE

When the University of Chicago was reorganized in 1890, its first president, William Rainey Harper, immediately launched a series of educational reforms. One of these was a summer session, an innovation received with great skepticism throughout most of the country. Another was the introduction of a graduate program which was to train principally for academic research. An admirer of the German university, Harper hoped that he might in time eliminate the freshman and sophomore years of his curriculum and concentrate the attention of his institution upon advanced studies only. As a start in this direction, he organized the upper division (junior and senior years) at the University of Chicago into what he called the "university college" and the lower division into an "academic college." After four years, these names proving somewhat awkward, the designations of "senior college" and "junior college" were substituted. While this was not the first instance of an administrative separation between lower and upper divisions in collegiate institutions, it seems to have been the first in which the name of "junior college" was used.

Hoping ultimately to admit all students to the University of Chicago at the level of the junior year and thus to eliminate the so-called "junior college" from his own program, Harper thoughtfully proposed methods by which the hiatus between twelfth grade and the university could be filled. He suggested first that strong high schools and academies be permitted to extend their offerings into the thirteenth and fourteenth grades, thus producing six-year high schools. Secondly, he proposed that weak four-year colleges drop the junior and senior years from their curriculums and concentrate upon doing better work with freshmen and sophomores. He estimated that, at the turn of the century, there were in America not less than 200 small colleges in which the change from a four-year program to a two-year program would prove beneficial.

While many of the small colleges mentioned by Harper were deeply offended at his proposals and few showed any real willingness to follow his advice, a few of them demonstrated the wisdom of Harper's reasoning. A group of three Baptist colleges in Texas actually reduced their programs to two years in 1897. Fourteen or fifteen years later a movement in this direction began in Missouri.

The development of junior colleges through this means, which Walter Eells has called the "decapitation" method, has been, however, extremely small. Many private colleges today, in the face of rising costs and shrinking endowments, might still find it expedient to avoid financial catastrophe by adopting Harper's advice.

President Harper's proposals to the high schools and academies were accepted with better grace. By 1904 there were some two dozen six-year secondary schools in different parts of the country whose graduates expected to enter universities as juniors. A number of these were in direct affiliation with the University of Chicago.

Harper was one of the first American educators to argue in favor of the junior college as an educational unit. He summarized most of his ideas in his decennial presidential report in 1902. They include the following: (1) the end of the sophomore year is a convenient point for many students to terminate their college careers; (2) some students who do not wish to undertake four years of collegiate instruction may be willing to attempt the two-year programs; (3) as larger numbers of students can be persuaded to take two more years of schooling after high school, the standards of the professional schools, such as those for medicine and law, may be raised by requiring longer preprofessional study before admission; (4) if high schools and academies add the junior college unit and if some colleges reduce their programs from four years to two, greater economy in the financing of higher education will result; and (5) with opportunities for education beyond the twelfth grade made locally available, students may continue to live at home until greater maturity has been reached.

These are some of the arguments which Harper advanced, and they constitute the chief reasons which have impelled communities to found junior colleges since his day. Only his third argument no longer holds water: the professional schools have raised their admission requirements in many cases to four years of college and the bachelor's degree. We must remember, however, that in Harper's day many professional schools admitted students directly from the high schools and academies. Harper, because he was one of the first who used the term "junior college" and because of his immediate and widespread influence upon the reform of collegiate education in the United States, has often been called "the father of the junior college."

PRIVATE ACADEMIES AND SEMINARIES

The junior college movement, product of nearly half a century of discussion, became active only about 1900. Two early two-year institutions, Decatur Baptist College in Texas, which opened a two-year program under denominational control in 1897, and Joliet Junior College in Illinois, which organized under public control in 1902, often are designated as the first junior colleges remaining in continuous existence until the present day. Other institutions also have claimed the priority. Lewis Institute, founded in 1896, later changed into a four-year college and joined with the Armour Institute to form the Illinois Institute of Technology. Several two-year denominational colleges for Negroes existed in the South even earlier. Technically, the Negro colleges probably were the very first junior colleges operating in America. On the other hand, their founders undoubtedly intended them to be replicas of the traditional four-year liberal arts colleges attended by white students, and it was chance rather than design which restricted their curriculums to only two years of work. Which institution actually can be regarded as the first real junior college is, of course, not a matter of great importance.

We have mentioned already the fact that some high schools, under the influence of efforts to reform our educational system, offered work beyond the twelfth grade at least a decade before 1900. Many private academies and seminaries, particularly in the East and South, were doing so even earlier.

A good example of this trend is Bradford Junior College in Massachusetts. Founded in 1803 as Bradford Academy and coeducational until 1836, this institution, like many others of its time, supplied higher education to women students late in the nineteenth century by adding the thirteenth and fourteenth grades. It must be remembered that most colleges were established for men students only and that the academy therefore constituted a natural place for women to receive collegiate instruction. When the junior college had begun to emerge as a distinct and separate educational unit in 1902, a division was made at Bradford between the upper years and the academy proper. Enrollment in the academy gradually diminished. In 1932 the name was changed to Bradford Junior College, and two years later all instruction below the thirteenth grade ended.

Most of the nineteenth-century academies were either preparatory schools for boys or finishing schools for girls, though a number of exceptions might be cited. Those for boys have tended ever since to retain their original purpose of preparing boys for admission to private four-year colleges. Those for girls and some coeducational institutions have tended, on the other hand, to extend their offerings beyond the twelfth grade and in many instances to turn into junior colleges. The dearth of collegiate opportunities for women and the relative lack of interest by women students in education on the university level apparently brought about this condition. Such institutions as Stephens College in Missouri and Greenbrier College in West Virginia, both of which offer two years of high school and two years of college, reflect this philosophy. In the progress of time, as the public high schools began to attract more and more of the girls, enrollment in the lower grades of academies and seminaries fell off. Enrollment in the junior college years concurrently increased. This has been the history of a substantial number of Eastern and Southern private junior colleges which originated as academies.

MAIN PERIODS OF JUNIOR COLLEGE DEVELOPMENT

During the half-century between 1850 and 1900, there became evident many influences and changes which resulted in the eventual establishment of the junior college as a separate educational unit. These 50 years might be called, then, the Preparatory Period. Chief among the influences which had a bearing upon this emergence of junior colleges was the attempted, but only partially successful, reform of American university education. It should be noted incidentally that the junior colleges which grew directly out of this attempt at university reform were intended only to duplicate the first two years of the standard college curriculum. The earliest junior colleges organized were largely of this type.

The second stage in the junior college movement, between 1900 and 1920, may well be called the Formative Period. During this period a number of junior colleges were established, either as (1) extensions of work in the high schools or academies, or (2) new institutions formed by reducing some four-year colleges to two-year colleges, or (3) entirely separate two-year colleges. While a few universities experimented with the segregation of the freshman and sophomore years into a distinct administrative unit, such experiments, until recently, seldom resulted in true junior college programs.

The variety of sources and theories which characterized the junior college movement in this formative period prompted Alexis F. Lange, then dean of the school of education at the University of California, to raise in 1917 his three famous questions: Shall certain colleges have their heads cut off, and, if so, by whom? Shall the American university-college have its legs cut off, and, if so, where? Shall the American four-year high schools be stretched, and, if so, how? [1] Lange, it may be observed, was a leading exponent of the theory that public secondary education should be extended upward through the fourteenth grade.

By 1920, when representatives of 34 junior colleges formed the American Association of Junior Colleges, the movement may be said to have come of age. There had been 50 years of discussion and experiment followed by 20 years of rapid growth. Colvert states that only eight junior colleges existed in 1900, with approximately 100 students among them. [2] By 1920 there were nearly 200 institutions and 15,000 students.

Development of two-year colleges within the next two decades came at an even faster pace. The period from 1920 to 1940 was

[1] A. F. Lange, "The Junior College as an Integral Part of the Public School System," *School Review*, XXV (September, 1917), 465–479.

[2] C. C. Colvert, "A Half-Century of Junior Colleges," *Junior College Journal*, XVII (February, 1947), 244.

marked particularly by two new characteristics. In the first place, the publicly supported junior colleges took a commanding lead in student enrollment, probably for economic reasons. In the second place, many institutions that specialized in vocational and adult education entered the field. This might be called the Period of Diversification. While the early junior colleges had merely imitated the first two years of university work, the 1920's and 1930's witnessed the addition to the junior college group of institutions of many types. A great many had been in existence before under other names, as business schools, trade schools, and the like. Now they assumed new functions and also took on academic respectability by calling themselves junior colleges and requiring graduation from the twelfth grade for admission.

After a brief lull during World War II, a final stage in the development of two-year colleges occurred. The period after 1945 may be regarded as the real starting point for the community college, for it was about this time that the community-serving function of the two-year college was widely recognized and accepted. Thus we might call the years from 1940 to the present the Period of the Community College.

The history of the junior college movement in the United States may be summarized, then, as follows: while institutions of several types offered the equivalent of the first two years of college during a substantial portion of the nineteenth century, the attempts to reform American university education seem to have been responsible for the earliest steps in the direction of the modern junior college. As a result of the desire to reorganize our universities in the German pattern, some high schools and academies extended their curriculums to the thirteenth and fourteenth grades, and some separate junior colleges were established. During the Preparatory Period and the Formative Period (1850–1900 and 1900–1920, respectively) there was little attention paid either to vocational and adult education or to community service as we now understand it, and the curriculum of the typical junior college was derived almost entirely from the freshman and sophomore years of the standard liberal arts college. The emphasis upon two-year vocational programs and upon adult education came during the Period of Diversification (1920–1940). The concept of the community-serving two-year college came to the fore during the most recent stage of development, the Period of the Community College.

VOCATIONAL AND ADULT EDUCATION

Oddly enough, historians of the junior college movement have hitherto ignored the important influence upon the two-year institution which has been exercised by American vocational and adult education as it has developed within the past century. The large number of technical and commercial schools which, for one reason or another, changed into junior colleges between 1920 and 1940 brought a significant new factor into the movement. Without it, the community college of today would have much less reason for existence.

VOCATIONAL EDUCATION

When Hanus declared in 1908 that an "efficient public-school system should include adequate provision for vocational training for persons of both sexes over fourteen years of age" and complained that, "while the schools have laid stress on culture as the end of education, they have laid almost no stress on preparation for a vocation," [3] he was not stating an entirely new idea. The academies proposed by Benjamin Franklin recognized vocational elements in education and were intended in part to make the school program more useful and practical; our public school system had admitted manual training courses into the curriculum before 1900. Yet by the time of Hanus there could be found very little actual support for the idea that the school system should accept responsibility for the vocational training of American students.

Hanus held office as chairman of the Commission on Industrial

[3] Paul H. Hanus, *Beginnings in Industrial Education*, Houghton Mifflin, 1908, p. 3.

Education, appointed by the Governor of Massachusetts to assist in setting up within that state a program which would provide young people with better opportunities to secure training for industrial occupations. In the course of his work with the Commission, Hanus visited Germany and inspected the industrial "continuation" schools of that country. These were schools in which the student could receive occupational training after he had completed his regular academic schooling. In Munich, for example, he saw 40 different kinds of public schools offering specialized instruction (much of it on a part-time arrangement) for such trades as those of shoemaker, jeweler, carpenter, printer, bookbinder, machinist, blacksmith, coachman, hotel and restaurant waiter, and the like. Few public schools offering similar training could have been found in cities of the United States at the time. He also saw, on a somewhat higher level of education, technical schools giving training for occupations of a managerial or semiprofessional type in commerce and industry. To this diversified system of occupational training Hanus ascribed the phenomenal growth of Germany as an industrial power.

Other educators of the early twentieth century, impressed by the tremendous waste of our human resources in the form of boys and girls who left our schools unprepared for any remunerative occupations, urged the establishment in our own public school system of something similar to the German continuation school (the *Fortbildungsschule,* a secondary school for special vocational training, usually in close association with apprenticeship in a specified trade). The results of this concern on the part of American educators and the public have become apparent chiefly in two ways. First, many of our public high schools have introduced programs of training for commerce or the skilled trades. Secondly, some of our states have established systems of separate trade schools on the secondary level. A number of these have become junior colleges or two-year (collegiate-level) technical institutes.

Vocational Education in Private Schools. While vocational training, as we have said, failed to win public acceptance as a recognized feature of our public school system until well along in the twentieth century, this does not mean that the obvious need for education of this type went unnoticed. Under the old guild system, stemming from the development of skilled artisanship in the Middle Ages, trades were learned through direct apprenticeship. A boy would serve with a master craftsman until he himself had become a master. Following the invention and widespread use of power-driven machinery, however, methods of manufacturing were radically altered. Machines accomplished on a larger scale the work previously performed by carefully trained hands. Thus the apprentice plan of training in many fields rapidly declined. There soon came a period of reliance upon, as well as unscrupulous exploitation of, young and unskilled laborers. During this period no special skill was thought to be required for the operation of industrial machines. Finally, however, the increasing complexity of industrial equipment and the financial organization of large corporations began to call for workmen with special skills and greater knowledge. In some cases manufacturers, conscious of the need for vocational training, experimented with schools in their own plants. In other cases philanthropic agencies and individuals undertook to provide instruction of a practical type to young men (and later to young women) who had left school early to seek employment.

Private philanthropy sponsored the development of such important institutions for vocational training as the various educational divisions in branches of the Young Men's Christian Association, the Carnegie Institute of Technology in Pittsburgh, Pratt Institute in Brooklyn, Wentworth Institute in Boston, The Dunwoody Institute in Minneapolis, Rochester Mechanics Institute in Rochester, New York, The Lewis Institute in Chicago, The Ralph Sellew Institute in St. Louis, and the Williamson Free School of Mechanical Trades in Williams, Pennsylvania—to mention only a few. At the same time and in some cases even earlier, private (usually profit-making) schools for commercial and industrial training had been springing up in all parts of the country.

Vocational Education and the Federal Government. In spite of rather general opposition to the idea of federal interference in education, there have been proposals, almost constantly from 1783 on, for federal aid as well as for federal participation in education. No bill succeeded in gaining enactment, however, until the First Morrill Act (1862), which had been proposed four years earlier (and once vetoed) as a means of encouraging the development of the agricultural and mechanical arts. (Politically considered, the bill seems to have been intended as a gesture to win the votes of the farmers.) To help establish colleges for the study of agriculture and mechanics, the states and territories were granted large gifts of public lands. The proceeds from such lands were to be used in founding these colleges. The First Morrill Act was followed in subsequent years by various amendments and by the Hatch Act (1887), the Second Morrill Act (1890), the Nelson Act (1907), and the Agricultural Extension Act (1914). While the original purpose appears to have been merely to "do something for the farmer," these bills resulted in a vast expansion of technical education, agricultural extension work, and agricultural research.

The Smith-Hughes Act (1917) was aimed chiefly at supporting vocational education in the secondary schools. It also provided funds for training teachers in vocational subjects. The act came as the result of creation by Congress in 1914 of a Commission on Vocational Education. Other acts extending federal support of training in the trades and commercial subjects, as well as in home-making, have become laws since 1917.

The principal interest of the federal government in education, at least until World War II, has been in agricultural and mechanical training. This was an area in which neither the public schools nor the colleges and universities had much interest in the nineteenth century. Both groups had been willing, until attracted by federal subsidies, to leave this kind of education in the hands of private agencies. With such incentives, however, as the establishment of state colleges of agriculture and mechanics under the Morrill Act, the spread of technological schools founded by private charity, the rise of private commercial schools, the introduction of occupational training into high schools through the Smith-Hughes Act, and the organization of trade schools (later technical institutes) in some of the states upon the example of the German pattern of industrial education, by 1920 vocational education in the United States had achieved a fairly prominent place in our system.

ADULT EDUCATION

By adult education we ordinarily mean programs of self-improvement, either cultural or vocational (though sometimes merely recreational), pursued after the completion of formal schooling. Most of the students in such programs probably are 18 years of age or older.

Presumably the first forms of adult education in this country consisted of clubs, lecture series, public forums, and the like, rather than organized classes. During the late eighteenth and early nineteenth centuries, for example, many clubs existed for the discussion of the new and exciting scientific discoveries of that age. There were also debating societies and reading clubs (often known as "young men's institutes") which collected books, read and talked about them, and encouraged literary activities among their members. Considerable numbers of these young men's institutes (like that at New Haven, Connecticut) later evolved into free public libraries.

Among other examples of adult education are the lyceums, or lecture societies, the first of which appears to have been organized in Milbury, Massachusetts, in 1826. Lyceums took fees from their members, with which they hired prominent speakers on topics of current interest. Until after the Civil War, they offered one of the chief and most agreeable methods by which a citizen could inform himself with regard to intellectual subjects. Popular among nearly all classes of people, they tended unconsciously to stir public sympathy in favor of support and improvement of the common schools. By bringing educational problems before the public, they cleared the way for later school reformers like Horace Mann and for the full support of the schools through taxation. After 1868 commercial lecture bureaus, operated for a profit, began to take over the functions of the voluntary, nonprofit lyceums, and the character of the whole movement underwent a change.

In 1871 the Chautauqua Institution opened in upper New York State as a summer training camp for Methodist Sunday School teachers. Combining lectures, exhibits, music, drama, and study sessions of several kinds, the venture included both educational and recreational activities. Its original purposes have been obscured in the popular mind by the adoption of the name *chautauqua* in connection with traveling commercial shows which became increasingly devoted to entertainment rather than to instruction. William Rainey Harper, incidentally, drew upon his experiences at Chautauqua when he started summer sessions and correspondence courses at the University of Chicago.

At the turn of the century women became gradually more important in strengthening and improving adult education. They faithfully supported the lecture programs. Many of them had become teachers, and more and more were beginning to receive some form of higher education. As women grew economically independent and exercised an interest in civic affairs, they sought opportunities for self-instruction and exchange of information through many informal means, including especially the women's clubs.

In the public schools, before 1917, what little adult education existed was aimed at teaching illiterates and the foreign-born how to read and write and at supplying occasional occupational courses for young adults. With increasing immigration and the spirit of nationalism aroused by World War I, attention was momentarily directed toward "Americanization" classes—the study of the American constitution and social order and the English language.

Mergence of Vocational and Adult Education

By the 1920's what had been sporadic and informal attempts at adult education began to change into an organized pattern within both our public school system and many of our collegiate institutions, particularly those in the larger cities. Bryson says that modern adult education may be dated from about 1926.[4] Evening classes and correspondence courses are now available in all parts of the nation. The concern once felt for the Americanization of recent immigrants has now given place to more essential consideration of the continued vocational and cultural advancement of our native citizens.

Thus vocational and adult education, developing along somewhat independent lines and in diverse forms, have merged into the general pattern of a broadening educational system. The influence of these two forces has thoroughly permeated the entire structure of our American schools, with the major emphasis being brought to bear at the secondary and collegiate levels. The junior college, in the process of its development as the community or "people's" college, has quickly taken the lead in organizing and improving opportunities for training in these areas.

Vocational and Adult Education in the Community College

As the needs of students for increasingly complex types of occupational training and the interest of adults in higher and broader forms of education have emerged, the two-year community college has found itself in the most fortunate position for meeting the challenge.

In the first place, while other collegiate institutions appeared reluctant to make changes in their traditional programs to supply the vocational and adult education demanded by the public, the community college has willingly accepted this task. When, for instance, the need for two-year vocational programs on the post-secondary level developed, community colleges (under the names of junior college, technical institute, and the like) filled the gap. In the second place, the community colleges by boldly discarding tradition have become peculiarly sensitive to the conditions within their own constituencies. Partly because of the desire to serve as many students as possible, they have elected to extend their offerings into

---

[4] Lyman Bryson, *Adult Education,* American Book Co., 1936, p. 24.

nearly every field in which local instruction was not already available or in which interest could be stimulated.

An interesting and significant fact, not generally noticed by historians of the junior college movement, is that many of our present community colleges have grown out of schools and institutes originally established solely for vocational and adult education. This development occurred on an extensive scale in the 1930's, and it clearly demonstrates the close connection between vocational and adult education and the community-serving institution. As an example of the many institutions which originally were organized for other purposes but have now joined the junior college movement as community colleges, one of the educational programs begun by the Young Men's Christian Association will be examined. The example chosen is Hillyer College in Connecticut.

In 1883, like many other branches of the nation-wide Y.M.C.A., the branch at Hartford started supplying part-time instruction of a rather informal nature to boys of the area. The purpose was partly vocational and partly character-building, as it was believed that constructive activity would help to curb delinquency. Instruction centered chiefly around the woodworking and metalworking trades. It aimed not so much at preparing boys for jobs as at encouraging them to develop hobbies, though the vocational usefulness of the information was not ignored. As time went on, the work was extended and formalized. Then the Hillyer family of Hartford donated $100,000 to support the program, and subsequently the school (or, more properly, the educational division of the Hartford Y.M.C.A.) took the name of Hillyer Institute. Courses in commercial and general subjects gradually were added, including after 1921 some on the collegiate level. Women students were first admitted in 1926.

As the Hartford school system increased its holding power over the high school students, in part by the addition of purely vocational subjects, and with the establishment of an excellent state trade school in the city, Hillyer Institute found itself able to attract fewer and fewer students in its high school and trades courses and more and more students in its collegiate program. By 1939 the curriculum had moved upward so far that only post-secondary students were being enrolled. At this point in its history the school formally entered the junior college fellowship and became known as Hillyer Junior College. Previously its classes had met largely in the evening; now it established a full-time day division as well.

While continuing a standard (university-parallel) program of the liberal arts on the freshman and sophomore level, Hillyer directed its major efforts at meeting vocational needs. It conducted such two-year courses of study as those in the fields of accounting, junior engineering, secretarial science, and others of a similar nature, plus a long list of even shorter programs, such as real estate, salesmanship, credit management, machine design, commercial art, and the like, all aimed at improving the student's vocational proficiency. In 1947, when its graduates were having difficulty continuing their college work elsewhere because of the postwar "educational bulge" in American institutions of higher learning, it finally entered the senior college field by adding the junior and senior years and changed its name to Hillyer College. It has since introduced a few graduate courses and has entirely severed its connection with the Y.M.C.A.

The histories of many other Y.M.C.A. schools closely parallel the development of Hillyer College. Dayton College in Ohio grew out of an educational program started in 1887, with a School of Commerce and Finance (junior college level) organized in 1924, a School of Liberal Arts (in association with Wittenberg College) added in 1927, and a Technical School added in 1938.

VOCATIONAL AND ADULT EDUCATION IN AGRICULTURAL AND TRADE SCHOOLS

Examples of some other types of vocational schools transformed into junior colleges are found in the agricultural high schools of Mississippi and New York State and the trade schools of Connecticut.

In Mississippi, legislation was enacted in 1910 permitting the establishment by each county of an agricultural high school for white children and a similar school for Negro children. Under this bill

54 of the state's 84 counties built schools of this kind. When, a decade later, improved methods of transportation made it possible to form new, standard high schools by consolidating local school districts, enrollment in the county agricultural schools dwindled. Mississippi then very wisely launched a state-wide program of converting these county school plants into junior colleges. Under the leadership of Knox M. Broom of the state department of education, Mississippi was divided into 13 junior college districts. The Hinds and Pearl River agricultural schools became junior colleges in 1922, and others rapidly followed their example. A Commission on Junior Colleges was organized six years later for the purpose of establishing and accrediting the new institutions. Emphasis upon agricultural training was retained in the curriculum.

Several of the four-year colleges in Mississippi, incidentally, had expressed fears during the early phases of this development that the new junior colleges would reduce enrollments in the older institutions. Contrary to their expectations, however, enrollments in Mississippi colleges of nearly every type increased markedly after these new two-year colleges were in operation.

At about the same period in which Mississippi was beginning to set up county high schools for agricultural training, the state of New York opened a number of schools of agriculture under state supervision. Some of these quickly introduced programs in homemaking and in industrial trades. Within a few years they were offering more and more advanced work, and during the late 1930's and early 1940's they joined the ranks of the junior colleges. The agricultural and technical institutes of New York are terminal in character, that is, they are intended for students who do not plan to continue beyond two years of college.

In Connecticut, with its numerous manufacturing industries requiring skilled workmen, the development of trade schools under the control of the state department of education was a logical move. Shortly after the agricultural schools of New York changed into technical institutes, the trade schools of Connecticut also began to extend their programs into technical education on the collegiate

level. Although for various reasons these are not officially designated as junior colleges but are called "technical schools" or
"technical institutes," the upper levels of their instruction actually
constitute public junior college work of the vocational type. In practice, their development resembles very closely that of the vocational
institutions of New York State and Mississippi, except for the fact
that no agricultural training is offered.

Certainly among the most vital forces in the formation of our
modern junior and community colleges have been the twin movements of vocational and adult education. The most noticeably rapid
period of growth in both these movements came between World
War I and World War II. Their influence, imposed upon that of the
two-year college which resulted from the attempts of nineteenth
century educators to reform the American university, effectively
brought out the community-serving potentialities of a new educational pattern for the United States. Perhaps it is not too much to
say that without the influence of vocational and adult education the
typical two-year college today might still be offering merely the
lower portion of a standard four-year collegiate program. Instead,
a much broader and more flexible curriculum has been produced.
The intertwining of the three vigorous roots of *university reform,*
adult education, and *vocational education* into a flourishing new
species of educational plant has given us the modern community
college. One other influence of deep significance remains to be acknowledged. This is the American ideal of extending educational
opportunity to all our citizens.

AMERICAN DEMOCRACY

Although the need for the education of all children was recognized in America as early as 1647, when the famous "Old Deluder"
act was passed by the colonial government of Massachusetts, a long
time went by before our people generally were willing to accept
education completely as a public responsibility. The motives behind
the Massachusetts law lay primarily in religious feeling. The Protes-

tants who occupied the colony believed that every person should be able to read the Bible. In this way the ignorance upon which that "Old Deluder," Satan, prospered could be alleviated. Throughout most of the colonies, however, education was commonly regarded either as a private matter or as the function of church groups. Not until the second quarter of the nineteenth century did interest in public support for the schools really awaken.

Cubberley in his great *History of Education* describes the seven important battles which had to be won in the long struggle for equality of educational opportunity.[5] As he interprets educational history, these were: (1) the battle for tax support; (2) the battle to eliminate the pauper school idea; (3) the battle to make the schools entirely free; (4) the battle to establish state supervision; (5) the battle to eliminate sectarianism from the schools; (6) the battle to extend the system upward; and (7) the addition of the state university to crown the system. The sixth of Cubberley's great battles—the one concerned with upward extension of the American educational system—has an important bearing on the development of two-year colleges.

For many generations free public education in the United States consisted in only a few years of elementary or common schooling. In most rural areas of the early nineteenth century, children learned little more in school than the rudiments of reading, writing, and simple arithmetic—the traditional "three R's." About 1820 the system in the more populated sections was extended *downward* into the primary grades for younger children. Kindergartens and even nursery schools have now become rather common, at least in our larger cities. But the normal extent of public education during the nineteenth century was no more than six or eight years for the average American. Those who could afford to continue beyond the common school attended academies or preparatory schools, at which fees were paid. These institutions and the colleges, for the most

[5] Ellwood P. Cubberley, *The History of Education,* Houghton Mifflin, 1920, pp. 676–710.

part, remained under private control. Only a small number of publicly supported secondary schools existed.

The private academies, of course, were eventually replaced by the public high schools. The first of these high schools was the English Classical School organized in 1821 in Boston. A similar school in Portland, Maine, opened not long after this, and several cities in Massachusetts were quick to follow the example set by the capital metropolis. In 1827 the legislature of Massachusetts passed a law requiring a high school to be provided in every town with 500 families or more. This law probably marks the real beginning of the free public high school as an essential part of our school system.

The upward extension of public education took place, however, somewhat slowly. In many states legislation to set up high schools financed by taxation was attacked in the courts as unconstitutional and as an invasion of private privilege. In Michigan, the famous Kalamazoo Case (1872) finally solved the situation by providing a legal precedent, followed in later cases, which held that the high school is a proper and legitimate part of any public school system.

Our battle for free public elementary schools was won by about 1850. The battle for high schools was won by 1900. After World War I enrollments on the secondary level increased enormously, so that pressure began to grow for better educational opportunity on still higher levels. Educators and other citizens now began to ask: Why should not the principle of free public education be applied as well to *every kind* of schooling needed by our citizens? A few states, notably California, have taken long strides in this direction. Others have declared the principle to be visionary and beyond achievement. The chief question being raised at the moment is whether the states can improve the quality of their elementary and secondary schools and at the same time extend the system upward. Federal subsidies have been suggested, though centralized control of our educational system by the federal government is popularly regarded as a real danger, especially when the possible results of centralized control have been demonstrated so forcefully and tragically in the schools of Nazi Germany and Communist Russia. There is now apparent among our forty-eight states a wide variation in willingness as well as financial ability to extend free public education beyond the twelfth grade.

FREE PUBLIC EDUCATION IN CALIFORNIA

The principle of upward extension of free public education as an application of American democracy has perhaps found its most enthusiastic acceptance in California, though movements in this direction have taken place in the other states as well. While California does not have as yet a fully planned state-wide system of public junior colleges, free education through the fourteenth grade exists as a recognized practice and is available to a large proportion of California's young people.[6]

The first legislation in California to affect the junior colleges directly was a bill passed in 1907, which, although it granted no financial aid, authorized the establishment of junior colleges by local high school districts. The intention seems to have been to encourage high schools to extend their work into the thirteenth and fourteenth grades. Beginning with Fresno High School in 1910, 16 districts organized locally financed junior college units within the next six years. Then, in 1917 provisions were made for state and county support of the junior college departments within the high schools. Another law was passed in 1921 which granted increased support and permitted the organization of separate junior college districts.

A decade later ten junior college districts had been formed to replace the original high school districts in which junior colleges had been organized previously. Seven new junior college districts also had been added. By 1947, although 24 junior colleges established by high school districts had been discontinued (some of them, however, were reopened after a period of suspended operation), all institutions administered by the junior college districts were still functioning. The principal reason for failure of those which closed

[6] Frank B. Lindsay, "California Junior Colleges: Past and Present," *California Journal of Secondary Education*, XXII (March, 1947), 137–142.

appears to have been insufficient or unwise planning. In most cases the assessed valuation of taxable property in the district proved too small to carry the financial burden.

Within the 30 years following 1917 (when state and county financial aid had become available) 92 junior colleges were organized in California, 68 in high school districts and 24 in 22 junior college districts (a district may operate more than one institution). Of the former, 12 were later incorporated into junior college districts, 21 have operated successfully during the entire period as originally administered, and 18 are dead. These figures may serve to indicate something of the struggle which has taken place in the upward extension of educational opportunity in California and also something of the vigorous, optimistic spirit behind the junior college movement in that state.

THE NATIONAL GOAL

Nowhere is the American goal of equal and full educational opportunity for all more clearly stated than in the report of the President's Commission on Higher Education. The Commission says very frankly:

> The American people should set as their ultimate goal an educational system in which at no level—high school, college, graduate school, or professional school—will a qualified individual in any part of the country encounter an insuperable economic barrier to the attainment of the kind of education suited to his aptitudes and interests.
>
> This means that we shall aim at making higher education equally available to all young people, as we now do education in the elementary and high schools, to the extent that their capacity warrants a further social investment in their training.[7]

While the Commission acknowledges that "this desirable realization of our ideal of equal educational opportunity cannot be attained immediately," it is convinced that, if we move toward such a goal as fast as our economic resources permit, attainment should not lie too far in the future. At any rate, the Commission believes, the time has

---

[7] *Higher Education for American Democracy*, Harper & Brothers, 1948, I, 36.

now come to go at least a good share of the way, "to make education through the fourteenth grade available in the same way that
high school education is now available." The Commission further
states:

> This means that tuition-free education should be available in public
> institutions to all youth for the traditional freshman and sophomore years
> or for the traditional 2-year junior college course.
>
> To achieve this, it will be necessary to develop much more extensively
> than at present such opportunities as are now provided in local com-
> munities by the 2-year junior college, community institute, community
> college, or institute of arts and sciences. The name used does not matter,
> though community college seems to describe these schools best; the im-
> portant thing is that the services they perform be recognized and vastly
> extended.
>
> Such institutions make post-high-school education available to a much
> larger percentage of young people than otherwise could afford it. Indeed,
> . . . such community colleges probably will have to carry a large part of
> the responsibility for expanding opportunities in higher education.[8]

If the Commission is right in its observations, the best way to extend
our educational system upward and thus increase educational opportunities for all Americans will be through the community colleges.

Does the point of view expressed by the President's Commission
on Higher Education really reflect the thinking of the American
people? Are we ready as a nation to go this far in improving and
expanding educational facilities? The list of members of the Commission is an impressive one, including university presidents, leaders
of educational and religious groups, and men and women prominent
in civic affairs. It seems likely that their judgment of American public opinion is sound and that they represent, therefore, the advance
guard of our educational planning and progress. Furthermore, the
whole history of our nation has demonstrated a growing faith in the
importance of education. Abraham Lincoln called education "the
most important subject which we as a people can be engaged in,"
and most Americans agree. We have striven constantly to improve

[8] *Ibid.*, I, 37.

the opportunities provided for our children. Thus the story of our public school system over the years is one of steady expansion.

The tendency of our people, it seems clear, is to move ahead in the direction of more extensive educational growth. It is doubtless only a matter of time before the fourteenth grade instead of the twelfth will be commonly accepted as the normal stopping place for free public education. This is already true in California and is approaching realization in several other states.

The Next Few Years

The tremendous flow of young war veterans into our colleges after World War II brought home sharply to American educators the need for more local two-year collegiate institutions. A large number of new junior and community colleges sprang up, and several universities established permanent or temporary two-year branches.

When this period of crowded enrollments was over, the Korean War began to demand a fairly large proportion of our young men for military service, and a heavy drain was made upon our national income for military defense. The result was a temporary decrease in the total number of college students. This picture was colored also by the low birth rate of the 1930's. The enthusiasm for organizing new community colleges, at its height in the late 1940's, rather abruptly subsided. We must not, however, make the mistake of assuming that the need for expanding our educational facilities has now passed. The "war babies" of the 1940's are now in high school and will soon reach our colleges. It should also be kept in mind that, though the total number of two-year colleges in the United States actually decreased in the past few years, total enrollments have continued their steady rise.

It is a safe guess that the democratic spirit of our citizens will make the continued expansion of educational opportunity an eventual certainty. That being true, the desirability of establishing a great many more community colleges within the near future seems unquestionable. Careful surveys have been conducted in several states to determine immediate educational needs. Overwhelmingly they point in one direction: state-wide systems of junior and community colleges. For a development as inevitable as this, it would seem only good sense to begin preparing at once.

We have seen that the junior college movement can be traced directly to firm roots in the American democratic tradition. Our basic belief in the intrinsic value of education, our increasing concern for the equalization of educational opportunity, and our constant efforts to extend our public school system so that it will more effectively meet the needs of our citizens—these factors all help to account for the amazing growth of the American junior college movement in the twentieth century.

III

The Goals of the Two-Year College

AN EDUCATIONAL movement as widespread and fast-growing as that of the junior and community college must be founded upon clear ideas as to its aims and functions. Without clearly understood and expressed aims which fit the pattern of modern American life, no new educational movement can long survive. The monitorial system of teaching, immensely but briefly popular in this country during the opening years of the nineteenth century, is a case in point. It failed because its basic philosophy proved unsound.

Much has been written about the philosophy of the junior and community college. Not all authorities have been in agreement as to particular aims and functions. A number of the more common reasons given in support of the general movement for two-year colleges have already been mentioned in the preceding chapters. The philosophy of the two-year college, however, needs to be considered in more detail.

PHILOSOPHY OF THE TWO-YEAR COLLEGE

EARLY DEFINITIONS OF FUNCTIONS

No definite statement regarding the philosophy of the two-year college came to public attention until after 1920. One of the earliest efforts to define the proper functions of the two-year college was made by Frank W. Thomas.[1] Thomas investigated the aims which had led to the establishment of existing junior colleges and also the social and educational needs, not then being met by other institutions, which the junior college could fulfill, and then tested these aims and functions by considering whether they agreed with those advocated by leading educators familiar with college problems. He concluded that the proper functions of junior colleges may be identified as follows: (1) the preparatory function, (2) the popularizing function, (3) the terminal function, and (4) the guidance function.

The Preparatory Function. By the preparatory function Thomas meant that of preparing students for advanced work in the upper divisions of universities. This implies a close resemblance, if not actual duplication, between subjects offered in the junior college and those found in the freshman and sophomore years of the four-year program. This function, in fact, was apparently what Folwell, Tappan, Harper, and other university presidents had chiefly in mind when they proposed the transfer of their lower divisions to the secondary schools.

Since this function tends to add prestige to the junior college in the sense that it links the institution closely with senior colleges, it has been stressed in junior college publicity and catalogs. Actually, it has tended to hamper the development of programs better suited to the real needs of students. In the same way that college entrance requirements have caused high schools to concentrate their efforts on courses which are of use to only a minority of their students, the transfer requirements imposed upon junior colleges have forced the two-year institutions to build their curricular offerings along traditional lines. With clearer understanding of the junior colleges by the senior institutions and with increasing evidence of successful transfer by thousands of junior college graduates, this problem bids fair to being solved.

[1] Frank Waters Thomas, "The Functions of the Junior College," in William Martin Proctor (ed.), *The Junior College: Its Organization and Administration,* Stanford University Press, 1927, pp. 11–25.

Because a fairly large proportion of junior college graduates do continue their education in the upper divisions of universities and colleges, the preparatory function remains important. For greater clarity and precision, however, it might well be called the duplicating function. It has also been spoken of frequently as the transfer function. Thomas believed that this purpose is justified in part by overcrowded conditions in the four-year colleges.

The Popularizing Function. What Thomas called the popularizing function we are more likely to describe today as the community function. The junior college, because it is usually located near the student's home, supplies higher education at less expense. The cost of room and board in a dormitory is eliminated. Thus, by providing educational opportunities to those who might not otherwise attend college, the two-year college popularizes higher education—that is, it encourages more students to attempt it.

The founders of many of our earliest junior colleges appear to have had this function in mind when establishing their institutions. Some frankly stated that the new colleges were for young people who could not otherwise afford further education. Unfortunately, many people have taken this to mean that an inferior brand of instruction would be perfectly adequate for such underprivileged students. Newer concepts of the community function, based on a standard of the best possible service to the community by the institution, have now largely done away with this undemocratic attitude, just as our nation did away earlier with the notion that free public education was only for paupers.

Thomas rightly pointed out the fact that distance from a college acts as an effective deterrent for many students who might profit by more education. When a college is located in the immediate vicinity, though it may offer no more than two years of work, larger numbers of students are encouraged by the accessibility of academic facilities to seek additional training.

This function also serves for those young people who, as Dean Alexis F. Lange of the University of California frequently said of them in his efforts to promote the extension of junior college departments among the high schools of his state, "cannot, will not, and should not become university students." The person who desires only two years of higher education instead of the usual four may leave the university in the middle of its four-year program with a sense of incompleteness and failure. In the junior college, after two years, he can experience a sense of accomplishment.

The popularizing function, as Thomas described it, removes those barriers to educational opportunity raised by location, economic strictures, home obligations, and the like.

The Terminal Function. Thomas recognized the need for instruction in preparation for the so-called semiprofessions, those occupations requiring more training than the high school can give but less than the traditional four years of college. Positions of this type abound in the fields of engineering, agriculture, commerce, and personal service. It has been estimated that, for every position requiring full professional training (engineer, lawyer, physician, dentist, and the like) there are at least five or six requiring not more than two years of collegiate preparation (draftsman, junior engineer, accountant, medical assistant, secretary, and so on). Since the traditional college ordinarily makes no provision for such training, this function is left to the junior college.

Thomas questioned whether students could be interested in such terminal courses. His data, when analyzed, revealed enough evidence of student interest to justify the terminal function. The experience of recent years has indicated an increasing demand for two-year programs, especially those of a vocational character. Studies made from time to time of enrollment in such programs report steady growth in the number and proportion of terminal students.

One group of educators has objected rather strongly to the use of the word "terminal" to denominate these courses. "Terminal" suggests a definite closing of the door to further educational opportunity. In theory, the terminal student's need for college work presumably terminates after two years. In actual fact, many terminal students go on to further training and continue to be successful in their studies. There is strong reason to believe that those courses desig-

nated as terminal discourage the educational ambitions of young
people. In America we profess belief in the continuing value of
education throughout every citizen's life; we often declare that,
ideally, no one's education should ever terminate. Thus "terminal"
would seem to be a word not conformable to our basic educational
concepts; and since many of the courses we have been discussing are
vocation-centered, it might be better practice to call them simply
vocational programs. With regard to nonvocational courses, the
junior college years offer, at the very least, a *continuation* beyond
high school.

The Guidance Function. To Thomas, the guidance function
implied assistance mainly to the less capable students, those who
could not ordinarily achieve admission to the standard universities
and who might need to be directed into suitable terminal programs
consistent with restricted academic ability. In view of the important
contributions recently made to our knowledge of psychology, this
probably constitutes an erroneous conception of guidance.

A conviction has been growing slowly to the effect that colleges
have three unavoidable obligations: (1) to admit only students who
can profit by the work offered, (2) to provide instruction of high
quality, and (3) to give every student the information and counseling he requires to make certain of selecting the most appropriate
course of study. Some institutions will say that the last obligation
proposed is the business of the student and not of the college, but
more and more colleges are beginning to recognize the importance
of guidance activities. At the time of Thomas' study, the principles
of modern guidance had not yet been firmly established, so that he
cannot be blamed for not being familiar with them. Since the colleges of a generation ago did not regard guidance as a function of
higher education, it was perfectly right for him to claim it as one of
the unique aims of the junior college.

We have now begun to regard guidance as a necessary function
of all educational institutions, at least up to the point at which the
student has entered professional or advanced training. The place of

guidance in our junior and community colleges will receive detailed attention in a later chapter.

SUBSEQUENT DEFINITIONS OF FUNCTIONS

The Function of Superior Teaching. One function which was not listed by Thomas but which has been counted important by others who have studied the junior college movement is that of superior teaching. While good teaching probably is assumed for most of the recognized senior colleges, in actual fact interest on the part of higher education has traditionally been not in students but in subject matter. John Erskine used to regard good teaching in our colleges as "so rare that the news of it spreads with the speed of scandal." Promotions of members of the faculty are still consistently made not for teaching ability but as a reward for notable research and publications. In the junior college, on the other hand, faculty members have not been judged by their research activities but almost entirely by their ability to teach.

Does the two-year college really do a better job of teaching? We have no clear evidence on this point. Theoretically, the fact would be perfectly possible, even probable. An institution which concentrates upon teaching seems likely, by and large, to teach better than one which concentrates upon research. The difficulty in coming to any sound conclusion on this matter lies in the fact that most judgments regarding the effectiveness of teaching have been subjective rather than scientific. Most junior colleges do claim superiority of teaching, however, as one of their special assets.

When McDowell made a study in 1919 of the reasons for which junior colleges were being organized, this function received no recognition.[2] In most later studies it has been considered important. As contrasted with institutions which regard the advancement of knowledge (that is, research) as a primary function, the junior and community colleges rank as teaching institutions almost exclusively.

The Function of Individualized Instruction. Many junior col-

[2] F. M. McDowell, *The Junior College*, Bulletin of the U.S. Bureau of Education, No. 35, U.S. Government Printing Office, 1919.

leges point out with great pride in their catalogues and other literature that, because of smaller classes, the student receives more individual attention than is possible in the larger colleges. This claim held
much truth during the formative years before the junior college had
become as popular as it is today. As a special function, however,
individualized instruction can be claimed by the junior college no
more than by any small college. The accident or circumstance of size
rather than any distinct philosophy of education seems to determine
the policy of each institution on this question. Some institutions
(but universities as well as junior colleges) provide individualized
instruction by keeping their classes reasonably small and by encouraging close personal relations between students and faculty.

The rising enrollments in junior colleges, especially the publicly
supported institutions, have made it expedient to place more
students in the average class. Perhaps the typical junior college
maintains a smaller average class than the typical senior college.
(One prominent university after World War II was placing as many
as 2,000 students in a single class—a practice frowned on by most
educators.) Yet to claim individualized instruction as a particular
function of the junior college is unquestionably going too far.

The relatively more homogeneous age groupings within the two-
year institution may offer some advantages in the improvement of
instruction. By focusing attention upon the needs of a limited age
group, as contrasted with the more varied age group in the senior
college student body, it is possible that the impact and unity of the
program may be intensified. These advantages, however, since they
have not been tested and proved scientifically, must be regarded as
theoretical. Individualized instruction was one of the functions
gleaned from a study of junior college catalogues by Koos in 1922.[3]

The Function of Providing Opportunities for Exploration. Many
junior colleges offer to a student the opportunity of exploring several
fields of study during his two-year program in the belief that he may
by this method ultimately select his own proper field. While this

---

[3] Leonard V. Koos, *The Junior-College Movement,* Ginn & Co., 1925, p. 23.

process consumes a considerable amount of time, it is reported exceedingly effective in some cases, especially among women students.

With modern techniques of guidance now available, it would seem that a more efficient system of selecting goals might be preferred.[4] This function still plays a prominent role in junior college literature.

The Function of Character Building. Particularly among junior colleges established by religious groups, character building or moral and religious training has been regarded as a primary function. In this respect, however, the junior college is hardly different from other colleges founded by churches. To most people, character building would seem to be an essential and implied function of every type of education. Outright instruction in religious principles, of course, has been largely avoided in all public institutions for quite obvious reasons.

The Function of Continuing Home Influence. Some authorities suggest that students graduating from high school are still rather immature and that an additional two years of home influence is often desirable. This may be the case for many, but it remains to be proved for the majority. There may even be reason to think that most young people mature somewhat more quickly when removed from the home and permitted to exercise a degree of independence in judgment. Whatever the true facts may be, the local junior college has frequently been recommended to parents by this characteristic of keeping children under home influence for a longer period of time.

Other Suggested Functions. A great many additional reasons for junior colleges have been proposed. Students, when canvassed, have expressed gratitude for the generally more liberal admission policies of the junior college and for opportunities of repairing scholastic deficiencies, as well as for cordial and sympathetic attitudes between teachers and students. Among other functions which have been claimed are a special research function, that of providing

---

[4] Tyrus Hillway, "Counseling with Testing versus Exploration," *Junior College Journal,* XVII (April, 1947), 316–318.

general and cultural education (as apart from vocational or specialized programs), and that of reorganizing the whole pattern of our educational system.[5]

THE PRESIDENT'S COMMISSION

A consideration of the aims of community colleges (the Commission's name for the two-year community-serving institutions) and some strong recommendations for future development are included in Volume I of the report made in 1947 by the President's Commission on Higher Education.

The Commission proposed reduced emphasis upon the preparatory or transfer function and more upon the terminal function. Its principal reasons for this recommendation are contained in the following statement:

In the past the junior college has most commonly sought to provide within the local community the freshman and sophomore courses of the traditional college curriculum. With notable exceptions, it has concentrated on preparing students for further study in the junior and senior years of liberal arts colleges or professional schools.

But preparatory programs looking to the more advanced courses of the senior college are not complete and rounded in themselves, and they usually do not serve well the purpose of those who must terminate their schooling at the end of the fourteenth grade. Half the young people who go to college find themselves unable to complete the full 4-year course, and for a long time to come more students will end their formal education in the junior college years than will prolong it into the senior college. These 2-year graduates would gain more from a terminal program planned specifically to meet their needs than from the first half of a 4-year curriculum.

For this reason, the Commission recommends that the community college emphasize programs of terminal education.

These terminal programs should include both general education and vocational training. They should be designed both for young people who want to secure as good a general education as possible by the end of the fourteenth grade and for those who wish to fit themselves for semiprofessional occupations.

Semiprofessional training, properly conceived and organized, can make

[5] Walter Crosby Eells, *The Junior College*, Houghton Mifflin, 1931, pp. 334–350.

a significant contribution to education for society's occupational requirements. In not providing this sort of training anywhere in existing programs, the educational system is out of step with the demands of the
twentieth century American economy.

Because of advancing technology, the occupation center of our
economic system is shifting away from the major producing industries.
The proportion of the working population engaged in these industries has
decreased, while the proportion in the distributive and service trades has
increased. In 1880, for instance, about one-half of all workers were engaged in agriculture; in 1947, less than one-seventh of the workers were
so engaged.

One result of this development is a new and rapidly growing need for
trained semiprofessional workers in these distributive and service occupations. To meet the needs of the economy our schools must train many
more young people for employment as medical secretaries, recreational
leaders, hotel and restaurant managers, aviators, salesmen in fields like
life insurance and real estate, photographers, automotive and electrical
technicians, and so on through a long list of positions in the business and
professional world.

Education on the technician level—that is, the training of medical technicians, dental hygienists, nurses' aides, laboratory technicians—offers one
practical solution for the acute shortage of professional personnel in
medicine, dentistry, and nursing. An adequate staff of well-trained assistants can substantially increase the number of patients one doctor,
dentist, or nurse can handle.

For these semiprofessional occupations a full 4 years of college training
is not necessary. It is estimated that in many fields of work there are *five*
jobs requiring 2 years of college preparation for every *one* that requires
4 years. Training for these more numerous jobs is the kind the community
college should provide.

If the semiprofessional curriculum is to accomplish its purpose, however, it must not be crowded with vocational and technical courses to the
exclusion of general education. It must aim at developing a combination
of social understanding and technical competence. Semiprofessional
education should mix a goodly amount of general education for personal
and social development with technical education that is intensive, accurate, and comprehensive enough to give the student command of
marketable abilities.[6]

[6] *Higher Education for American Democracy*, Harper & Brothers, 1948, I,
68–69.

Thus the President's Commission, in perhaps the most authoritative statement on the functions of the modern community college, stressed the needs of young people who will never complete more than two years of college, and the responsibility of the institution to meet those needs. It would, however, give these students not only vocational training but a rich admixture of general cultural education.[7] Presumably, on the other hand, the community college program should not be planned exclusively for the terminal student and should continue to make provision for those who will transfer to senior colleges and universities for advanced work.

The Commission proposed adult education as another highly important function. Late-afternoon and evening courses can serve the community by offering useful instruction to persons who have completed their formal education. Furthermore, through adult courses the college can keep intellectual curiosity alive in out-of-school citizens, stimulate their zest for learning, and improve their lives as individuals and as citizens.

To the President's Commission on Higher Education, then, the primary functions of the two-year college appear to be these: (1) training for the semiprofessions, or those occupations requiring no more than two years of college; (2) general education for students who will complete their formal education at the end of the fourteenth grade; (3) adult education in late-afternoon and evening classes; and (4) some provision for those young people who will transfer after two years to colleges offering more advanced studies.

SECONDARY OR HIGHER EDUCATION?

The idea that the thirteenth and fourteenth grades are by their nature a part of secondary education and not really to be regarded as higher education is, of course, not at all a new idea. As already mentioned, Henry Tappan was preaching this doctrine a century ago. He and others pointed to the German school system as a model for our own. "A College in distinction from a University is an ele-

---

[7] Tyrus Hillway, "Enriching the Vocational Program," *Educational Supervision and Administration*, XXVIII (December, 1942), 663–671.

mentary and a preparatory school," Tappan declared. "In Germany the Gymnasia are really the Colleges. The education which they furnish is more thorough, we believe, than what is obtained at the Colleges of either England or of our own country." [8]

During the early years of the junior college, both expediency and the educational theories of some of the founders resulted in the development of two-year collegiate programs as postgraduate additions to the high school. Dean Lange saw junior college work as an extension of secondary education. All those who admired the German *Gymnasium* and the French *lycée* tended to agree with him.

Several of the private junior colleges for women, such as Stephens College in Missouri and Greenbrier College in West Virginia (both founded in the nineteenth century as academies for girls), entered the collegiate field by shifting the level of their work upward. They now offer the junior and senior years of high school and the freshman and sophomore years of college.

Gradually there developed the concept of the four-year junior college as a separate educational unit. This type of institution, while usually called a college, has been generally regarded as the final stage of secondary education.

The Four-year Junior College. The arguments in favor of the four-year junior or community college have been well presented. The basic premise is that the first two years of college really are a part of secondary education. This belief, as we have said, goes back at least a century in our educational history. Proponents of the four-year junior college assert that the rapid growth of this type of institution has been prevented only by tradition and prejudice. When one considers how quickly the two-year junior college has grown in spite of strong traditions opposing it, however, this assertion loses a little of its force.[9]

---

[8] Henry P. Tappan, *University Education*, Putnam, 1851, pp. 48–49.

[9] For a full description of the four-year junior college plan, see John A. Sexson and John W. Harbeson, *The New American College*, Harper & Brothers, 1946.

In 1929, William J. Cooper, then United States Commissioner of Education, summarized supporting arguments for the four-year unit.[10] Secondary education, he said, could better serve young people if it were divided into two sections: the first (grades 7 to 10) geared to the needs of early adolescence, and the second (grades 11 to 14) geared to the needs of middle adolescence. The basic needs of these two periods in a student's mental, physical, and psychological growth, he stated, are essentially different.

Besides this major theory, Cooper advanced several other arguments. According to his reasoning, problems of articulation between the various levels of education, such as the duplication of courses in high school and college, would be minimized by the plan. The brighter students would be enabled to make better progress and might be graduated a year earlier. The program could be reorganized to offer training for the semiprofessions as a regular part of public secondary education. Furthermore, there would be substantial savings in financing junior college work, since the upper grades of high school and the lower years of college would be combined under one administration, and the resulting institution would attract a large enough student body to effect many economies in operation.

Among other arguments presented in favor of the plan have been the possibility of improved guidance facilities, the increased flexibility of the curriculum, its influence toward keeping children in school for a longer period of time, and the probability of attracting better teachers. On the whole, most of these arguments are effective and have been proved in actual practice.

With all these advantages, why have so few four-year junior colleges appeared on the American scene? Eells gathered and listed most of the arguments against the plan in 1931.[11] He found, for example, that many of its advantages could apply with equal justice to the two-year junior college. The theoretical division of

[10] William J. Cooper, "Some Advantages Expected to Result from Administering Secondary Education in Two Units of Four Years Each," *School Review,* XXXVII (May, 1929), 335–346.

[11] Eells, *The Junior College, op. cit.,* pp. 683–719.

adolescence into an early and middle period, he said, cannot be substantiated by psychological studies. As far as duplication or overlapping of courses in the high school and college is concerned, a certain amount of it may actually be desirable. The assumed saving in cost is probably much less than would be supposed and is likely to be possible only in the large metropolitan school system.

Eells marshaled the arguments against the plan in a very thorough manner. He named the following difficulties facing the four-year junior college: (1) arranging for satisfactory collegiate competition; (2) adjustment to existing administrative practices; (3) the feasibility of the plan in sparsely populated areas; (4) the great variety in students' ages (the marked disparity between the characteristics of eleventh graders and fourteenth graders); (5) the adjustment of instruction to these different levels; and (6) the likelihood that students might leave school earlier rather than later under this plan.

Because few four-year junior colleges were in existence when Eells surveyed the situation in 1931, most of the arguments both pro and con of that period must be looked upon as theoretical, but we have since had more than two decades in which to examine the effectiveness of the four-year unit in practice.

Public four-year junior colleges, while they began to appear in the western states from 1923 onward, did not really become established until around 1930. Some of the early ones (like those at Hillsboro and Edinburg, Texas) gave up the four-year organization after a few years of trial.

EXTENSION OF THE SECONDARY SCHOOL

George A. Merrill, director of the California School of Mechanical Arts in San Francisco, had begun to urge the reorganization of public education as early as 1894. He was concerned mainly with training offered in the trades, and he argued that the system would be more effective if boys could be admitted into vocational training at the end of the tenth grade instead of at the end of the eighth. The prevailing pattern of elementary education at that time was based upon eight grades. By setting up four-year programs of study in the trades following ten years of general or common schooling, the arrangement would create a new type of high school, one which would begin with the eleventh grade and continue through the fourteenth.

In speeches and reports during the first decade of the twentieth century, Merrill suggested that all elementary schools end their work at the sixth grade and that there be established an intermediate school offering grades seven through ten and a secondary school offering grades eleven through fourteen. Students learning trades could thus be better prepared for actual jobs. Because this theory of reorganization was intended principally to fit the needs for training in the trades, it was obviously a far cry from the earlier proposals of Tappan, Folwell, and Harper. In one respect, nevertheless, the two points of view coincided: both proposed that secondary education be extended into the fourteenth grade.

The 6–4–4 Plan.   Merrill's principle of school reorganization has come to be known as the 6–4–4 plan. It includes a six-year elementary school, a four-year junior high school, and a four-year combination of senior high school and junior college (frequently referred to simply as a college). The adoption of this plan, starting in the 1920's, has progressed slowly. Those who support it are vehemently enthusiastic and regard it as a very natural and logical division of our public school programs. The prevailing type of school organization in our cities today still is the 6–3–3 plan, with a six-year elementary school, a three-year junior high school, and a three-year senior high school. A two-year junior college is often added, its students being drawn usually from three or four local high schools within a union district. This division of the various schools comprises a 6–3–3–2 plan. Another common form of organization is the 8–4–2 type, with eight years of elementary school, four years of high school, and two years of junior college.

The 6–4–4 plan operated successfully in several cities for a number of years. Among the best known of the public junior or community colleges associated with the plan were those at Pasadena, Ventura, and Compton, California. Stephens College in Missouri has already been mentioned as a private junior college representing a similar kind of organization. In 1950, the public four-year junior college at Compton, after 19 years of highly satisfactory operation, reverted suddenly to the two-year pattern. This event, more than any other, probably has discouraged additional communities from trying the 6–4–4 plan in the future. In fact, one may almost predict the ultimate failure of the four-year unit. This fact, of course, does not in itself settle the question of whether the junior college can properly be classified as offering secondary education.

Why did Compton College give up its four-year plan of organization? If we examine the situation closely, we find that a dividing line between the lower division of the institution (grades 11 and 12) and the upper division (grades 13 and 14) had gradually been growing more marked. Instead of a closely integrated four-year unit, the college seemed more like two two-year units housed together. There were separate social groups, separate athletic teams, separate assembly programs, and separate systems of records. Furthermore, parents greatly wanted to see their children receive high school diplomas at the end of the twelfth grade, as children in other communities do. There were minor difficulties as well.

Compton College was altered from a four-year junior college to a two-year junior college by vote of the union district in which it is located. The district then resumed the 6–3–3–2 plan of organization. Since many educators had used Compton as a prime example of the successful four-year institution, the decision to change came as a shock. The "New American College" so strongly advocated by both practitioners and theorists in education seems now unlikely to achieve the magnificent growth predicted for it.

THE TWO-YEAR COLLEGE AND SECONDARY EDUCATION

The battle of descriptive terms goes on. Junior college administrators in general, hoping to identify their institutions in the public mind with higher education, and pointing to the fact that their work is on the collegiate level and acceptable as transfer credit at most universities, resist the efforts to include the junior college as a part of secondary education. Others believe that the freshman and sophomore years are not logically a part of college or university work. If all senior colleges and universities would eliminate the freshman and sophomore years from their programs and admit students at the junior level only, the situation might be clarified. But this is not likely to occur. All evidence points toward continuation of the four-year program in the liberal arts colleges, although such colleges will undoubtedly accept many transfer students in the junior year. The present confusion of terms, then, will probably be perpetuated unless a special descriptive term can be substituted which will prove acceptable to everyone.

Eells proposed rather lukewarmly the use of "collegiate education" to describe the first two years of college and "university" or "higher" education to designate everything beyond the sophomore level. This idea, as we have already seen, he derived from William Rainey Harper's division of the program at the University of Chicago. Stoddard suggested "tertiary education" as a compromise term to cover the junior college program,[12] but no one seems to have adopted the suggestion.

To be realistic, we must recognize all such terms as largely arbitrary. The junior college movement will continue to grow regardless of its classification as secondary education, higher education, or something else. Now that "community college" is coming into vogue as the name for a particular kind of institution, the term "junior college" itself may be in danger. For the time being, however, it might be well to lay aside all arguments over terms and speak simply of "junior college education," keeping in mind that "junior college" has for half a century served adequately as the generic name for this unique American contribution to educational progress.

PRESENT FUNCTIONS OF TWO-YEAR COLLEGES

In dealing with purposes and functions of the two-year college, it is essential to remember that all these institutions are not alike.

---

[12] George D. Stoddard, *Tertiary Education*, Harvard University Press, 1944.

Far from it. Among no other group of educational institutions will so much variety be found as among junior and community colleges. One institution may be established exclusively for technological training; another may offer general cultural education only. In the emerging form of two-year institution which we call the community college, however, there seems to be a fairly unanimous agreement as to the major purpose—that of providing whatever educational services are needed in a particular community. And it is this philosophy of the community-serving institution of higher learning which appears likely to affect the educational pattern in the United States most profoundly during the next few decades.

EQUALIZING OPPORTUNITY

Without much question, the democratization of higher education ranks as the single most significant purpose or function of the two-year college. Very simply, this entails the provision of better opportunities for more students to enter collegiate courses of study. Basically the problem or barrier which this type of institution attempts to overcome is one of finances. By saving money for the student both on tuition costs and, especially in the local community college, on the cost of room and board in a dormitory, the new institution makes it possible for some students to attend college who might not otherwise be able to do so. Since the average young person is more likely to enter a college near home than one at a distance, convenience of location plays a vital role in this function of democratizing higher education. Even the student who has decided upon four years of college or more can benefit from the fact that money saved on the first two years of study can be used in financing his later, more expensive years of education. He will insure his chances of advancing higher on the educational ladder by reason of his financial savings in the freshman and sophomore years.

Since it is evident, as the President's Commission on Higher Education emphasizes in its report, that lack of money constitutes the principal barrier to educational opportunity, the community college movement stands in a position of real leadership in the battle to equalize this opportunity for all citizens. "Low family income, together with the rising costs of education, constitutes an almost impossible barrier to college education for many young people. . . . Nor are tuition costs the whole of it. There are not enough colleges and universities in the country, and they are not distributed evenly enough to bring them within reach of all young people. Relatively few students can attend college in their home communities. So to the expense of a college education for most youth must be added transportation and living costs—by no means a small item."[13] A large part of the solution to this problem, says the Commission, will come through the establishment of a great many more community colleges.

Who Should Attend College?   Appraising the talent of America's young people, the President's Commission declares that at least 49 percent of our citizens have the mental ability to profit by 14 years of schooling, while not less than 32 percent seem capable of succeeding in advanced liberal arts or professional education.[14] This amounts to double or three times the number who actually attend college at the present time.

Furthermore, the Commission states, the nation as a whole desperately requires a greatly increased number of college-trained persons for the successful conduct of its affairs and the maintenance of its economic position. Thus both individual needs and the basic needs of the country demand expanding opportunities for tuition-free education.

The democratization of higher education, through its capacity to lower economic barriers and the barrier of location, then, must be regarded as the most vital purpose or function which the community college performs.

COMMUNITY SERVICE

A second essential function, and one of which we have only recently become widely conscious, is that of community service. A

---

[13] *Higher Education for American Democracy, op. cit.,* I, 28.
[14] *Ibid.,* I, 41.

community-serving institution ought to be one in which the students are recruited largely from the local area. When this is true, the curriculum can be planned not upon the basis of a fixed pattern imposed by tradition or by abstract educational theory but upon the basis of the students' demonstrable needs.

The President's Commission believes that a restricted curriculum, one influenced by tradition and aimed at the needs of only one type of student, presents another significant barrier to educational opportunity. Most colleges, in other words, try to be like other colleges. "Traditionally," says the Commission, "the colleges have sifted out as their special clientele persons possessing verbal aptitudes and a capacity for grasping abstractions. But many other aptitudes—such as social sensitivity and versatility, artistic ability, motor skill and dexterity, and mechanical aptitude and ingenuity—also should be cultivated in a society depending, as ours does, on the minute division of labor and at the same time upon the orchestration of an enormous variety of talents."[15]

Community service may, of course, involve activities in addition to the curriculum. The true community college becomes an integral part of the social and intellectual life of its locality. Through lectures, musical programs, community surveys, informal study groups, cooperation with employers and placement agencies, donation of its facilities for civic functions, and a hundred similar methods, the institution raises the cultural, social, and economic level of its town or district.

Yet its most potent influence for good lies in the curriculum itself. Here the community college makes the greatest contribution to society's welfare by searching out and undertaking the kind of instruction that will be socially and intellectually profitable for the students whom it serves. To use an extreme example, if courses in bricklaying are demanded, the community college will not hesitate to offer them; on the other hand, it may decide that what its area needs is a program in the Great Books. Both offerings fall within the province of the community-serving institution. The only really

[15] *Ibid.*, I, 32.

important consideration for such a college must be the actual educational requirements of its community. Thus each one of these institutions, because of differences in communities, may be in some respects different from all the others.

The ideal of community service liberalizes, in the broadest sense, the curriculum which can be offered.

VOCATIONAL TRAINING FOR THE SEMIPROFESSIONS

Because the traditional college has made little effort to supply the kind of training which is useful with respect to the semiprofessional occupations, this necessary function falls logically to the junior and community college. This constitutes a third vital purpose for which these institutions are organized.

Most young people cannot be trained for the semiprofessions in high school. An additional two years of special training can give them the preparation and background required. Its ability and willingness to provide such preparation account in very large part for the present success and popularity of the two-year college. As previously stated, education of this kind, while specialized and aimed at a vocational objective, should include generous amounts of liberal arts course work which will aid the student in improving himself socially, culturally, and spiritually as well as vocationally; and it should leave the door open for further educational advancement if the student wishes it.

ADULT EDUCATION

Perhaps no institution of higher learning is better suited than the community college for the development of effective adult education. As a community-centered institution, it must be concerned with the needs of the local constituency. Its program does not end with an associate degree for the 20-year-old, nor its daily schedule at four o'clock in the afternoon.

If a school or college really intends to serve its community, it must be ready to meet every type of educational need that can be detected. This invariably includes those of the adult student. Since most people numbered in this classification earn their living at full-time jobs, adult classes usually are conducted in the late afternoon and evening. There is a rich opportunity here, fully in keeping with our American ideals of continuing education, for community service of the very finest kind.

GUIDANCE AND REHABILITATION

While guidance, as we have already said, ought not to be regarded as an exclusive function of the junior and community college but should be a distinguishing feature of every worth-while educational institution, perhaps a special kind of guidance program should be included among the purposes which we are discussing. This is the academic rehabilitation of students with scholastic deficiencies.

The tradition of selectivity in many of the older colleges prevents the admission of students with questionable records. The motive is a sound one, for very often such a college maintains a limited enrollment and can produce better work with selected students. Yet a considerable number of young people, because of factors other than mental ability, do poorly in the secondary school. Sometimes they begin to show signs of improvement as they near maturity. The tendency of tradition-bound educators, however, has been to think of them as "not college material." For such young people there has always been a place in the junior college. Often, with proper guidance and some remedial studies, they turn into excellent scholars and go on into the universities and professional schools.

As our techniques of understanding adolescence and of detecting latent abilities advance, this function may become obsolete and ultimately vanish. For the time-being it remains important. The junior college clearly has done much toward breaking down the undemocratic notion that a student who has made poor use of his previous educational opportunities deserves no second chance.

SUMMARY OF PURPOSES

The philosophy of the modern two-year college, while there

are wide variations among the specific programs, mainly centers around: (1) the democratization of higher education through the extension of greater opportunity to all youth; (2) community service; (3) vocational training for the semiprofessions; (4) more effective adult education; and (5) guidance and rehabilitation. The so-called preparatory or transfer function simply amounts to increasing the number of convenient locations in which freshman and sophomore collegiate courses are made available, and we may therefore include it in the democratizing function. The terminal function, if we agree with our basic American concepts in relation to the values of education, has no place on our list, unless we mean by it chiefly vocational training for the semiprofessions. Termination in our American system is a misnomer. As an undercurrent running through all these vital purposes we may recognize still another: the identification of the junior and community college as an institution devoted not to scholarly investigation and research (as are the universities) but rather to sound and meaningful teaching directed at the production of well-informed, competent citizens of a democratic nation.

IV

Students in the Two-Year College

EVEN such an astute and well-informed observer of the American educational scene as James Bryant Conant seems to think of the two-year college primarily as an institution for students who do not have sufficient ability to "make the grade" at regular four-year colleges. This is a basic misconception which might in the future do much harm to the development of junior and community college programs.

A misconception of this kind seems to arise from two natural but wholly mistaken attitudes on the part of some American educators. The first of these, unfortunately, is pure snobbery—the snobbery of the respected, long-established institution of learning toward the young upstart which has dared to assume some of the older college's functions. Time and the successful products of the junior college have almost, though not entirely, negated this point of view. The other attitude seems far more logical but is equally mistaken. This is the idea that every person should have as much education as his mental ability will permit him to acquire and that those who, for one reason or another, abandon their college careers before completion of the senior year necessarily indicate thereby their lack of real fitness for study.

One has only to look briefly at the records of successful men in the recent history of the United States to recognize the fact that outstanding achievement is possible even without a college education. Thomas Edison, often spoken of as one of the greatest Americans of all time, did not attend college and had little desire to do so. Hundreds of other examples might be cited. This is not, of course, to belittle the importance of college work or in any way to suggest that higher education may not be worth-while. Far from it. The point is that other factors besides mental ability help to determine whether a young person can and should enter college. The young person may have great mental capacity but no desire or need for what college can offer him, and attending college might even be a complete waste of time for him. We have learned from psychological studies that the emotional make-up of an individual, as well as his environmental influences, may have quite as much effect upon his actions as the quality of his brain matter.

MENTAL ABILITY OF JUNIOR COLLEGE STUDENTS

What is the actual mental ability of students now enrolled in junior colleges? How do these young people compare with students in other types of institutions for higher learning? There is ample evidence showing that junior college students compare very favorably with other students.

The Psychological Examination of the American Council on Education, a test devised by L. L. Thurstone and Thelma Gwinn Thurstone, is one that colleges and universities throughout the United States use constantly in testing the scholastic aptitude of their freshmen. Some interesting and useful figures are provided in the bulletins which accompany the annual editions of this examination. In 1943, for example, the scores achieved by freshmen in four-year colleges, in junior colleges, and in teachers colleges were recorded. The average raw score on the examination for freshmen in the four-year colleges was 107.24. The average raw score for junior college freshmen was 101.80. This would seem to indicate that students admitted into the junior colleges rank, on the average, slightly lower in scholastic aptitude than do students in the four-year colleges. But the raw score for students in teachers colleges for 1943 was only 92.83, considerably below that of the junior college group. At the same time, variations among the different institutions indicated that junior colleges by no means all have the same standards. In some junior colleges the average raw score was as high as 125.53, far above the four-year college mean. In other junior colleges the average score was as low as 77.09. The scores for all four-year colleges in which the tests were given ranged from a high of 129.50 to a low of 32.55, the latter being far lower than the lowest average recorded for any junior college. Scores in the teachers colleges ranged from 115.46 to 40.86.

The scores on this examination did tend to show that the four-year colleges, on the whole, admit more of the students with exceptionally high ability. Scores in the highest quartile among the four-year college people fell between 130 and 139, while those in the highest quartile of the junior college people fell between 120 and 129—a difference of roughly ten points. But scores in the lowest quartile for both groups were exactly the same, falling between 90 and 99. Thus it would seem clear that the average of scholastic aptitude, as measured by the A.C.E. Psychological Examination, is not much lower for junior college freshmen than it is for freshmen in standard four-year colleges and universities. Furthermore, vast variations exist among individual institutions in this respect.

Further evidence showing that junior college students are not inferior to other college students is provided by the records of those who transfer to four-year colleges as juniors after graduation from a two-year institution. DeRidder, summarizing the statistics compiled by Congdon, Eells, Sammartino, and Pendorf, discovered that junior college transfer students actually demonstrate marked superiority over comparable groups of students who have entered four-year colleges and universities as freshmen.[1] Eells found that even the students who had graduated from the so-called terminal courses

[1] Lawrence M. DeRidder, "Comparative Scholastic Achievement of Native and Transfer Students," *Junior College Journal*, XXII (October, 1951), 83.

(supposedly nontransferable) in junior colleges did well in later college and university work. Of 1,177 students transferring from terminal courses, Eells reported that 46 percent succeeded in obtaining better than average grades in the university, and only 16 percent received grades below average.[2]

Such clear evidence as this would seem to indicate that the two-year college is not merely a place to send students with insufficient ability to succeed in the work of the four-year college, and the sooner we can eliminate this mistaken idea from our thoughts the better it will be for American education. Yet we must also avoid going to the opposite extreme and assuming that the two-year institution is actually a *superior* choice for the average college freshman. If we assume this, we are equally mistaken. For the student who is absolutely certain that he desires four years of college or more, the standard four-year program still would seem to be the correct choice. Yet for many students the junior college is preferable.

TYPES OF TWO-YEAR STUDENTS

Many students are what one might call "two-year students." This does not imply any lack of ability or ambition. The student may simply be impatient for independence and thus prefer to enter as quickly as possible upon his career. He may actually be more mature in many ways than the usual high school graduate. Such a person will find the two-year college exactly the kind of educational institution suited to his individual needs. He commits himself to only two years of study. Should his ideas change during these two years, he has not in any way handicapped himself with regard to further education. The door is still open for him. On the other hand, should he continue of the same opinion and remain in college for no more than two years, he will have completed a recognizable unit of study. He will not have experienced the frustration of having to drop out

[2] Walter Crosby Eells, "Success of Transferring Graduates of Junior College Terminal Curricula," *American Association of Collegiate Registrars Journal,* XVIII (July, 1943), 372–398.

in the middle of a four-year program. The two-year program has been planned as an integrated unit, and the student may even have acquired an associate degree as proof of success.

Again, the student may be one who plans to enter one of the occupations for which the two-year college offers preparation. He is not likely to find a program to meet this need in the standard four-year college. Katz and Allport some years ago ascertained that the principal reasons impelling students to enter college and remain there are, first, that of preparing for a particular vocation and, secondly, that of general improvement in culture and ideals. According to their calculations fully 73 percent of college students declare the vocational goal to be the most important reason for attending college.[3] If the results of such a study can be accepted, they explain the special appeal of the two-year institution to the young person who has set his sights on one of the semiprofessional occupations. For such a student the junior college must be regarded as distinctly preferable to the four-year college.

Another type of student for whom the two-year college offers a particular advantage is the person who has not yet made up his mind regarding future plans. Two years of an exploratory nature, especially if the college provides expert counseling and guidance, may be just what such a student needs in planning his career. Instead of remaining entirely out of education, he spends two years furthering his training and discovering his aptitudes. At the end of this time he will usually be ready to decide whether he should go on to the university or professional school or terminate his formal education entirely. In either case, he has lost no valuable time.

If there is a two-year community college in his home town, a student may wish to attend it simply to save money. Regardless of whether he desires two years of college or a great deal more, the question of cost can be a very important consideration for the average young American. This point is much emphasized in the

[3] Daniel Katz and Floyd Henry Allport, *Students' Attitudes*, The Craftsman Press, 1931.

report of the President's Commission on Higher Education. In fact, the Commission believes that lack of money is the chief barrier to further education for most of our young people. It also believes that community colleges ought to be established in all areas not already served by local collegiate institutions. In time it may be customary for a student to complete 14 grades of school in his local district before entering the university or professional school. If a sufficient number of two-year community colleges were established and if other states besides Arizona, California, Kansas, and Mississippi would banish tuition fees in these institutions, there seems little question that such a situation would rapidly develop. This may or may not be the ideal arrangement. In the minds of many educators, however, it looks like the inevitable pattern of the future.

As we have seen, the student who is relatively immature when he graduates from the twelfth grade may profit from attendance at a local junior or community college. Also, the student who has been studying in a very large high school may prefer to enroll in a small college (and many junior colleges have remained quite small) rather than going to a large state university. By doing so he may receive more personal attention from the faculty and greater opportunity to develop his personality and social abilities. The same advantage, of course, might be obtained in a small four-year college.

In general, then, we may say that the student who should attend the two-year college is definitely not the student with inferior ability. He is, instead, (1) the student who, for any reason, does not wish to commit himself immediately to more than two years of collegiate education; (2) the student who plans to enter one of the semiprofessions; (3) the student who has not yet made up his mind with regard to his future plans; (4) the student who cannot afford to attend college away from home or who wishes to save money for his later education; or (5) the student who still is relatively immature and who for that reason should live at home for another two years. There are other types of young people for whom the junior college is beneficial, but these five are the main groups.

RECRUITMENT OF STUDENTS

One of the sadder aspects of higher education is the disproportionately large amount of effort which many institutions put into the recruitment of students. This effort, unfortunately, is not confined merely to the recruiting of good athletes but is encouraged as a general policy. It seems to be based upon the false premise that mere size is a measure of success.

If education is a service and not a commercial product, there would seem to be no reason to spend money and time in recruiting students. Yet formidable amounts are expended each year for no other purpose than to secure more and more students, and the money and time spent in this way must be deducted from the educational services of the institution. If legislatures and other sources of educational funds were to become aware of the huge loss which occurs as the result of investments in advertising activities rather than in constructive educational work, there seems little doubt that steps would be taken at once to correct this abuse of public trust.

Yet junior colleges, like other institutions, appear to believe that student recruiting is essential for various reasons. For the public junior college, the number of students enrolled may affect the amount of money appropriated by the district board or the legislature. Thus there is an incentive for the administration to gather together as large a student body as possible in order to secure larger funds for operation. This develops a vicious cycle. More students require more money, which in turn is used as a means of attracting more students, and so on *ad infinitum*. Until there is emphasis upon quality rather than mere quantity, the urge to recruit constantly growing numbers presents a serious danger to all higher education. In a private junior college, in which over 80 percent of operating funds may be derived from student fees, the same incentive to obtain larger amounts of money for conducting the institution's work tends to place emphasis upon student-recruiting efforts.

Too many institutions of higher learning appear to compete with other colleges. While a certain amount of competition may stimulate improvement in the educational program, it should be competition aimed at producing a better product. Instead, much of the competitive spirit between colleges makes itself apparent in the search for students. College representatives visit high schools and talk with prospective students. If the object is merely to enroll the student rather than to counsel him and to appraise his aptitude, this procedure may be detrimental and unfair to the student.

Obviously the two-year college which draws nearly all its new students from the immediate neighorhood has little need to advertise its wares. Local students will know the institution and be in a good position to judge its effectiveness. Junior colleges which draw from a wider area, however, have a more difficult problem in making their services known. In their case an extensive public relations program would appear to be justified. But public relations does not mean the same thing as recruiting. The recruiting of students through paid advertising, institutional representatives who visit prospective students and their parents as out-and-out salesmen, scholarships offered not on the basis of need but as a special inducement to enroll (especially when funds for scholarships of this kind come from the general budget and are therefore paid for largely by the other students), paid bands and other performers, and similar practices can hardly be justified from the point of view of educational service.

The efforts of every two-year college (and this is true for all other educational institutions as well) ought to be directed at providing a program of the highest quality and usefulness for whatever constituency is being served. Only those applicants for admission who can definitely profit by the program should be encouraged to enroll. In general, higher education would undoubtedly benefit if it were to abandon present recruiting practices, which, after all, fail to consider the welfare of the student and are concerned only with the welfare of the administration. In addition to planning a program which will meet the needs of the student body, the college ought to see that the student body enrolled actually is one for which the particular program of the institution is fitted. Any other approach to the matter must needs be dishonest.

PUBLIC RELATIONS

As pointed out above, recruiting and public relations are different things. Every college has the responsibility to report regularly to its constituency. The public has the right to know what a college is doing, what its present status is, and what problems it faces. Education in the United States today is a public service rather than an individual profit-making enterprise. For this reason the public should have an honest report of what is going on in institutions.

The principal agency of public relations is, of course, the official bulletin describing courses, fees, and policies of a college. In addition to the catalogue issue of the bulletin, many institutions publish picture books or other items of information which describe the kind of work and atmosphere which the prospective student may expect on the campus. If these are presented as honest announcements rather than as commercialized advertising matter, there can be no objection to such items. Public relations entails the dissemination of *information*. When information is dishonest, however, either because it creates a false impression or because it makes unjustified claims, it ceases to be worthy of an educational organization. It should be ruled out by any respectable college.

A news bureau also is useful in the dissemination of information about an institution's work and problems. It should be operated as a means of distributing news and not merely as an advertising bureau. The soap or cigarette company may increase its total sales and its profits by an effective campaign of advertising and propaganda. The public expects a certain amount of exaggeration and artificialty in this kind of activity. But an educational institution must guard against this type of approach to the news-dispensing responsibility. A college must remember its obligation to serve the public, which does not include the right to profit at the expense of the public.

The annual report of the president, a publication which nearly all reputable institutions of higher learning publish, ought to be considered an essential factor in public relations. Again, this is not an advertising item, and any effort to make it one cannot be other than dishonest. It should be a frank and complete report of the operations during a given year, with a full statement of the financial transactions of the college. Every junior college president, if not already required to submit such a report, should accept the duty to do so.

The major item of good public relations is an effective educational program. This entails knowing thoroughly the constituency to be served, planning the curriculum with care, selecting the best possible staff and faculty, maintaining financial stability, and directing the efforts of the staff and faculty toward a common goal. The institution in which this kind of situation can be found hardly needs a special public relations program. Unless it is a very new or a remotely located college, it certainly needs no expensive plan of recruiting students. On the whole, that institution is best which can spend the most on educational service without wasting money on extraneous activities.

In selecting a junior college, the student might well keep such questions in mind. He may be able to judge from the approach made by the institution whether it is trying to sell him admission by means of high-pressure salesmanship or whether it is really concerned about his educational welfare. Since not all two-year colleges are alike any more than all four-year colleges are alike, it is wise for the student to take special pains in learning about the actual services provided by the institution in which he plans to study.

Founders and administrators of present and future two-year colleges might also do well to keep such questions in mind while settling upon policies for their institutions. Merely adding to the number of our colleges will not solve America's educational problems. One of our aims appear to be that of providing college opportunities for more students. Undoubtedly this aim is an extremely important one for American education. As we strive to achieve it, however, we must keep in mind that we must have not merely quantity but quality as well.

V

General and Vocational Education

THE descriptions of the two-year college which have been given and the discussions which have been presented regarding the services they render and the students they serve has no doubt made abundantly clear the tremendous amount of institutional variety that exists in the junior college movement. This variety has come both from the diversity of the roots from which the modern two-year college has grown and from the attempts made by individual institutions to meet the educational needs of particular communities.

Because junior and community colleges developed out of so many different sources (*e.g.*, academies, high schools, technical schools, agricultural schools, evening schools, and commercial schools) and because they have been established in communities widely different from one another in their economic and sociological characteristics, this tendency toward great variety has long been one of the chief distinguishing features of the movement. Within the past few years, however, a change in the direction of greater unity with respect to certain phases of the curriculum has appeared. This came about mainly through an emphasis upon the kind of program we are now calling "general education."

The Harvard Committee on the Objectives of General Education in a Free Society, in its excellent and much quoted report, makes a distinction between two types of educational experience. "The term, general education," explains this report, "is . . . used to indicate that part of a student's whole education which looks first of all to his life as a responsible human being and citizen; while the term, special education, indicates that part which looks to the student's competence in some occupation." [1] Upon these definitions most educators would agree. They would probably agree also that in a democratic society each of these aspects of education has an important place and that our schools must give attention to both phases.

GENERAL EDUCATION

For some centuries that portion or type of education which consists of intellectual disciplines rather than of training for a vocation was known, at least on the collegiate level, as the liberal arts. Historically this term goes back to the classical age of Greece, when only the free man, or *liberus* in the Latin, had the privilege of being educated for citizenship. He learned those arts in which the free man was expected to be accomplished. By tradition, then, this phase of education has been associated both with leisure (as opposed to purely vocational) activities and with specific intellectual pursuits. During the Middle Ages the liberal arts were formalized into the so-called *trivium* (grammar, logic, and rhetoric) and *quadrivium* (arithmetic, geometry, astronomy, and music). The liberal arts have since been regarded variously as training for the life of a gentleman, as the foundation for later professional schooling, or as preparation for effective citizenship. While opinions as to the purpose of these studies have changed somewhat from time to time, and while the subject matter included under the term has been extended and amplified over the years (as when courses in the modern sciences were added late in the nineteenth century), until very recent years collegiate programs in the liberal arts have

[1] The Harvard Committee on the Objectives of General Education in a Free Society, *General Education in a Free Society*, Harvard University Press, 1946, p. 51.

been fairly well standardized as to content. Now, however, changes have occurred which would appear to justify substituting for the liberal arts the term "general education."

Colleges and universities today are just as concerned as ever with the problem of introducing the student to a generous and broad sampling of every major field of human knowledge. But more than in the past today's educators wish to make this process a thoroughly integrated educational experience. Three principal evils were discovered in the standard liberal arts program. First, the subject matter was being taught for its own sake rather than for what it might mean in the life of the student. Secondly, every subject was taught as if it were an isolated body of knowledge with no relation to any other subject. Thirdly, classes were taught as if every student were a specialist in the subject. The subject matter was presented largely as preparation for further work in the same department. These evils—or supposed evils—led the colleges to attempt a reform in the liberal arts curriculum, and it is this reform which has become known as general education.

One of the major evidences of the reform has been a broadening of the subject matter offered in the freshman and sophomore years of college. For example, it was long customary in the traditional curriculum of the liberal arts college to require every student to take at least one course in a laboratory science. It might be biology, chemistry, or physics. In the modern collegiate program of general studies, on the other hand, it is more usual to give the student a much broader introduction to scientific facts and methods through such courses as the Survey of Biological Sciences and the Survey of Physical Sciences. The former of these ordinarily consists of a combination of botany, zoölogy, anthropology and the like; the latter of the most important aspects of astronomy, chemistry, geology, physics, and so on. Such courses, while not concentrated upon any one department of scientific knowledge as intensively as those formerly given, are intended to give the student a general and well-integrated acquaintance with science as a whole, and to demonstrate the value of this knowledge in the life of an intelligent citizen.

College professors, because of their training and their strong but specialized interest in a single narrow field of knowledge, are inclined to teach every subject as if the students were expecting to become specialists in the same field. To a certain extent every teacher tries to remake students in his own image. General education represents a reaction against this tendency toward specialization. It seeks to encourage educational experiences along broader lines, to foster an acquaintance by the student with many areas of knowledge.

What place has the study of ancient history in the life of the educated American citizen? If one searches for the answer, he may soon uncover adequate reasons for devoting time to the subject. But is knowledge merely of the *facts* of ancient history what makes the study valuable to a student? The proponents of general education say that it is not. They believe that the teacher must somehow relate the facts of ancient history to the student's twentieth-century life. Furthermore, while studying the history of ancient civilizations, why not study art and literature and politics and sociology and science and a hundred other branches of human knowledge? Why confine the investigation to the dates of important battles and the reigns of particular kings, as historians have in courses of the past? By using the approach of modern general education, the student may memorize fewer details, but he will have a better grasp of relationships among the different subjects. Better still, he may see how the various kinds of knowledge affect his own life.

AIMS OF GENERAL EDUCATION

Perhaps the actual aims of general education are not much different from those claimed for the liberal arts. The Harvard Committee has declared that general education is ordinarily understood to be aimed at conveying knowledge which is useful to the student in his personal, social, and civic development. It is intended to assist him in becoming a well-informed and cultured person, a well-adjusted member of society, and an effective citizen.

Educators believe that these aims can be achieved by exposure to several foundation courses in the earlier years of college that provide a general survey of the essential fields of learning; these fields are sometimes classified as communication, the humanities, science, and the social studies. Communication involves the use of language in reading, listening, speaking, and writing. The humanities ordinarily include the studies aimed at personal self-realization through knowledge of art, literature, music, and philosophy. Science covers all areas of scientific activity. The social studies encompass economics, history, sociology, and related subjects. To these might be added a fifth area, that of health and recreation.

Another way of describing this matter is to say that general education concerns itself with the study of man in relation to his physical world, man in relation to society, and man in relation to the esthetic and spiritual aspects of his universe.

All this brings up the age-old question of what actually constitutes the well-educated person. There would seem to be a substantial amount of agreement about the characteristics of general competence and culture but considerable disagreement as to how the desired results may best be achieved. The well-educated individual, most people would say, should have at least the following minimum qualifications: (1) the ability to use effectively language and mathematics, the common tools of communication; (2) a comprehensive and usable knowledge of nature and science; (3) an understanding of human society and its development; (4) acquaintance with and appreciation for the fine arts; (5) ethically sound attitudes toward his fellow men; (6) deep loyalty to the worth-while institutions of contemporary society; and (7) confidence in man's capacity for improving his world.[2] Such attitudes, knowledge, and skills are commonly regarded as the objectives of general education in the modern college and university. That similar objectives may also be considered important at every level of education needs hardly to be added.

[2] For a more detailed list, see George A. Coe, *What Ails Our Youth?* Scribner, 1925, pp. 39–41.

GENERAL EDUCATION AND THE JUNIOR COLLEGE

Having summarized briefly the nature and aims of general education as we now understand them, we next approach the problem of how general education fits into the program of the junior and community college. There are two principal aspects of this question.

One aspect pertains to the fact that junior colleges actually were among the first collegiate institutions in America to introduce the type of course we now associate with general education into their programs of study. Such courses as those in the humanities, surveys of science, and surveys of the social studies were being offered by junior colleges a few decades ago (especially in the 1930's), but were looked upon with suspicion by the standard four-year institutions. In fact, many junior college graduates who sought admission as transfer students to the senior colleges were denied credit for such courses. After a few years, however, when interest in general education had spread throughout the collegiate world, an increasing number of institutions of every kind began to introduce identical courses into their own programs. Such courses are now fairly widespread and to a certain degree may be regarded as one of the distinct contributions of the junior college.

A second aspect is the growing tendency to regard the fourteenth grade (or the sophomore year of college) as the logical terminating point for all general education. In one sense, this may be a reversion to the ideas of Tappan and others who hoped that our secondary schools would become like the German *Gymnasium*. In another sense, it represents the changing concept of the American people with regard to the amount of education believed desirable for our youth. At one period in our history we thought it sufficient if a majority of our children received nothing more than elementary schooling. In the years following World War I we came to expect most students to complete at least the second year of the high school. Now we are beginning to consider 12 to 14 grades of schooling as the birthright and, indeed, the necessary minimum of instruction for nearly everyone. The growing complexity of our industrialized civilization, of course, has made a longer span of education appear to be more and more essential to effective living.

For many modern educators, then, the junior college constitutes the logical capstone of general education—that is, the final stage in the intelligent person's preparation for useful citizenship. When this general part of his education has been completed, it is assumed that the student will be ready for specialization in the field of his particular interest or occupational need. He may then continue his training in a technical or professional school; he may pursue a special interest in one of the areas of knowledge with which he has become acquainted; or he may enter directly into his vocation.

Since general education is aimed primarily at the objective of increasing the student's understanding of himself and his world as well as at satisfactory adjustment through desirable attitudes, it might be called, perhaps even more appropriately, "developmental education." In its broadest sense, it seeks to guarantee an educational environment leading to the student's greatest possible self-development and self-realization and his highest usefulness as a citizen and member of society.

THE TERMINATION OF GENERAL EDUCATION

The objection may be raised that, far from completing 14 grades of school, many students never get beyond the tenth grade. Indeed, it is at this point that the diversification of study programs chiefly begins. In our high schools a boy or girl decides at about this time, if not earlier, whether to take a college preparatory course, whether to prepare for apprenticeship in one of the trades, or whether to enter secretarial training. As a matter of fact, once they have reached the age set by law, large numbers of students drop out of school entirely at the end of the tenth grade. The question may be raised, therefore, whether the tenth grade rather than the fourteenth may not be regarded most logically as the terminal point of general education.

Theories as to when general education should end are probably based not so much upon the present situation as upon what we envision for the future. In the opinion of many leading educators, the time will come eventually when the majority of our students will complete the work of the junior college. For the moment, it is true, this can be thought of only as a remote possibility.

Under conditions which will no doubt prevail for some time to come, however, it seems clear that junior and community colleges, if they wish to serve the needs of youth in their own communities, cannot confine their offerings, except in unusual circumstances, to general education alone. For some students general education may end at the eighth grade, for others at the tenth, for still others at the twelfth, and so on. Thus general education is a matter which concerns not one but nearly every level of our educational system. While we may agree that the curriculum should be substantially the same for all children in the elementary grades, we do not agree that it should continue to remain unified throughout the junior and senior high school grades. In present practice, a branching out into diversified programs of study begins during these latter years of the system. Whether general education should continue for all students up through the twelfth or fourteenth grade is left for future educators to decide.[3] What should be kept in mind is the fact that the concept of general education as a part of the collegiate program has been a very recent innovation in our educational history.

GENERAL EDUCATION AS A JUNIOR COLLEGE PROGRAM

Some junior colleges operate on the principle of general education as a sole objective. As we have already stated, this cannot very well be true of those institutions which are trying to serve the varying needs of a particular community. It is true, however, of some private junior colleges not primarily concerned with community service.

At Pine Manor Junior College in Wellesley, Massachusetts, for example, the entire course of study consists of a two-year program of general education. Some election of courses in fields of the student's own interest is permitted, though none of these aims at a vocational objective. All students take four basic required subjects:

[3] Earl J. McGrath *et al., Toward General Education,* Macmillan, 1948, p. 7.

(1) a general course in English (Introduction to Writing), which must be taken during the freshman year; (2) a survey course in the humanities (Our Cultural Heritage), which comes during the second year; (3) a course in history (The United States in a World Setting); and (4) a course in science (Introduction to Science). Elective subjects are available in the departments of art, Bible, chemistry, economics, English, French, German, history, mathematics, music, physical education, physiology, psychology, sociology, Spanish, and speech. The entire curriculum at Pine Manor, according to a recent catalog description, "is based on the belief that courses should be developed as integral parts of a body of knowledge essential to personal competence and intelligent community living." It may be added that this institution is not in any sense a community college but a privately controlled junior college for women which has a student body of a more or less homogeneous type from all parts of the United States.

The College of General Education at Boston University (see pp. 28–29) attempts to achieve what it calls the "total integration" of its two-year academic program. Its aim, according to official public statements, "is to unify [all] courses of instruction so that they constitute, in effect, one single course, in which the material drawn from *all fields* is synchronized and correlated at every feasible point to emphasize significant relationships and to promote meaningful generalizations, consistent knowledgeable attitudes, and critical appreciation."

This institution regards its program of general education primarily as preparation for later specialization, or at least as a suitable foundation for it. Guidance intended to assist the student in arriving at a satisfactory life goal is made a part of general education. On the theory that, without proper guidance, nearly half of our college graduates enter occupations for which their college training did not prepare them, the program seeks to put off any decision as to a final field of specialization until general education has been completed. The curriculum includes materials from five major areas of human interest, "taught without reference to the lines of demarkation which normally set off one subject from another." These fields are natural science (biology, geology, physics, chemistry, and astronomy), human relations (psychology, sociology, and anthropology), English and the humanities (composition, literature, music, and art), political economy (government and economics), and guidance.

"The aim is *fusion* within each of these broad fields, and careful *integration* among all fields. The subject matter of physics, chemistry, and biology thus are fused into the single course in science, and science is correlated in turn with history and government and the social sciences, with English literature and the humanities, and with guidance." So states the official announcement of the college.

The institution describes its plan of instruction as "the problem method," and it regards this method as essential to profitable study in a program of general education. Lectures at the regular class sessions are supplemented by smaller conference meetings, at which the students and faculty discuss and apply the principles and facts making up the subject matter of each course. Actual cases and problems—situations drawn from life—are brought before students in these discussion groups, where they serve the purpose of helping the individuals to arrive at sound personal conclusions.

Neither of the institutions mentioned here maintains that its curriculum is the only type valid for the junior college student, but each believes that its program fits admirably the particular kind of student which it enrolls.

VOCATIONAL EDUCATION

Practically all of our early colleges offered vocational education exclusively. Harvard College, for instance, was organized originally to supply trained clergymen for the colonies. Nowadays, however, we expect professional men and women—ministers, physicians, teachers, engineers, etc.—to be trained at professional schools. This specialized kind of education is no longer considered the function of the typical four-year college.

As we have previously noted, the Harvard Committee defines "special" education as preparation for some specific occupation. We might with equal justice call this type of learning "occupational" or "vocational." The Committee, along with others, has named it "special" education presumably to distinguish it from "general" education. The terms used, of course, are not of primary significance except as they clarify the distinction between two areas of instruction.

Some educators hold the opinion that programs of general education or the liberal arts, because of the broad cultural development and increased power to learn which they supposedly bring about in the student, offer the best possible kind of preparation for any vocation. These educators quote business and industrial executives in declaring that the broadly educated person makes a more satisfactory employee than the person trained specifically for a given job. While impressive arguments may be advanced in support of such a theory, more and more occupational courses continue to be introduced each year into our schools and colleges. If students did not find such training of distinct use in securing remunerative positions, it could hardly have attained its present popularity.

VOCATIONAL EDUCATION IN A TECHNOLOGICAL SOCIETY

A century ago the economy of the United States was still predominantly agricultural, and about two-thirds of our population lived on farms. Today, with rapidly growing industrialization, the major part of our population has been drawn into urban areas, and the former proportions have been reversed. We live in an age of truly spectacular technological growth and change, with an industrialized economy which requires thousands of technically trained workers.

Anderson and Davidson analyzed the distribution of employment in the United States during 1940 as follows: total labor force, approximately 52,000,000; professional and semiprofessional workers, 3,500,000; proprietors, managers, and officials, 9,000,000; clerical and sales personnel, 8,300,000; craftsmen and foremen, 5,900,000; operatives (semiskilled), 9,400,000; protective service workers, 740,000; other service workers, 5,500,000; and unskilled laborers, 8,600,000.[4] The largest occupational group, according to the census figures available to these investigators, consists of those engaged in essentially manual work, ranging from unskilled and farm labor up through the ranks of semiskilled machine-tending operatives in shops and factories, craftsmen, foremen, domestic and service workers, and working farmers. This group, most of whom would not be interested in collegiate education, constituted about 56 percent of our labor force at the time of the study. The second largest group is that of proprietors, managers, and officials, including farm supervisors (over 17 percent). Clerical and sales workers make up another 16 percent; and professional and semiprofessional personnel, under 7 percent.[5]

Between 1870 and 1940, we are told, the number of agricultural workers decreased from nearly half the total American labor force to less than a fifth. The number of those in the purely clerical occupations increased over the same period from 2.5 percent to 10.5 percent, and those in professional services from 2.7 percent to 6.8 percent. Persons engaged in the transportation and communication industries, in commercial trade (including sales), and in public service accounted for only 8.4 percent in 1870 but for 25.9 percent by 1940.[6] These figures indicate in a general way the decreasing relative importance of the agricultural occupations in our present economy and the increasing relative importance of such fields as transportation and communication, clerical occupations, public service, the professions, and commercial trade. Even more significant, perhaps, is the technological complexity which has become characteristic of most of these occupations and the consequent need for workers trained in specialized skills.

[4] H. Dewey Anderson and Percy E. Davidson, *Recent Occupational Trends in American Labor,* Stanford University Press, 1945, p. 115. Figures quoted are in round numbers only.

[5] *Ibid.,* pp. 9–10.

[6] H. Dewey Anderson and Percy E. Davidson, *Occupational Trends in the United States,* Stanford University Press, 1940.

TECHNOLOGY AND THE JUNIOR COLLEGE

Since the liberal arts college no longer considers vocational or special education as its proper function and since training for the professions (*e.g.*, architecture, dentistry, engineering, law, medicine, teaching, etc.) is now provided by the professional schools, the junior college has been left with responsibility for special education in those fields requiring more training than the high school can give and yet less than that usually required for the recognized professions. As we have seen, these are precisely the fields in which employment has risen in the most noticeable degree during the past three-quarters of a century.

Within the area claimed by the junior college there is tremendous variety. To give some idea of this variety, among the occupations for which training programs may be found in junior colleges today are advertising art, automobile mechanics, aviation, banking, building trades, credit management, drafting, engineering technology, home economics, horology, hotel and restaurant management, insurance, medical laboratory assistantship, real estate, recreational leadership, refrigeration, secretarial work, and so on. The list is by no means exhaustive.

For the most part, students enrolled in programs offering training for the occupations mentioned above intend to complete their formal education in the junior college. Such programs, therefore, are often spoken of as terminal education. We have already discussed reasons why this appears to be a somewhat unhappy term: It implies a closing of the door to further educational opportunity. Most educators who speak of terminal education mean occupational training on the junior college level, though two-year programs of general education, when the student intends to go no further, may also be included.[7]

THE SEMIPROFESSIONS

The areas of employment for which the junior colleges can pre-

[7] Phebe Ward, *Terminal Education in the Junior College,* Harper & Brothers, 1947.

pare their students in a two-year course of study are sometimes referred to as the semiprofessions. In many instances these vocations may be directly related to the recognized professions, as drafting is related to engineering. (It has been estimated that, for each fully trained professional engineer employed by American industry, five or six technicians with less extensive training are needed.) In other instances the same term is used for occupations not connected with the professions in any real sense. It is not uncommon to hear "semi-profession" applied to the work of managers, accountants, clerical workers, and secretaries. Koos once distinguished between the professions and the semiprofessions by stating merely that preparation for the former requires at least four years of college and preparation for the latter only two; at the same time he proposed that clerical and trades training should be limited to the high schools, trade schools, or commercial schools.[8] Koos also recommended to the junior colleges a long list of occupations which he regarded as semiprofessions and as entirely suitable for training programs two years in length. Among them are the following:

Agriculture
Florist
Foreman, truck farm
Forest ranger
Lumber salesman
Manager, butter and cheese factory
Maker, butter, cheese, ice cream
Poultryman
Tester, cow test association
Woods superintendent

Art
Designer, commercial
Designer, costume
Designer, jewelry
Designer, stage
Engraver, jewelry
Engraver, lithography
Engraver, photography
Glass cutter
Glass designer
Glass painter
Illustrator, commercial
Interior decorator
Map-maker

Commercial
Chief clerk
Credit man
Department store buyer
Insurance agent and adjuster
Jobbing, wholesale merchant

[8] Leonard Vincent Koos, *The Junior College,* University of Minnesota Press, 1924, p. 153.

Commercial (Continued)
  Shipping department head
  Statistical clerk
  Storekeeper

Engineering
  Cement tester
  Chemical laboratory worker
  Contractor
  Draftsman, architectural
  Draftsman, mechanical
  Draftsman, mining
  Draftsman, structural
  Electrician
  Inspector
  Superintendent
  Surveyor

Home Economics
  Cafeteria manager
  Dietitian
  Professional shopper

Medical
  Chiropodist
  Dental mechanic
  Masseur
  Nurse
  Pharmacist
  Veterinarian

Miscellaneous
  Musician
  Teacher
  Welfare supervisor

The information upon which Koos based the above list was gathered in 1922 and must, therefore, be considered as no longer strictly up to date; but it offers an idea of the numerous kinds of special education thought appropriate for the junior colleges at a time when the movement was in its formative years.[9]

POPULARITY OF THE VOCATIONAL PROGRAM

It has already been indicated that the opportunities for employment in those occupations lying somewhere between unskilled and semiskilled labor, on the one hand, and the professions, on the other, have increased enormously since 1870, and in all likelihood this trend will continue for some time to come. Technologists for many fields will be needed in the future. This fact already has been recognized by young men and women preparing for careers. As the result, there has been, ever since the junior colleges began their major de-

[9] *Ibid.*, pp. 156–164.

velopment in the 1920's, a fairly steady increase in the proportion of junior college students interested primarily in vocational training.

An additional factor is the tendency for students who might formerly have sought such training in the job itself to seek it now in the two-year institution. Many of these young men and women, because of their lack of interest or specific ability in the purely academic subjects, would probably never be admitted to the standard four-year college. This does not imply that the two-year vocational course of study in such fields as accounting or engineering technology is any less difficult than the first two years of the usual collegiate program. Since it ordinarily includes a large proportion of advanced specialized study, it may, in fact, prove even more difficult. The technical program in the junior college—and this point needs particular emphasis—is not for the student who has less ability than the average college freshman but rather for the student whose *interests* are specialized and who wishes to depart from wholly general education at a comparatively early stage in his educational career. This fact is frequently misunderstood. Educators as well as the public in general often make the mistake of assuming that the length of time devoted to a student's formal education depends entirely upon his intellectual ability. As a matter of actual fact, it should and does depend much more largely upon his basic interests and needs. Many students of outstanding academic ability deliberately select the shorter program in order to enter productive work more quickly.

Transfer from the Vocational Program

It is extremely desirable in our American system of education to make every attempt at keeping open the door to further educational opportunity. Even students who undertake a strictly vocational program in the junior college may ultimately change their minds and decide to continue further college work. A number have done this in the past sufficient to make awareness of the problem unavoidable. Can students who alter their plans in this way manage the upper years of collegiate work successfully?

The meager evidence we have suggests very definitely that they can. At the New Haven Junior College, for example, studies have been made (the most extensive one in 1946) to determine the degree of success of the institution's graduates in their later collegiate careers. Although every one of these graduates had completed a vocational, or "terminal," program with no thought of planning for future transfer, a considerable number (about 15 percent of the total) did achieve satisfactory transfer as juniors and in practically every case performed at least as well as the average college student.[10] Eells previously reported that, although senior colleges in some instances are prejudiced against the "terminal" student as a transferee, those colleges and universities which had accepted this type of student generally found him as well prepared for advanced work as transfer students taking university-parallel courses in the junior college.[11]

On the basis of this and other evidence, we may safely say that academic success in the upper years of college depends more on ability and willingness to learn than upon the precise nature of the program studied in the lower years.

Limitation of the Vocational Areas of the Junior College

The question has often been raised whether such instruction as that in automobile mechanics or the building trades can properly be offered by a collegiate institution. Are such courses actually of "collegiate grade," or should they be relegated because of their intrinsic nature to some other level of our education system?

The rather large group of junior colleges which offer courses of this type would reply firmly that a community-serving institution must offer those programs actually needed by its students. If the community requires training for bookbinders or mechanics, and if no other institution in the locality provides it, then the true community

[10] Jesse P. Bogue (ed.), *American Junior Colleges,* American Council on Education, 1948, p. 7.

[11] Walter Crosby Eells, "Success of Transferring Graduates of Junior College Terminal Curricula," *American Association of Collegiate Registrars Journal,* XVIII (July, 1943), 372–398.

college must undertake the responsibility. Furthermore, they would point out, instruction in such fields can be aimed at a level higher than that sufficient merely for the production of manual skills. Such training can be extended and broadened in a number of directions and should prepare students not solely for basic trades and crafts but for supervisory positions as well. Most junior and community colleges would consider themselves untrue to their function if they did not maintain higher academic standards and cover a wider scope of subject matter than the trade schools. Another way of putting this is to define the aim of junior college vocational courses as the training not of craftsmen but of technologists. The capable technologist understands, besides the fundamental skills and procedures of his vocation, its broader aspects and its place and worth in human society.

Perhaps, however, the primary consideration in determining whether certain courses of study may be accepted as proper for the junior and community college should not be academic tradition but— far more important—sound knowledge of the various types of educational opportunity which will prove really useful to the high school graduates of the community and to the area's economy.

TRENDS IN VOCATIONAL EDUCATION

Within the past few years a number of states, partly as the result of the federal government's example, have made exhaustive studies of their problems and resources with respect to higher education. The state of New York began such a study in 1945 and used its findings as the basis for a reorganized and expanded educational program. One of the most careful and complete surveys of this kind was conducted at about the same time in Minnesota.[12] As part of the Minnesota survey, a committee of prominent educators explored "the need in this state for terminal occupational curricula."

The Minnesota Study. Most of the conclusions reached by the committee studying this problem in Minnesota would no doubt

---

[12] Minnesota Commission on Higher Education, *Higher Education in Minnesota,* University of Minnesota Press, 1950.

apply to similar situations in the other states. The committee learned, for one thing, "that there are many occupations in Minnesota, both agricultural and nonagricultural, for which . . . [two-year] occupational preparatory educational programs at the college level would be feasible." But it also cautioned that too many persons might be prepared in certain vocations of this type unless the schools could keep vigilant contact with the replacement needs of agricultural and industrial employment. "[T]he establishment of a junior college type of occupational preparatory program is justified only if the number of estimated annual replacements is large enough to provide placement opportunities for trainees. . . ." It noted, in addition, that "a close coordination of training programs for different occupational groups" is both possible and highly desirable.

One of the interesting and significant phenomena which the committee observed in the course of its study was the "steady upward trend in the amount of general and occupational education required for vocational competence" in our present century. "The growth of modern scientific knowledge and the rapid technological advances in all vocational fields have accelerated the demand for workers who are not only technically trained but capable of handling tasks that require a high level of judgment and discretion. A growing proportion of our working population, then, will be occupied in jobs that necessitate more technical skills and a broader educational background." These are the conditions which the committee found in the present economic structure of our society.[13]

The committee recommended the establishment of so-called "terminal technical programs" at the post-high-school level throughout the state. The means by which these programs might be set up were carefully and intelligently detailed as follows:

1. Representative committees on a community or regional basis should appraise the facts and agree on recommendations for instituting or enlarging the technical or semiprofessional curriculums.
2. Determination of courses should be on the basis of job opportunities in given communities through conference surveys with employer and

[13] *Ibid.,* pp. 159–160.

employee consultants. The course content for subprofessional and technical training should be checked by qualified persons from the occupational field.

3. Occupational training or vocational education must be specific. Preparation should be for real, not imaginary, jobs. Real learning situations are always patterned after existing conditions in the occupation.

4. Statewide coordination of the regional programs must be maintained. Approval of the State Department of Education in the establishment of new or expanded course offerings should minimize these problems.

5. Vocational education of less than college grade, conducted in the secondary schools, will continue to be necessary for a large number of youth who do not find it possible to take advanced training.

6. Community resources and cooperative work plans providing experiences under actual working conditions should supplement the school program.

7. Teachers and instructors should have occupational competency and occupational standing based on several years of successful employment in their fields. Administrators and supervisors must understand the philosophies and specific nature of vocational and technical education and have a high interest in the success of the program.

8. The learning process needs to provide student participation and experience in terms of related and technical knowledge. Facilities, equipment, and devices used in the learning experience should be real, diversified, and similar to those of the occupation.

9. The entire program should be coordinated continuously with the occupational field by instructors, coordinators, supervisors, and consultants through active contact, placement, and follow-up procedures. The special interests of employers and labor groups should be constantly evaluated concerning the use of the graduate.

10. Course offerings should be limited in keeping with available facilities rather than to attempt to offer a great number of courses with attendant poor results in an overstretched program. Mediocre, low-cost instruction by methods designed to save money at the sacrifice of effective teaching procedures will quickly reflect the inadvisability of attempting offerings unless sufficient funds are available to do a job to high standards.[14]

[14] *Ibid.*, pp. 161–162. The major points in the committee's report are summarized in H. T. Morse and John A. Butler, "Survey of the Need for Terminal Occupational Curriculums," *Higher Education in Minnesota*, pp. 145–163.

Community Surveys. As emphasized by the Minnesota committee, the types of occupational programs needed by various regions or communities can best be determined by means of systematic surveys. Efforts to devise and carry on such occupational surveys are now being made with more and more frequency and effectiveness by the community colleges. While no more than a start in the right direction can be said to have been made, and while techniques of conducting the surveys have not yet been perfected, the future of this development shows considerable promise. An approach to the survey method made at the San Francisco Junior College (now City College of San Francisco), an institution in which nearly 80 percent of the students are normally enrolled in "terminal" courses of study, is described in Miss Ward's *Terminal Education in the Junior College*,[15] an excellent source of information about the present status of special education at the junior college level.

Planning the Curriculum

The danger inherent in too great an enthusiasm toward the development of special education lies, of course, in the possibility of training vocational specialists without a broad understanding of life or a sense of social responsibility. To avoid this danger, it is widely agreed among informed educators that programs of special education in the junior college must contain a general leaven of general education.

An examination of recent catalogues of American community colleges reveals the reassuring fact that most institutions recognize the danger and require, therefore, at least a third to a half of the vocational student's courses to be of a general or cultural nature. Thus nearly every institution insists upon one or more courses in the correct use of written and spoken English. Many require some subject matter to be studied in the fields of the social studies, science, and the humanities. A few also have requirements in psychology or philosophy.

[15] *Op. cit.*, pp. 142–147.

As an example of the way in which general education is arranged in a program of which the major pattern is special education, a typical course of study actually prescribed by a junior college is outlined below. This program is in the field of business administration and seeks to prepare students for positions as department heads, salesmen, junior executives, and the like.

Business Administration Program

First Year		Second Year	
	Sem.		*Sem.*
General Courses:	*Hrs.*	*General Courses:*	*Hrs.*
General English	6	World Literature	6
Intro. to Social Studies	6	Survey of Science	6
Introductory Psychology	6	Physical Education	2
Physical Education	2	*Special Courses:*	
Special Courses:		Marketing and Sales-	
Elementary Accounting	6	manship	6
Business Mathematics	6	Business Law	6
	—	Economic Geography	3
	32	Elective subject	3
			—
			32

This course of study is similar to those found in a large number of junior and community colleges. While titles of courses may vary among the different institutions, and while some junior colleges and some vocational fields allow less time for general education, the aim of combining education for occupational efficiency with education for personal competence and good citizenship is a common one among the vast majority of junior and community colleges.

While general education terminates at different points for different students, its importance during the years covered by the curriculum of the junior college is universally recognized. More and more educators are now thinking of the sophomore year of college (or the fourteenth grade) as the logical place for completion of all general education. As increasing numbers of our young people continue their educational careers beyond the high school, this viewpoint undoubtedly will be strengthened.

Junior and community colleges, however, cannot be concerned exclusively with general education, but must meet the needs of their students for vocational training as well. The specific nature of the vocational programs offered by a particular institution should be determined by careful surveys of the region or community in which the institution is located. For the community college, facts ascertained through the survey method provide a better basis for curriculum planning than does educational tradition.

In planning a program of vocational education in any field, the college must recognize its responsibility to offer something beyond mere training in occupational skills. The graduate of such a program should be an *educated* as well as a *trained* person. To attain this objective, the institution must include a generous portion of broad, cultural subjects in every course of study. Most modern junior and community colleges accept this concept of their function and consciously integrate general education and special education within their various programs.

VI

Coöperative and Adult Education

Two of the many questions faced by the American school system within recent years—questions which the junior and community colleges have made some notable attempts to answer—have been these: How can the industrial and commercial resources of the community be better utilized as a means of supplementing the school shops and laboratories for vocational training? How can educational opportunities be extended more effectively to students in full-time jobs? To answer these questions, the two-year colleges of the United States have experimented in the fields commonly designated as coöperative education and adult education.

The special adaptability of the community-serving institution in dealing with the particular educational needs indicated above has been demonstrated convincingly in many parts of the country and in a variety of forms. Both coöperative and adult education seem to fit remarkably well into the pattern of this type of institution.

COÖPERATIVE EDUCATION

Coöperative or work-study education makes direct use of shops, factories, and community business and governmental offices to further the vocational training of the student. In its most prevalent form, coöperative education consists of alternating periods of class-room study and actual employment. The institution arranges with a local employer to provide the student with a learner's job in which he can develop familiarity with the real conditions of his chosen occupation. Usually such a job is directly related to the special field of study in which the student is enrolled. He may spend from six to ten weeks in regular classroom activities, then a similar amount of time on the job; and he shifts in this way from one phase of his training to another.

PRINCIPLES INVOLVED IN COÖPERATIVE EDUCATION

Two main advantages have been claimed for this type of program. One is that actual work experience, far more than the training received in a school shop or laboratory, soundly and quickly demonstrates to the student the practical applications of his course of study. Another is that it gives the student an opportunity to earn a small income while attending college. If the former constitutes the principal advantage of the plan, it is obvious that the work experience of the student must be in exactly the same academic area as his college major. If, on the other hand, the latter is more important, the amount of money which can be earned becomes the chief consideration.

Most educators who have studied coöperative education extensively praise it as a means of combining theoretical and practical training. The industrial shop or business office becomes, in effect, an outside laboratory for the college, and one in which the student can study under real rather than simulated conditions. Work experience, while valuable in itself, has much less value if it is not closely related to the academic subjects being studied in the classroom. The money earned by a student on the job, most educators assert, is only an agreeable by-product of the system and not one of its intrinsic advantages. As a matter of fact, some institutions which operate coöperative education programs will not permit their students to accept wages for their assigned jobs.

Nevertheless, an examination of junior college catalogues reveals that several institutions try to attract students into coöperative education by pointing to the immediate financial help which it provides. The chance to earn money in a position supplied by the college, these catalogues declare, is an ingredient ordinarily lacking from the regular collegiate program. To the layman, of course, this appeal of the "earn-while-you-learn" slogan may seem sufficient in itself to justify coöperative education. To the informed educator, however, a work-study plan derives its principal attractiveness from the fact that it brings existing community resources to bear on the educational program and enriches the learning process by combining theory and practice in the proper proportions.

Another advantage claimed for coöperative education involves placement after graduation. There can be no doubt that business and industrial firms generally support arrangements of this type with colleges because of the splendid opportunity it gives them to locate and look over potential employees. A significant number of students who enter programs of coöperative education ultimately accept permanent positions with the companies in whose plants their training courses are undertaken.

Development of Coöperative Education

While coöperative education is proving particularly suitable to the two-year vocational programs found in junior and community colleges, institutions of other types have also made use of this training plan. Probably the first college in this country to introduce the plan was the University of Cincinnati, where a coöperative program was initiated in 1906 at the suggestion of Professor (later President) Herman Schneider.

According to a dramatic account written later by one of his colleagues, Professor Schneider conceived the idea of a work-study plan as the result of his dissatisfaction with the inadequacy of school shops and laboratories for the training of engineers. How could practice best be combined with instruction in theory? he asked himself. The account of his discovery goes on to say:

A solution to this vexing problem came to Prof. Herman Schneider in a curious way. One evening as he was walking across the campus of an eastern university where he was teaching, he heard the answer in the blast of a Bessemer furnace at a neighboring steel plant. Instantly the idea appealed to him as perfectly simple and obvious. Here was something better than any conceivable school shop—a million-dollar laboratory, with unlimited possibilities for illustrating the applications of technical theory. In this plant many graduates of this same college would find employment, as others had done before them. Why should they not learn as students to translate their book knowledge into terms of industrial processes? [1]

Like most new ideas in education and other fields, coöperative education was finally attempted and proved successful at the University of Cincinnati only after it had met with considerable skepticism and opposition in academic circles.

Other colleges took up the plan in later years. Noteworthy developments, for example, occurred at Antioch College in Ohio and at Northeastern University in Massachusetts. Coöperative education was not adopted in junior colleges until the 1920's and then only on a small scale; its chief growth came during the 1930's, when the prospect of using it as a means of securing financial support for college careers and of locating permanent jobs (then extremely scarce because of the national economic depression) attracted large numbers of students into this type of training.

It should not be assumed that the movement is now widespread. The work-study plan has actually been tried by only a relatively small minority of the present junior and community colleges. Yet its possibilities for future development appear highly promising. Although, as reported by Miss Ward, only about one percent of all junior college students during 1941–1942 were enrolled in coöperative programs (chiefly in the publicly controlled institutions),[2] expansion of this training plan seems likely as two-year colleges

[1] Clyde William Park, *The Cooperative System of Education,* Bulletin of the United States Bureau of Education, U.S. Government Printing Office, 1916, p. 8. See also Henry H. Armsby, *Cooperative Education in the United States,* Bulletin of the U.S. Office of Education, U.S. Government Printing Office, 1954.

[2] Phebe Ward, *Terminal Education in the Junior College,* Harper & Brothers, 1947, p. 67.

increase their emphasis upon vocational training in the technical occupations.

VALUE OF COÖPERATIVE EDUCATION TO THE JUNIOR COLLEGE AND ITS STUDENTS

According to the analysis presented by Miss Ward and statements made by those junior colleges which have experimented with programs of coöperative education, benefits to the institution result principally from the following facts: (1) students enrolled under the work-study plan tend to drop out of college in proportionately smaller numbers than those taking the regular program; (2) the college is able to accommodate a somewhat larger enrollment of students without increasing the size of its plant or faculty; and (3) the practical nature of the work experience appears to strengthen the student's interest in his class work.

Students, Miss Ward indicates, like the coöperative plan of study because (1) it provides the opportunity to earn an income while attending college; (2) it stimulates academic interest and achievement; (3) it offers a very practical kind of training for the student's chosen vocation; and (4) it opens the way to permanent employment in the future.[3]

We may safely say, however, that the true success of any program of coöperative education depends almost entirely on the care and skill with which the college uses the resources available in its community. While perhaps work experience of any sort has its value for educational purposes, the work-study program should always provide for the highest possible correlation between class work and job. Merely to place the student in a remunerative position is not enough. There must be a definite and clearly understood relationship between the work of the classroom and that of the shop or office. It is educationally not nearly so important whether the student earns wages or a salary while engaged in his outside work as whether he will have sufficient opportunity to apply in practice the

[3] *Ibid.,* pp. 67–68.

theoretical knowledge he is acquiring on the campus. (This is the reason why some institutions, contrary to the more common practice, insist that their students, as learners under the coöperative system, accept no remuneration for their services.) This must not be regarded, however, as an argument in favor of eliminating the student's chance to earn a part of his educational expenses through employment under the coöperative plan. The essential point is that classroom activities and work experience must be coördinated into a constructive and unified educational program if they are to be of the greatest value to the student.

OPERATION OF THE COÖPERATIVE PLAN

Since part of the student's time has to be spent away from the campus, coöperative education usually requires a few more months for completion than the regular course of study. Institutions, therefore, arrange the schedule in such a way that the program either continues during the summer or is extended an extra semester or two. Under the plan, the student must undertake the same academic subjects as other students; his work experience makes an additional claim upon his time.

Groups of students enrolled under the coöperative system ordinarily are divided into two sections. While one section remains on the campus taking course work, the other is distributed throughout the community on training jobs. After a period of time—frequently six to ten weeks, but varying according to the preference of each institution—these groups exchange places. For example, Student A may work for several weeks as a machine operator in a factory; then, while his place at the machine is taken by Student B, his partner under the system, Student A returns to the campus for a period of class instruction. When he again resumes work at the factory, he will be placed on another job in which he can learn some new aspect of the industrial process. Many institutions, it should be stated, prefer the method of half-day alternation, one group of students remaining on the job during the morning, the other taking their places during the afternoon, and so on.

Keeping in close touch with students while they are on the job, helping them to solve the numerous problems which arise out of their employment, and securing reports of individual progress from the employers involves a great amount of skill, careful checking, and sympathetic understanding on the part of the college staff. These functions are normally performed for an institution by a member of the faculty known as a coördinator. Such a person spends most of his time consulting with employers about possible placement opportunities, visiting students on their jobs, and conducting student group sessions at which the problems of the job are discussed. The coordinator may also hold frequent meetings with committees of the leading employers in the community to stimulate their interest in the plan and to work out better methods of industry-college cooperation.

The major stumbling blocks in the path of successful operation of the coöperative plan of technical training seem to be (1) the proper selection and guidance of students who will benefit from the system; (2) location of training opportunities which will be practical and varied enough to provide a real introduction to the student's chosen vocation; and (3) coördination of work experience and class work.

The coöperative method has been effectively applied by junior colleges in such fields of study as accounting, agriculture, banking, engineering technology, library work, nursing, and retail merchandising.

Coöperative education, while not yet widely practiced by junior and community colleges, appears to have been established as a valid method of training for the technological and semiprofessional occupations. Its future growth seems assured and educationally desirable. It provides, above all, a means of using the community's commercial and industrial resources to supplement the facilities of the campus. Institutions which add programs of this type should see that the students are carefully selected and counseled, that the work experience provided is practical, and that there is maintained a close correlation between the academic program and the student's activities on his job.

ADULT EDUCATION

Adult education as one of the roots out of which the junior college movement grew has already been discussed. We need now to consider the importance of this phase of education in the present and future curriculum of the junior and community college.

By adult education we mean, of course, that kind of program which is offered for students who have completed their formal education in high school or college. Usually this type of student is 18 years of age or older. Most of the courses given in a program of adult education are scheduled after working hours—that is, in the late afternoon or evening.

Adult education as it now exists may actually include every conceivable sort of educational offering, from a short course in real estate appraisal or algebra to an extended series of courses leading eventually to an academic degree. The main practical difference between the regular collegiate program of studies and adult education is that part-time evening students do not ordinarily have the time to engage in campus activities other than the specific courses in which they are enrolled. They may also lack time for much outside study. The class work, however, is almost always basically the same as that offered in the daytime program, though there may be more variety in the adult courses.

NEED FOR ADULT EDUCATION

The President's Commission on Higher Education has pointed out the need for institutions of higher learning to assume additional responsibility for furthering the education of adults. Its report says in part:

Many factors make a broad program of adult education essential for our national well-being. Some of these arise out of a new concept of world community and others out of the problems of the domestic environment. The population of the United States is becoming an increasingly adult one . . . .

The increasing tempo of change in our technology is another factor which is increasing the demand for adult education. The human significance of social change is dramatically reflected in shifting occupational patterns . . . .

Increased technical efficiency has also made possible a drastic reduction in hours of work. In 1914 the average workweek in manufacturing was 49.4 hours, and by 1947 it had dropped to 40 hours or less. With further decline in the workweek, it will become increasingly important to learn how to make wiser use of leisure time.

The increasingly specialized nature of work has done more than increase the leisure time at the disposal of the worker; it has changed the kinds of activities in which individuals need to engage during their leisure hours. The very nature of the work frequently tends to fractionalize the experience of the worker and to draw on only a part of his personality. Repetitive and simple operations too frequently fail to give any satisfying sense of creativeness. Adult education may assist in offsetting these factors and in giving meaning to work experience as well.

. . . .

A further element in the need for expanding adult education is that adults desire to learn. The Gallup Poll for December 16, 1944, reported that 34 per cent of adults desired to enroll in adult education classes after the war. The greatest interest was shown by the age group from 20 to 29. The percentage of those interested in adult education was even higher when the poll was again reported on July 6, 1947; 41 per cent, or more than two of every five adults in the voting population, expressed the desire to engage in some kind of study.[4]

Such evidence and opinion as that above would seem to argue for vast expansion of present opportunities in adult education.

Programs of this kind may be said to serve primarily the following purposes: (1) to offer a means of continuing their educations to those who have completed regular schooling and are working in full-time jobs or as housewives; (2) to supply supplementary vocational training for employed persons who wish to prepare for occupational advancement or to change their jobs; (3) to assist people in developing a constructive and satisfying pattern of leisure-time activities; (4) to develop special courses not ordinarily found in the regular curriculum; and (5) to offer instruction for adults in any field in which interest or need exists.

[4] *Higher Education for American Democracy*, Harper & Brothers, 1948, II, 60–61.

EXTENT OF ADULT EDUCATION IN TWO-YEAR COLLEGES

Nearly half of all the junior and community colleges in the United States operate programs of adult education, about a third of them (chiefly those in urban centers) offering rather substantial programs. In 1949–1950, when a total enrollment of over 558,000 students was reported for junior colleges in this country, nearly 213,000 of the total number consisted of part-time adult students. This gives some idea of the quantitative significance of these programs in the complete picture of junior college education.

Some institutions, indeed, have more evening students than full-time day students; and a few, such as the New Haven Junior College, exist primarily for the employed student. Ever since the 1930's, adult education has grown rapidly among the junior colleges, both because of increasing enrollments within established institutions (the evening student body at such an urban institution as Hillyer College in Hartford, Connecticut, for example, nearly doubled within two or three years during the 1940's) and because a number of evening schools of several kinds, not previously identified as junior colleges, entered the junior college field during this period.

Sexson and Harbeson have contended that as the logical center for adult education in a community, the junior or community college appears to be in a strategic position. It is, they say,

the logical organization to assume the responsibilities for adult education. The organization of an evening high school or school of adult education unnecessarily complicates the machinery of public education. In fact, the traditional distinction between regular and adult education should be abandoned. Adult persons who are free during the regular day should be permitted to enroll in day classes if they desire. Adolescent students might find it more convenient or profitable to enroll in the late afternoon or evening classes. What is needed is not a separate school of late afternoon and evening classes, but an extended day in the junior college— a day extending from 8:00 A. M. to 10:00 P. M.—chock-full of rich educational offerings for the entire community without regard to age or walk in life. This is indeed a significant function of the junior college . . . .[5]

[5] John A. Sexson and John W. Harbeson, *The New American College,* Harper & Brothers, 1946, p. 58.

While not all educators would share the enthusiasm of Sexson and Harbeson for some of their proposals, there seems to be much general support for the idea of centralizing the community program of adult education into a single educational unit. For this purpose the community college does indeed stand in a strategic position.

ADVANTAGES OF THE COMMUNITY COLLEGE FOR ADULT EDUCATION

There are at least four major advantages with respect to adult education which may be claimed for the community college. First, and probably most important, is the fact that the community college by its very nature must be familiar with its community and aware of the educational needs which exist there. Instead of determining the character of its offerings by academic tradition and the special qualifications of the various members of its regular faculty, it makes frequent investigations of what the economic and social structure of the area requires in the way of educational opportunity and then provides the necessary type of program. The institution concerns itself less with patterns of education established by other colleges and more with local conditions. Thus a program of adult education in one community college may differ markedly from that in another.

Secondly, the community college maintains a flexible curriculum, sensitive to the changing needs of local students. The curriculum lends itself to innovations and changes dictated by changing circumstances. Changes to meet new needs are likely to occur very slowly in the traditional college.

Thirdly, the junior and community colleges have probably had more experience with evening courses than almost any other type of educational institution. While schools and colleges of all sorts now engage in adult education, few have had more extensive experience in this field than the urban two-year colleges.

Finally, the junior and community colleges have accepted as their own special area for instruction those occupational fields in which the greatest need for adult education appears to be felt—the technical vocations and the semiprofessions. The two-year colleges obviously are better equipped than other institutions to supply training at this level.

The Adult Student

We have already said that adults desire further education of innumerable types and for many different reasons. The attitude of the typical adult student may be illustrated by the two following case histories, both true except for the names used:

When Henry Jones died in 1934, he left behind for his wife and son a small insurance policy, a house, an automobile, and some scattered property. His wife, Mary, was thirty-two years old at the time of Henry's death. The son, Henry junior, was nine. There were no other immediate relatives.

Luckily for Mary and Junior, they possessed a roof over their heads which was clear of mortgage. But what about clothes and food and the expenses of Junior's education? Following the funeral, there was enough of the insurance money left to provide somewhat less than three years of security. Beyond that, no prospects of a regular income were in sight.

Mary was a brave woman, but there seemed little she could do in the way of self-support except housework. Never in her life had she worked at a job outside the home, and she hardly knew how to begin.

A friend suggested that Mary might realize a few hundred dollars from the sale of the miscellaneous property. Mary tried. She found prospective buyers; and she consulted with lawyers about prices, deeds, and bills of sale. She began to see how little she knew about business in general and the real estate business in particular. But the experience fascinated her, and the activity took her mind from her troubles.

There was a college near-by where courses in real estate were offered. Mary decided hesitantly that she might have a chance of success in real estate, that she owed herself the opportunity to get a thorough training in the subject. She registered for the required courses, determined that she would make every sacrifice necessary to succeed. After a year of study, she was ready to enter into business as an independent agent.

Mary is today one of the few women real estate agents in her neighborhood. She is earning a good living. Her son Henry, now in high school, will be going to college in a few years.

The case of Mary Jones is not very different from those of a thousand others in the United States who each year face problems similar to hers.

She represents the person who needs practical occupational training on the college level, the adult with a recognizable educational problem.

Joseph Cernovic is another example. A machinist by trade, he has been working in the same factory for thirteen years. He has been considered several times for promotion to a supervisory position. But Joseph's technical education has been sadly neglected. He needs to know something more of mathematics, of blueprint reading, of elementary physics. Younger, better trained men are being promoted over his head. There should be some way, he tells himself, for him to obtain the training that he knows would open the blocked passage of advancement.

Joseph is looking for a technical school where he can study in the evenings, and where a year of training will give him the qualifications he needs for that supervisory position.[6]

While not all adults have educational problems as readily discernible as those described above, there are many who do. A great many more have at least an interest in further education. Whether the student has a serious need, a desire for further knowledge, or merely an interest in cultural activities, the community college's program of adult education should make provisions to accommodate him.

TEACHERS IN AN EVENING PROGRAM

Evening classes are most often conducted by the regular faculty of an institution. Many colleges pay members of the faculty an extra fee for evening teaching. When such work is added to the individual's usual full schedule, however, there is always danger of overloading and, consequently, of a slackening of effort and lowering of the quality of instruction. In some cases, evening divisions make use of teachers from other nearby schools and colleges; and this method, while widely used, also has its disadvantages if it gives those teachers a heavier work load than is advisable. The teachers themselves, of course, cannot be expected to decide wisely and objectively whether to accept additional hours of teaching, for they are tempted to undertake such extra assignments by the attraction of added income.

[6] Tyrus Hillway, "The Junior College and the Adult Student," *Journal of Adult Education,* XIII (October, 1941), 1–4.

In a community college, probably the best method, if a high quality of instruction is to be maintained, consists of distributing the teaching hours of each member of the faculty in such a way that both day and evening classes combine to make no more than a normal work load. Some teachers will object to evening teaching under any circumstances, but these are in the minority.

Another excellent source of evening teachers, especially for vocational subjects, is the specialist in business or industry. Experts in various occupations frequently enjoy and actually derive benefit from teaching the principles of their work. Teaching, because it constitutes a change, often amounts to relaxation for these specialists. Some community colleges follow the practice (unless restricted by certification laws) of determining first who are the most successful and respected men and women in the community in certain occupations—the best accountants, the best engineers, the best commercial artists, etc.—and then putting forth effort to securing these people as evening teachers. Students invariably appreciate this policy and are impressed by such a teacher's reputation and practical competence. When this method is used, however, the institution has the responsibility of guiding such teachers and of training them in the most effective teaching procedures. Unfortunately, most institutions at present neither accept nor even recognize this responsibility.

VARIETIES OF ADULT EDUCATION

We cannot assume that adult education should be a function of the junior and community colleges exclusively. Many other agencies or institutions can make effective contributions in this field. The community college, on the other hand, seems to be especially well-qualified for the task.

In addition to class instruction, a program of adult education may include many varied activities. The President's Commission on Higher Education declares:

The community college seeks to become a center of learning for the entire community, with or without the restrictions that surround formal course work in traditional institutions of higher education. It gears its programs and services to the needs and wishes of the people it serves, and its offerings may range from workshops in painting or singing or play writing for fun to refresher courses in journalism or child psychology.

If the health of the community can be improved by teaching restaurant managers something about the bacteriology of food, the community college sets up such a course and seeks to enroll as many of those employed in food service as it can muster. If the community happens to be a center for travelers from Latin America, the college provides classes in Spanish for salespeople, waitresses, bellboys, and taxicab drivers.

The potential effects of the community college in keeping intellectual curiosity alive in out-of-school citizens, of stimulating their zest for learning, of improving the quality of their lives as individuals and as citizens are limited only by the vision, the energy, and the ingenuity of the college staff—and by the size of the college budget. But the people will take care of the budget if the staff provides them with vital and worthwhile educational services.[7]

Among a few of the nonclass activities through which programs of adult education serve their constituencies are lectures, public forums, concerts, exhibitions, community surveys, publications, tutoring, nutrition and health conferences, child-care laboratories, rehabilitation programs for the physically handicapped, speech clinics, and the like.

Community Needs and Adult Education

Important help in determining what activities are desirable and useful in a community can be derived from consultations with committees of interested citizens. Through this means the college can keep in close touch with the wishes and needs of the people it serves.

Sexson and Harbeson describe the method used at one institution as follows:

In the Pasadena Junior College the following civic organizations have representation on the Citizens' Advisory Committee: Alumni Association of Pasadena Junior College, American Legion, Professional Business Women's Club, Chamber of Commerce, City Board of Directors, Civic

---

[7] *Higher Education for American Democracy, op. cit.,* I, 69–70.

League, Junior Chamber of Commerce, Knights of Columbus, Masonic Bodies, Merchants' Association, Metropolitan Business Men's Association, Pasadena Central Labor Union, Pasadena Junior College Patrons' Association, Pastors' Union, Pasadena Federation of Parents and Teachers, Realty Board, Shakespeare Club, United Service Clubs, Pasadena *Star-News,* and *Post,* Pasadena *Independent,* Property Owners' Division of Realty Board, Young Men's Christian Association, Young Women's Christian Association, and Boy Scouts.

This group meets at the college for a luncheon about six times per year to discuss the offerings and ways and means by which the college may more adequately serve the educational needs of the community. The enthusiasm of the group is unbounded, and each member goes back to his civic body a living apostle of lifelong learning through the agency of the community college.

In addition to the organization of the Citizen's Advisory Committee there should be frequent meetings of representatives of the leading vocations carried on in the community with the administration staff of the college. Practicing lawyers and doctors as well as other professional and vocational groups should meet with members of the college staff to discuss the offerings and their content and the training that should be given in preparation for their respective fields. In Pasadena it is planned to have each of these groups meet at least once per year for luncheon and discussion. The community will thereby be made junior college conscious and employers will naturally look to the junior college as a source of supply for recruits.[8]

Maintaining these contacts with community life aids not only in the developing an effective program of adult education, but also in improving all phases of the institution's work.

A recent study sponsored by the United States Office of Education attempted to measure the most successful methods used by public school and community college directors of adult education to identify the interests and needs of adult students in their communities. This report states:

The best ways of identifying educational needs and interests of adults were these in rank order of merit:
   1. Cultivation of "coordinators" or liaison people in industry, busi-

[8] Sexson and Harbeson, *op. cit.,* pp. 125–126.

ness, and community organizations who watch for opportunities for education to perform a service.

2. Receiving requests from business, industrial, labor, and community groups.

3. Study of deficiencies of adults.

4. Maintenance of extensive personal acquaintance with community leaders and groups.

5. Examination of census and similar data.

6. Making systematic surveys of industrial, business, civic, and [social] life of the community.

7. Examination of published surveys of other communities and similar literature.

8. Examination of catalogs, schedules, publicity materials, and programs of comparable institutions.

9. Acting on hunch.

10. Being sensitive to civic, personal, and social problems of people which can be alleviated by education.

11. Checking on known interests of people.

12. Utilization of checklists and other interest finders.

13. Receiving individual requests.

No method tested was valueless, although some widely used had least value and some used by only a few directors were of most value.

In *building community awareness of the possibilities of new courses and additional educational services,* personal approaches to leaders and groups ranked highest. Bringing leaders and groups to visit activities at the school plant and notification of leaders and groups by mail of possibilities were next most useful. General publicity expressing willingness to offer any course for which enough registrants and a qualified teacher could be obtained was used most frequently and had least value, although it was of positive benefit.

Content, methods, and organization of courses to meet needs and interests of adults were determined best by these practices ranked in order of merit:

1. Discussing content with authorities in the field.

2. Reviewing content and methods at the end of the term and revising accordingly.

3. Setting up advisory committees to work out course content and suggesting methods.

4. Obtaining experience of others in the same or similar courses.

5. Letting outside regulations or agencies determine content.

6. Engaging practitioners in the field to teach courses.

7. Determining content by consulting with members of the [student] group.

8. Letting instructor determine content, methods, and organization after considering knowledge, skills, habits, and attitudes desired.

9. Using textbooks when available as guides to content.

In general, the most effective methods of identifying educational needs and interests of adults require the association of specialized professional educators with a wide range of lay people. Study of systematic data obtained from the census, surveys, and similar sources supplement extensive human contacts.[9]

Revelation of Needs Through Guidance.   One excellent method of determining the educational needs of students, which was not specifically mentioned above, is the use of guidance records. A good program of guidance will reveal not only what those who use the service are interested in but also the things for which their native ability fits them. A community center of guidance and information, whether operated by the college or by some other agency, can supply excellent recommendations to school administrators regarding adult courses and other educational activities of value to the community.

In 1945, for example, when Public Law 16 and Public Law 346 (the so-called "G.I. Bill of Rights") made free education available to veterans for World War II, most people, including the vast majority of educators, believed that veterans would be much more interested in jobs than in college study. Guidance officials, however, knew that the opposite was true and with considerable difficulty persuaded schools and colleges to prepare for the huge influx of veterans who entered our educational institutions in 1946.

Need versus Desire.   As a vital principle of adult education, it should be kept in mind that what people of the community want in the way of educational service is perhaps even more important than what they apparently need. A community college ought not to adopt the attitude that it can infallibly determine educational needs through surveys and that the establishment of a program to meet

[9] Homer Kempfer, *Identifying Educational Needs of Adults,* U.S. Government Printing Office, 1951, pp. 63–64.

these needs will guarantee the enrollment of students. To the cold logic of surveys must be added the psychology of recognizing and catering to the community's desires.

The people have the unquestionable right of saying just what services they wish to have provided for them by their institutions, and no community college can be said to be truly democratic or of maximal benefit to its constituency which does not respect and fulfill these wishes.

Adult education has become well-established as a program of the junior and community college. At least a third of the institutions operate extensive evening programs. The community college has a particular advantage in that it is familiar with its community and the needs of adult students, it maintains a flexible curriculum, it has had considerable experience with adult education during the past quarter-century, and it offers instruction in those areas of study for which adult needs appear to be greatest. The community college, furthermore, seeks to make itself the center of learning for the entire area which it serves and is ready to sponsor any constructive activity which may be of use to the people of that locality.

OTHER PROGRAMS OF TWO-YEAR COLLEGES

We have seen that both general and special education have a place in the proper functioning of the two-year college. The division of the curriculum under these two headings, of course, is made in order to distinguish between certain types of subject matter and certain objectives. The special education offered in the typical junior or community college, for example, usually has as its objective preparation for one or more of the semiprofessions. Coöperative education, on the other hand, represents a device or plan for improving special education of certain types by making better use of community facilities for training and is not, therefore, so much different in purpose as it is different in method from the ordinary academic program. Adult education includes both general and special education and, broadly considered, is aimed at the same objectives as the regular part of the curriculum, but the courses are offered at different hours and for a different group of students.

Thus, while probably all programs organized in the junior and community college can be classified, as far as their objectives are concerned, as either general or special education, much variation exists within these programs with respect to the methods employed in presenting them. Two or three additional methods may be mentioned.

EXTENSION CENTERS

Extension work, or off-campus courses, ordinarily are not a characteristic activity of the community college. For one thing, an institution is not likely to be as familiar with other communities as it is with its own. On the whole, it would seem wise to leave the function of establishing extension centers to the universities. Extension courses are best justified when offered in communities which are at some distance from adequate educational facilities on the collegiate level and which are not large or wealthy enough to afford colleges of their own. In some cases, when training of a particular type is required in a community, it may be desirable to secure it through the extension division of some specialized institution. Advanced courses for teachers may be provided, for example, by a college of education.

A few community colleges, because of unusual circumstances, operate extension centers in neighboring areas. Mitchell College in New London, Connecticut, began in 1949 to offer afternoon and evening courses at Norwich, 15 miles from the campus. This came about because many students in the Norwich area found it inconvenient, especially during the winter months, to travel in the time available to them between their homes and the college. Classes for nursing students were started in the Norwich hospital, and other courses were offered at the high school.

Some community colleges located in large cities have considered the possibility of decentralizing their programs in adult education. This would mean establishing evening extension centers at convenient locations throughout the city. While there are disadvantages in such a plan, it might very well result in considerably greater accessibility and popularity of the courses.

There have been frequent instances of the organization of junior colleges as extension centers of major universities. When a sufficient measure of local control can be exercised and when the teachers become residents of the community, such an institution can approximate the advantages of the community college. Drawbacks may be recognized, however, in the difficulties which an extension center faces when the question of relating its work to the real needs of the community is raised. Vital decisions usually cannot be made on the local level but must be referred to the main campus and must be in harmony with policies in force at the mother institution. Since the center's ultimate control remains in the hands of administrators who are miles away and to whom the problems of the community must be of secondary importance, it is not easy for such a center to serve the community as well as it should. Furthermore, common practice under this arrangement has been for the university to send instructors from the main campus to teach these classes on a part-time arrangement. A part-time teacher, spending no more than a few hours each week in the community, cannot be expected to familiarize himself thoroughly with local needs.

Typically, the university extension center offers the same courses as those given on the central campus, and often they are taught by the same teachers. Although this procedure helps to maintain academic standards, it also prevents adaptation of the curriculum to the special requirements of the community.

The University of Wisconsin Plan. When communities do not or cannot provide local college facilities for their young people, however, an extension center operated by a reputable university may be a gratifying substitute. This appears to be the situation in Wisconsin, where the state university after World War II established as many as 34 separate centers of education in various places throughout the state. These offered in some cases one and in other cases two years of collegiate instruction. Though some of them were closed when the postwar demands of the veterans had been satisfied, about half of the University of Wisconsin extension centers have remained active and in many of their aspects resemble the typical junior or community college. Ten of them (at Fond du Lac, Green Bay, Kenosha, Manitowoc, Marinette, Menasha, Milwaukee, Racine, Sheboygan, and Wausau) give two full years of regular collegiate courses.

The principal difference between the community college and the two-year university extension center would seem to lie in the closer ties which the latter necessarily has with the university curriculum. It cannot be as free to adjust its program to the real needs of the community in which it is located. One is inclined to recommend that the university extension center, if it is to provide the broadest kind of service to the American public, should either be given administrative autonomy within the structure of the university or be separated entirely from its affiliation. Wilkes College in Pennsylvania, formerly a junior college under the supervision of Bucknell University but now legally independent of the parent institution, illustrates how a university may serve as the breeder of strong educational offspring which eventually learn to stand on their own feet and serve their own communities.

Extension Programs for Workers.   A community college may find many opportunities to assist the larger commercial and industrial firms in its area by taking instruction directly to workers in the plant. Since most of the better manufacturing and business concerns operate programs of in-service training for their employees, what the college can do is to relieve the company of administrative problems with respect to such programs and to insure that effective modern teaching methods will be used. In addition, there are many instances in which arrangements can be made to grant academic degrees for completion of a planned sequence of courses taken in the student's place of employment.

Examples of this type of offering among the junior colleges are not numerous. The New Haven Junior College in Connecticut carries on a considerable amount of this work, and other community colleges are beginning to experiment with it. The plan involves drawing up an agreement between the college and one or more business firms to institute courses which are directly related to the needs of the company and which will prepare employees for higher positions. The company releases employees from their usual duties during the hours at which classes meet and supplies a classroom, textbooks, and equipment. The company often pays all or at least a part of the cost of instruction.

There seems to be great promise in the development of many more programs of this kind, though some companies prefer to manage their own educational work. When community colleges break away from traditional notions regarding curriculum, they find that the can supply highly satisfactory educational service in many untried ways.

COÖPERATION WITH PROFESSIONAL ORGANIZATIONS

Various professional organizations (the American Association of Bank Clerks, the American Society of Tool Engineers, the National Association of Credit Men, and the National Association of Purchasing Agents, to mention only a few) conduct educational activities through their local chapters, and many of them go as far as to sponsor formal classes. The community college not only can offer a convenient location for the educational work of these groups, but in some cases the curriculum of the institution can be made to fit readily into their special training programs.

The program of the National Association of Credit Men is an example of how coöperation between college and professional society of this kind actually works. One of the authors of the program, while a junior college administrator in Connecticut some years ago, had a most satisfactory experience with this organization. He described it as follows:

[The National Association of Credit Men] has created a department of its work which it calls the National Institute of Credit. This is an agency for setting up educational standards and for supervising the training of newcomers to the credit business. It has fixed upon what it considers the minimum essentials of college work for successful credit men. These essentials include the satisfactory completion of college-level courses in Economics, Credits and Collections, Fundamentals of Accounting, Business English, Business Law, Marketing, Public Speaking, and Problems of Credit Management. In many instances the local chapters of the association directly provide this training to students; in others the classes are part of the regular curriculum in an approved college. Where the latter arrangement exists, the student matriculates as a regular student of the college concerned and must, of course, meet the admission requirements of that institution. By completing the first four of the courses prescribed by the National Institute of Credit, the student becomes eligible for the award of Associate in the Institute. By completing all eight of the prescribed courses, he becomes eligible for the award of Fellow. At the same time, to be sure, he is not prevented from taking the regular college degrees.

Students in the business administration of Hillyer Junior College are given the opportunity, when they register, of applying at once for membership in the National Institute of Credit. This application costs them two dollars in addition to the regular fees of the college. Those who desire to take only the courses required for the award of Associate or Fellow in the Institute are permitted to do so, and fees in these cases are proportional. Such students ordinarily would not become candidates for the degree of Associate in Science.

The local chapter of the National Association of Credit Men assists the program of the college in several ways. Occasionally it furnishes visiting lecturers for the credit classes. It offers advice, chiefly through its educational committee, in the general planning of course content in certain subjects. It makes available to the classes various types of office records for study and helps in the conduct of study trips through credit offices and departments. It publicizes the credit courses throughout the state, both among its neighboring local chapters and among the general public. It cooperates in finding positions in credit offices for the successful graduates of the courses.

The effect of this relationship, of course, is to make the student's work more practical, to increase the services and the prestige of the junior college, and to insure permanence in the educational activities of the credit group.[10]

Coöperation with professional societies would seem to offer an

[10] Tyrus Hillway, "Junior Colleges and Professional Societies," *Junior College Journal*, XII (May, 1942), 508–510.

excellent means of increasing the interest and usefulness of the community college curriculum.

CORRESPONDENCE COURSES

While a few junior colleges have at various times offered home-study courses, no strong program of correspondence work seems to have been developed among the institutions generally. On the whole, it would appear preferable to allow this function to remain with large universities and the special correspondence schools. It is the nature of the community-serving institution to prefer direct contact with students, and most of the curriculum development within the junior colleges at present is definitely in the direction of increasing and improving community service rather than extending programs beyond the community. As a useful method for the junior and community college, therefore, correspondence study cannot be recommended.

Future trends with respect to the junior college curriculum are likely to include: (1) increasing emphasis upon two-year vocational programs; (2) further extension of opportunities in adult education; (3) continuation of current tendencies toward the inclusion of general education in all courses of study; and (4) more and better use of community facilities through cöoperative education, in-service training programs for workers and collaboration with the local chapters of professional societies.

VII

Guidance and Student Welfare

WHEN Frank Waters Thomas, 30 years ago, designated guidance as one of the four principal functions of the junior college (along with what he called the preparatory, popularizing, and terminal functions), he stressed the need for special help and advice to the student whose lack of academic ability denies him admission to the standard college or university.[1] Such a student, since he cannot hope for success in a four-year program, becomes the problem and responsibility of the two-year institution. "The junior college," Thomas insisted, "must accept the duty of guiding these [less capable students] into lines of study for which they are fitted and which they can profitably pursue."[2]

This point of view with regard to the guidance function, when judged by modern ideas on the subject, must be considered extremely old-fashioned. Both the concept and methods of guidance have changed markedly since Thomas' analysis was made. We no longer think of guidance merely as a means of rescuing the student who is in academic difficulties. The current notion is more nearly that guidance constitutes an important educational service—including accurate information, psychological testing, and professional coun-

[1] Frank Waters Thomas, "The Functions of the Junior College," in William Martin Proctor (ed.), *The Junior College: Its Organization and Administration,* Stanford University Press, 1927, pp. 11–25.

[2] *Ibid.,* p. 24.

142

seling—to which every student in our schools is entitled. It presents the advantage of offering advice of a disinterested and specially informed nature to objectify and strengthen the vital decisions which every student must make regarding certain aspects of his life.

Not only the student of limited academic ability, or the student with emotional or behavior problems, but every one in our educational system, can profit from intelligent guidance and counseling. Furthermore, since demonstrably effective techniques in this field are now generally available, anyone who is prevented from receiving the benefits of an adequate counseling service may justly complain of being short-changed by the school authorities. Most modern school systems, of course, now acknowledge this fact by instituting such programs as a regular part of total educational service.

GUIDANCE IN TWO-YEAR COLLEGES

Junior colleges as a group have been, on the whole, more interested in providing some form of counseling to their students than have the traditional colleges. This interest has no doubt resulted, as Thomas implies, partly from the more highly selective admissions practices of the older institutions, and partly from the widespread academic habit of conservatism. Besides these factors, the junior colleges appear to have recognized quite early in their development the need for special measures to serve effectively the more heterogeneous group of students which they enroll. In addition, because the two-year student actually has less time at his disposal to make the proper choice of objective than the four-year student, his problem of determining the direction of his training is a more urgent one.

All these factors have had some influence upon the establishment of guidance programs in the junior colleges. Even more significant, however, is the fact that the period between the ages of 18 and 20— the normal junior college years—is commonly the one in which most final decisions with regard to careers and further educational plans are made.

PSYCHOLOGY OF THE JUNIOR COLLEGE STUDENT

The young person at the usual junior college age is approaching adulthood. Physically and mentally he has attained nearly the summit of his powers, though he may continue to mature along both lines for a few more years. In certain respects, of course, he retains the characteristics of an adolescent; for his experience usually has been insufficient for the development of social and other kinds of maturity.

The emotional difficulties and instabilities of early adolescence, however, are at this period largely a thing of the past, even though the junior college student may frequently revert to his younger attitudes and habits of behavior. His attention is directed toward the problems of adult life—especially those of a career and marriage—to a far greater degree than that of the high school student. Many of his contemporaries already have left school to seek jobs or to start families. Economic matters loom large on the horizon, and the young person feels markedly at this time an increasing sense of responsibility for his own future and, in spite of many moments of uncertainty, a growing surge of confidence in his own powers. He is probably already contributing something to the family finances and, in particular, to the cost of his education.

The feeling of independence has ordinarily grown strong at the junior college age. Among all American youth aged 18 to 20, at least a third no longer live with their parents. About half of this latter group have become heads of households; the rest are living alone or attending college away from home. About 71 percent of young men between 18 and 20, and about 45 percent of young women in the same age group have entered the labor force in one capacity or another.[3] There also seems to be a tendency to change residence rather freely at this age; many young people move during these years from the farm to the city or from one city to another at a considerable distance—another evidence of the prevailing spirit of self-confidence and independence.

[3] Metropolitan Life Insurance Company, *Statistical Bulletin*, May, 1951.

Generally speaking, the junior college period is one of great physical well-being, with the frequency of both illness and mortality at a very low point. Perhaps associated with the excellent health of this time of life is the feeling of energy and ambition that noticeably characterizes this age group, in so marked a contrast to the lassitude or purposeless activity of the earlier adolescent years. The junior college student in most instances has recognized the need for directing his energies toward an intelligent goal.

The aim which appears most practical as well as most urgent for young people in the junior college is, of course, a satisfactory choice of occupation. Children and early adolescents cannot, as a rule, make wise vocational decisions, with or without guidance. There is neither an understanding of the world of work nor the desire for self-sufficiency. In the late high school years we begin to see the development of the desire to earn money and assume independent responsibility, but a detailed knowledge of occupations and the activities they entail is usually lacking. When the student enters the junior college, he is ready with respect both to emotional fitness and to work experience for a serious decision regarding his career. This, then, is the period at which vocational guidance normally proves most useful and meaningful.

Ideas about marriage are beginning at this age to take the form of an actual searching for a life partner. This development also seems to be associated with an increasing sense of responsibility and independence. Young people, especially girls, have at this period begun to think of the opposite sex not merely in terms of a social and recreational pastime but in the much more serious terms of marriage and family.

Many of the prominent characteristics of earlier adolescence, of course, remain important. The marked romanticism of the young women and the idealism of the young men have been somewhat modified by experience and maturity but not submerged. Religious doubts and questions of personal ethics and morality may be the excuses for extensive soul-searching at this period.

REASONS FOR GUIDANCE

As long as young people have problems and decisions to make, the establishment of personnel services in colleges to assist in meeting them is amply justified. Although guidance in some form has existed among educational institutions from very early times, it has been only recently that we have succeeded in developing techniques which are demonstrably effective and scientific. Since we have them, there seems no reason why they should not be made available to all persons who can benefit from them.

Many reasons exist why guidance is perhaps more necessary in the modern world than ever before. Guy C. Mitchell has admirably summarized a number of them. He points out, for example, that young people of today are subjected by the circumstances of their world to much greater emotional strains than were previous generations. Furthermore, and possibly because of this, students are now entering college with a noticeable desire—indeed, a drive—for life planning. Vocational selection has been generally delayed because employers seem to expect more education of young people and because the professional schools now require more lengthy training. The tremendous upsurge in collegiate enrollments during recent years has apparently brought into college great numbers of students not innately equipped with the ability to profit by the traditional kind of education which most colleges provide. With expanding curricular offerings, elective courses, and activities of all sorts, the student needs more and better guidance in making suitable choices among them. The seriousness of this problem, says Mitchell, is indicated by the fact that about half of all college students make one or more major curriculum changes.

Mitchell believes that colleges are beginning to recognize their responsibility with respect to the high drop-out rate of present students. While, according to the President's Commission on Higher Education, approximately 50 percent of the population could profit by at least two years of collegiate instruction, many are now entering the wrong institution or the wrong program. Such a situation calls for more effort in the field of guidance, as does the fact that the growing complexity of civilization itself necessitates more strenuous attention toward helping youth to solve their many problems.

In addition, Mitchell declares, war and the military experiences of hosts of our young men have convinced them of the usefulness of guidance and have therefore created a demand for it.[4]

Administrative Problems of Guidance

How can the various desires and needs of junior college youth, over and above mere classroom instruction, best be met? The first step seems to be the determination by the faculty and administration to look at students not merely as members of a group, but as individuals. In most school programs the students are taught and otherwise dealt with only in groups; their individuality is emphasized by the nature of guidance and what is often spoken of as the "student personnel point of view."

Guidance programs, of course, differ from one another both as to their emphasis and as to their methods. Not all guidance at the junior college level, as we have already implied, can be restricted entirely to problems of occupational choice and preparation for marriage. Many other vital questions—moral, social, educational, religious, and personal—may be involved. Not every institution organizes its program in exactly the same way. In some, counseling is almost completely separate from the instructional program and is regarded as a separate (often optional) service of the institution; in others, guidance and classroom instruction are integrated and regarded as parts of the same whole, all teachers being required to understand something of guidance and to apply some of the approved techniques in their contacts with students.

In general, we may consider as ideal that arrangement in which professional counselors are available to coördinate the program and serve all students directly and in which the teachers understand and support the specalized work of the counselors without being

[4] Guy C. Mitchell, "Guidance in Higher Education," *Junior College Journal,* XXII (December, 1951), 207–208.

required to participate in actual guidance beyond the limits of their training and ability. The administration and interpretation of psychological tests, for example, should not be expected of the classroom teacher.

It is hard to see how any guidance program can function effectively without a full-time, well-trained psychologist as director. Yet M. A. Hillmer determined in 1950 that only about one-fourth of the public junior colleges employ full-time persons in this capacity. His figures probably can be applied with some degree of accuracy to junior colleges generally. As the result of his study, Hillmer concluded that junior college administrators have begun to recognize the need for well-planned programs of professional guidance but have not yet reached the point of making adequate budgetary provisions and of securing technically trained counselors.[5] In some junior colleges, on the other hand, excellent work is being performed in this field.

While many institutions appear to be doing more talking about good guidance than application of its basic principles, there is strong evidence of a growing desire on the part of administrators for professionalization and improvement of the counseling services. Student personnel problems are being carefully studied, and the American Association of Junior Colleges has for some time given attention to this matter through one of its committees. The findings of this committee are closely followed by persons in the field. The stumbling blocks to the improvement of counseling services seem to be: (1) the cost of a really effective guidance program; (2) the shortage of adequately trained counseling personnel; and (3) lack of knowledge as to how the student personnel program should be properly organized.

As J. Anthony Humphreys has declared: "This institution [i.e., the junior and community college] cannot live up to some of its primary purposes—helping the individual student explore his capacities and

---

[5] M. A. Hillmer, "Present Status of Administrative Organization of Student Personnel Programs in Public Junior Colleges," *Junior College Journal,* XXI (November, 1950), 143–144.

interests and helping him to find his own particular place in society—unless the junior college supports an active, adequate program of student personnel services. Any college owes to its clientele the periodic study of the requirements and content of offerings in relation to the educational and personal needs of its students." [6]

AIMS OF THE GUIDANCE PROGRAM

The essential aims of the guidance program are, in the broadest sense, those of education itself. Guidance is not something apart from the curriculum but an integral part of it.

The terms "guidance" and "student personnel work" have been used above somewhat interchangeably. As a matter of fact, the latter is the more inclusive term, describing all services of the institution which are concerned with the individual welfare of the student. Under student personnel services are included guidance, housing, health services, placement, and most other institutional services except actual classroom instruction and the library.

A committee of the American Council on Education a few years ago considered what the student personnel point of view (consideration of the student as an individual and as a whole person) might hope to accomplish. Pointing out that a student's development is conditioned by many factors (his background, abilities, attitudes, and expectancies brought with him to college, his classroom experiences, his classmates, and the like) and his individual reactions to all these factors, the committee in its report insisted that the student's growth in personal and social wisdom rests ultimately with himself. The college, at best, can only provide a favorable environment for such development.

The institution should strive, according to this committee's report, to create conditions which will help in bringing about the following results: The student will achieve orientation to his college environment. He will succeed in his studies. He will find satisfactory living conditions. He will achieve a sense of belonging to the college. He

[6] J. Anthony Humphreys, "Facts Concerning Student Personnel Programs," *Junior College Journal*, XIX (September, 1948), 8–13.

will learn balanced use of his physical capacities. He will progressively understand himself. He will understand and learn how to use his emotions. He will develop likely and significant interests. He will achieve understanding and control of his financial resources. He will progress toward appropriate vocational goals. He will develop individuality and responsibility. He will discover ethical and spiritual meaning in life. He will learn to live with others. He will progress toward satisfying and socially acceptable sexual adjustment. He will prepare for satisfying and constructive postcollege activity.[7] One may venture to assert that any college which provides the conditions for students to achieve even the major part of these goals is doing a superb job.

Having briefly discussed the nature of guidance work, the psychology of the junior college student, reasons for guidance in the junior college, a few aspects of the administrative problem, and the general aims of guidance, we may now turn our attention to the actual operation of guidance programs in the two-year institution.

AREAS OF GUIDANCE

The typical well-planned guidance program in the junior college attempts to provide assistance to the student in several areas. While nearly every educational institution administers activities or services of one kind or another in some of these areas, under a competent guidance director the services are carefully coördinated and are all part of a unified master plan for developing the best resources of the college in solving the student's educational, vocational, and other problems.

The first area of guidance, after admission to college, is *orientation* of the student. This involves registration, the proper selection of courses, familiarization with college rules and procedures, and making first acquaintances with college personnel and other students. Usually there is at least one assembly of new students at which matters of common interest are discussed and general instructions and

[7] E. G. Williamson *et al.*, *The Student Personnel Point of View*, American Council on Education, 1949, pp. 6–11.

advice given regarding collegiate life. Considerable emphasis frequently is placed on methods of study and wise budgeting of the student's time. Orientation is necessary chiefly during the early stages of collegiate experience but may continue into the later stages.

Closely allied with orientation is *group guidance.* The usual orientation program, indeed, may be considered largely this type or method—an approach to immediate problems through group instruction or discussion. In addition to the opening assembly which is aimed merely at a rapid introduction of the student to collegiate life, the institution usually provides other assembly programs dealing with topics of current interest and importance. When these are not offered simply as entertainment or as part of the curricular program, they should be included in the plan of group guidance. The student handbook, round table discussions of moral and ethical questions, forums, conferences of many kinds, career days, and the like all employ the group guidance techniques. In some institutions the vocational adviser may offer a series of lectures and conferences, or even formal classes, designed to assist students with problems concerning choice of occupation. A career-planning unit may occasionally be introduced as a portion of the course in elementary psychology.

Collection and analysis of personal data, a very necessary guidance activity, supplies the institution with accurate information that enables it to look at the student as an individual rather than simply as another member of the group. Test scores, academic marks, and personal and family data (such as health records) help in determining not only the student's abilities and probability of success but also his special problems and needs. Without such information, guidance would be at best extremely ineffectual.

One of the most useful steps in guidance is, of course, *individual psychological testing.* No standard battery of tests will serve equally well for all students; thus the tests given must be chosen by an expert psychologist in light of the individual situation of every student. The usual test includes measurement of academic intelligence, vocational preferences, personal and social adjustment, and occupational aptitudes. For satisfactory results, it is essential that such tests be administered and interpreted by someone adequately trained and experienced in their use.

The success of psychological testing depends almost entirely upon the skill with which the results are used in *individual counseling interviews*. Only through preliminary interviews can the psychologist determine which tests ought to be administered in each case, and interpretation of the results will have meaning for the student largely to the extent that the counselor succeeds in pointing out the relationship between the scores and the student's particular situation. The personal interview, in fact, constitutes the backbone of all effective counseling. Through competent use of a series of such interviews, the student can be aided in making wise decisions regarding his present course of action and his plans for the future.

Every guidance program worthy of the name has a library of *occupational information*. The student should be guided to the most recent and authoritative data available regarding the fields in which he is interested. Such information should include facts about remuneration to be expected, general nature and status of each occupation, descriptions of entrance jobs, possibilities of advancement, conditions of work to be found in each field, and the qualifications necessary for success. Ideally, the counselor should have some first-hand acquaintance with the major vocational areas and should know where jobs are to be secured.

Another desirable function of the guidance program is *placement*. The institution should be able to help the student in taking his next step after graduation, whether it involve transfer to another college for more advanced instruction or immediate entrance into his chosen field of work. Placement must be skillfully done, with careful consideration of the needs of both student and employer.

Most guidance authorities believe that the program should also include a *follow-up* of graduates to determine how accurate and effective the counseling procedures prove to be, as well as to help graduates advance in their vocations. Follow-up is necessary in order to provide information upon which to base an *evaluation* of the entire guidance program.

COUNSELING SERVICE TO THE COMMUNITY

Just as an institution should be interested in the continued progress and success of its graduates, it may also be concerned with supplying effective counseling to those who are not and never have been students of the college. This applies particularly to noncollege youth and adults in the community.

Unless there are other agencies offering such a service, the community college probably ought to accept responsibility for a community guidance program. Since the facilities required for such a service and the trained personnel are both rather expensive and not always easy to come by, many communities will be unable to afford more than one center for guidance. In such a community as Bridgeport, Connecticut, a unified counseling and information service has been set up in the Community Advisory Service Center, a private agency. Some guidance is also offered for special groups at the University of Bridgeport, in all the public schools, and elsewhere within the city. There seems to be no reason, except in a large urban center, why one guidance program cannot be organized which will care for all needs of this type in the area. Such a service, of course, must be on a highly professional level and somewhat more complete and specialized than the personal and social guidance included in the usual school program.

In many ways the community-serving collegiate institution seems the ideal place for centralizing the professional counseling and information services of the entire community. This arrangement, however, would not eliminate the need for continuing guidance on various levels throughout the public school curriculum, and its work should probably be limited to those who are primarily interested in problems of occupational choice, further education, or others of a decidedly serious nature. Its chief benefits will be for those who are old enough to profit by professional advice and information, though it may offer special help to the physically or mentally handicapped of all ages.

The community guidance center must maintain contact with all service agencies of the area—social agencies, churches, legal counselors, veterans' organizations, employers' groups, labor groups, and the like—and must be able to direct citizens to those agencies which can best serve them in solving their problems.

QUALIFICATIONS OF THE COUNSELOR

One of the greatest mistakes made in the establishment of school guidance programs is the assumption that anyone with a knowledge of teaching and a sympathetic understanding or feeling toward other people can become, with little effort, an effective counselor and that nearly every teacher can administer and interpret psychological examinations after reading a set of directions. No one knows how much damage has been caused by this belief.

The college counselor ought to be a full-fledged psychologist and one especially trained in the field of guidance. In addition to his academic preparation, he should possess actual experience in several fields of work. It would be helpful if all counselors could secure, as part of their training, rather extensive experience in employment agencies and personnel offices. Thus their preparation would be practical as well as theoretical. Probably not more than a handful of counselors now engaged have had the benefit of such experience.

To be realistic, however, some provisions for a guidance program, even when fully trained people cannot be secured, probably would be better than none at all. On the other hand, a strong community college, recognizing the importance of the guidance function in its total educational service, must be willing to make suitable provisions in its budget for adequate counseling facilities and adequately trained personnel.

Besides his qualifications as to training, the successful counselor must be energetic and intelligent, must have a genuine interest in people and their problems, must understand the psychology of human development, must have a grasp of the interrelationships among community agencies and activities, and must clearly display an optimistic outlook and philosophy.

OTHER PERSONNEL SERVICES

Besides guidance, a number of other functions are ordinarily performed by the two-year college among its customary student personnel services. These include admissions counseling, health services, proper supervision of living accommodations, employment and financial aid, various remedial services, and student activities. The last of these will be discussed in a separate chapter.

ADMISSIONS COUNSELING

The effective college admissions officer serves not merely to determine whether the prospective student can meet the minimum entrance requirements of the institution, but he must interpret for applicants the nature of the program and ascertain whether the potential student is actually likely to profit from the type of educational experience offered. In far too many cases, it is feared, the admissions office conceives of its duty in other terms. It may think of its primary function as recruiting, and encourage the enrollment of students who should be enrolled elsewhere.

The prospective student has the right to know the college to which he seeks admission—the scope and purpose of its curriculum, its particular educational aims, the type of student body already enrolled, the major occupations and further educational progress of its graduates, religious or social restrictions, and the character of student activities. At the same time, the admissions office must learn as much as possible about the prospective student, so that the advice it gives him will be sound and helpful. Since it is altogether too much to expect that any one institution can meet the needs of all students equally well, and since we have in America an abundant variety of educational programs, the admissions counselor must keep in mind that he often serves the student best by sending him elsewhere. To many college administrators this may sound like heresy;

for in the past the effort of most institutions has been to secure as many as possible of the students with outstanding ability, without any concern for the needs of the student or the direction in which his ability ought to be exerted.

In making sure that the individual requirements of every prospective student can be adequately met by the institution, as well as in providing complete and accurate information about the college to the young person, his family, and his high school teachers, the admissions office really takes the first important step toward the proper guidance of the student.

HEALTH SERVICES

In recent years all colleges have begun to assume certain responsibilities for the physical and mental welfare of their students. The health service ought to be regarded as an integral part of the student personnel program, though in most institutions it still remains a separate unit, often connected with the department of physical education.

Practically all junior colleges throughout the United States, in common with the senior institutions, make provision for at least one medical examination for every student at the beginning of each academic year. These examinations vary, however, in degree of thoroughness. Ideally, they may include, besides the routine tests, a chest X-ray, an audiometer test, the Kahn or Wassermann test, and a mental hygiene interview. Therapeutic and corrective treatment should be supplied whenever necessary.

Some junior colleges—chiefly those under private control—add medical fees to their annual charges to cover the cost of medical services, including use of an infirmary. This fee may be used by the institution to purchase medical reimbursement insurance. Whenever the college cannot afford an adequate infirmary or when most of the students reside with their parents, insurance of this type has proved very practical. Ordinarily it covers the expenses of all medical treatment and hospital or infirmary bills.

It is common among collegiate institutions of all types to offer a required course in personal hygiene. Unfortunately, instruction in this course appears to have little to recommend it at present, and there can be no question but that some better way of presenting materials on personal health needs to be devised. It would be desirable also if colleges were to employ not only registered nurses but public-health nurses, whose training has included work in preventive medicine and group therapy. A mere handful of junior colleges follow this practice now.

The typical health program in the American junior and community college consists only of: (1) required medical examinations, chiefly for new students; (2) facilities for first aid; (3) special examinations for participants in athletic events when required by state law; and (4) a bare minimum of treatment leading to the correction of defects. Obviously much more can be done in this area: there could be greater coördination between the health services and the program of physical education and recreation; there undoubtedly should be more definite provisions made for the problems of mental health.

Since the student's mental and physical health affects many aspects of his educational experience—academic success, outside employment, social participation, disciplinary coöperation, and the like, it should receive the attention of the institution as an important function of the student personnel service.

SUPERVISION OF LIVING ACCOMMODATIONS

In a college which maintains dormitories, the quarters provided and the food served can have a significant influence upon the student's morale and upon his personal and social adjustment. The dormitory should not be treated as if it were simply a convenience for students or a source of extra income for the college but as a real element in the educational program.

While the operation and control of dormitories usually are placed in the hands of the business manager, the student personnel office should have responsibility for such matters as the assignment of rooms, the selection and supervision of dormitory supervisors and counselors, and the development of social and educational activities within the housing units. The institution also should maintain some control, for the welfare of students, over conditions in the fraternities and sororities and in rooms or apartments rented by the students off the campus. In addition, special help and guidance of many kinds ought to be made available to married students and to students from foreign countries.

FINANCIAL AID AND EMPLOYMENT

Most educators believe that work experience *per se* is an excellent thing for young people. As a matter of fact, right or wrong, through choice or necessity, a large number of junior college students work. There are some jobs on the campus which can be performed well by students, and these may be allocated partly according to students' needs. Those who operate the student personnel services usually are in the best position to determine whether a student really needs financial help and whether he is capable of holding a job without allowing his academic efforts to slacken. Outside employment also may be obtained for students through the personnel office, though a great many college young people seem fairly competent in finding jobs without such assistance.

Loans and scholarship aids may be considered another logical responsibility of the personnel department or bureau. Some students are unable to continue their collegiate work without financial help. Whenever loans are made, they should be handled in a businesslike way, and no student should be encouraged to regard such a debt lightly. Scholarship funds, in an ideal situation, ought not to be narrowly restricted in their use but should be allocated in a manner which will recognize merit and also help to equalize educational opportunities. Occasionally students will apply for scholarships merely for the prestige involved and not because any financial assistance is necessary. In general, the granting of scholarships and loans by the college ought to be contingent upon both academic ability and actual need.

Since learning to control one's personal finances and developing financial responsibility should be a part of educational experience, the student personnel program should include facilities for counseling on financial problems.

REMEDIAL SERVICES

Nearly every junior college helps new students in the formation of good habits of study. This is often thought of as a part of the instructional curriculum, but the modern tendency is to classify it with student personnel work.

Students with curable personal defects—difficulties in reading, speech, and the like—should receive special attention and help in overcoming them. The well-equipped junior college provides programs for the improvement of reading habits, the correction of speech defects, and other forms of remedial work in addition to the program of improving study habits. The student personnel bureau should be primarily responsible for services of this kind.

ORGANIZATION OF PERSONNEL SERVICES

A study of 1951–1952 junior college catalogues reveals the fact that 54 percent of the junior colleges use various members of the faculty as part-time advisers or counselors in the guidance program. Only 34 percent employ specially trained persons for this purpose, and many of the latter do not spend their full time in guidance work. In about 47 percent of the institutions guidance is a primary responsibility of the dean of students (or of the dean of men and the dean of women together).[8] A few institutions may still be discovered in which the administrative head (president, principal, or dean) provides all the student counseling, but such examples are becoming rare.

These figures indicate, in the main, two things. The first is that considerable differences exist among the institutions with respect to organization and administration of guidance services. The other

[8] Figures supplied by Charles W. McLain, Division of Education, Colorado State College.

is that the services now being offered have not been fully professionalized, though we may perhaps assume some special training for
guidance on the part of many deans and even a number of the
faculty members who are used for counseling purposes. On the
whole, however, the situation seems to leave something to be desired if guidance in the junior colleges is to be truly and generally
effective.

How should student personnel services be organized and administered? Many different methods are now being used. Some of these
are described in a report issued by the American Council on Education:

> Some colleges have adopted a highly centralized system in which a
> dean of students or director of personnel and a small specialized staff
> perform all student personnel functions. Other institutions have appointed
> a dean or director with administrative control over some personnel func-
> tions and departments, and advisory or staff relations with agencies and
> departments performing additional personnel functions. In the small
> liberal arts college, the academic dean is frequently given the additional
> responsibility for the student personnel functions. Another organizational
> plan is to create a council or committee of the heads of student personnel
> departments, usually without any administrative control allocated to one
> person. Sometimes these councils or committees are composed of both
> personnel administrators and representatives of the instructional faculty,
> and serve in a policy making and coordinating capacity. A few institutions
> have designated one person to serve as coördinator, in some cases with
> responsibility for several personnel functions. By far the majority of
> institutions have failed to provide any administrative or coordinating di-
> rection for the various student personnel departments.[9]

While the information quoted above refers particularly to the situation in four-year colleges and universities, the statements apply as
well to junior and community college.

The kind of organization established will depend, of course, upon
the size of the institution and the number of administrative persons

[9] Willard W. Blaesser *et al.*, *Student Personnel Work in the Postwar College*,
American Council on Education, 1945, p. 85.

it can afford to hire. Certain procedures for organization, however, seem definitely preferable to others and can be briefly stated.

If possible, all student personnel services—guidance, health services, housing, and the others—probably should be placed, for proper coördination and efficiency, under the supervision of one person, usually the dean of students or director of personnel. In a very small institution the academic dean may be given this responsibility. The person placed in charge must coördinate and administer the services; he should not, except under unusual circumstances, perform the functions themselves but should be able to delegate these to specially trained members of the staff. He may have serving with him, or under his direction, a director of guidance, a director of student health, a director of housing, and so on. The titles and the staff itself may vary somewhat under situations in junior colleges of different sizes and kinds; the important thing is that all student personnel services be smoothly coördinated.

Such a program obviously must be operated in harmony with the general purposes of the college and the special nature of its work, but the brief outline given here will probably fit most institutions. The number and variety of assistants used to perform all the functions desirable in carrying on a satisfactory program of student personnel services (*e.g.*, vocational advisers, religious counselors, dormitory supervisors, advisers for student activities, public-health nurses, directors of remedial services, and the like) will be determined largely by the number of students to be served and the size of the annual budget.

THE STUDENT AS AN INDIVIDUAL

The real essentials of successful student personnel work are probably these: (1) willingness to regard the student not merely as a member of the group but as an individual with desires and needs different from those of others, and to help him achieve satisfactory self-realization; and (2) the employment of properly trained persons to perform the special functions involved. Junior colleges have long demonstrated an interest in the individuality of the student and a willingness to make adjustments in the curriculum to meet individual needs. Professionalization of the student personnel organization, especially that part of it which is concerned with guidance, has lagged behind. Now, however, professionalization seems to be taking place with signs of growing rapidity and should lead eventually to a vast enrichment and greater usefulness of the two-year college experience. As a matter of fact, what has been said in this respect of the two-year college might well apply to collegiate institutions of all types. In professional guidance and in other personnel services which affect the welfare of the student as an individual, there still remains much room for improvement. Since effective techniques have already been devised and since trained people are now becoming available in this field, it seems likely that progress during the next few years in this function of higher education will continue at a faster pace.

VIII

Student Organizations and Athletics

AMERICAN higher education has long since outgrown the notion that the purpose of a college program is merely to train the mind. Modern colleges accept mental training as only a part of their total educational objective; other phases of the student's development have come to have equal importance. Today's educators concern themselves not only with a student's acquisition of academic knowledge but with his physical, social, and spiritual growth as well. This is evident from the tremendous emphasis now being placed, both in the two-year and the four-year institution of higher learning, upon control and encouragement of student clubs, fraternities and sororities, student government, and athletics. The tendency at mid-century is to bring all such activities into closer association with the curriculum.

Although from extremely early times the American college faculty and administration have constantly tried to maintain some form of control over the student's behavior both on and off the campus and also, in varying degrees, over his religious life, many aspects of his life (such as participation in sports and social activities) were until quite recent years generally thought of as his own business. The junior and community college developed, however, at a time when all these activities have been more and more closely integrated into the total college program. Almost every two-year institution today not only controls much of the nonclassroom program of every student but actually encourages and directs these activities. The justification lies in a concern for the well-rounded growth of the "whole student."

TYPES OF ORGANIZATION

Direction of nonclass activities is normally exercised through the medium of officially sponsored and organized clubs. Ruth Strang classifies the chief student organizations in our educational institutions into eight principal types: (1) policy-making and governing organizations, like the student councils; (2) service groups, which offer various kinds of service to the college and the community free of charge; (3) social and recreational clubs, such as those dealing with hobbies and other special interests; (4) sororities and fraternities; (5) esthetic expression groups, such as the music clubs; (6) religious organizations; (7) departmental or academic interest clubs, whose purpose is usually individual self-improvement in some field of subject matter; and (8) groups organized for physical activities and athletics.[1] To these might be added the honor societies, which ordinarily seek to recognize academic achievement in general.

The American educational philosophies of the twentieth century and the natural inclinations at this period of both students and faculty have been highly favorable to the steady increase of student organizations on the two-year college campus. The number of such groups has multiplied rapidly since 1900. One strong objection which has been raised against the participation of students in many extracurricular activities is that their grades in the regular academic subjects may suffer. Time spent in social and other nonacademic pursuits conceivably reduces the time which a student can give to his studies. But this objection appears to be invalidated by the conclusions reached in several studies of the problem. With a few

[1] Ruth Strang, *Group Activities in College and Secondary School,* Harper & Brothers, 1941, pp. 86–90.

prominent exceptions, it has been found that the students most active in clubs and other organizations on the campus actually receive, on the average, higher grades than do students who spend little time in outside activities.[2] As was mentioned before, the two-year college seems to have an unusual opportunity to aid in the development of self-confidence and maturity in students by encouraging their active participation in organizations. Because the junior college student is inevitably forced into positions of leadership within two years, often as an officer in some campus group, he learns to accept responsibility more quickly than does the typical freshman or sophomore in a four-year college. This undoubtedly helps to give him a mature attitude and the experience of leadership —a most valuable asset for most young people.

STUDENT GOVERNMENT

The most common example of a student policy-making or governing body in the American two-year college is the well-known Student Council or some similar organization. Sometimes the entire student body of an institution constitutes a legal organization with definite powers and responsibilities.

It should be pointed out that any form of student government can have only such powers as are granted to it by the administration or by the trustees. The charter or constitution of such an organization serves much the same purpose as a contract between the students making up the group and the college authorities. For this reason a charter should be very carefully studied and prepared before it is put into effect. A charter or constitution should clearly define the purposes for which a student governing body is organized, its duties and powers and the limitations, if any, which are placed upon them, and (not least important) the role of the faculty. The terms of such a constitution ought to be clear as well as agreeable to the students, the faculty, and the administration. Many difficulties have been experienced by institutions in which this matter was not carefully at-

[2] O. Myking Mehus, "Extracurricular Activities and Academic Achievement," *Journal of Educational Sociology*, VI (November, 1932), 143–149.

tended to at the very beginning. An administration which cancels a student constitution because it was badly prepared puts itself into an embarrassing position. Most of the disputes over control of student affairs have come as the result of a lack of understanding regarding the exact allocation of authority. It goes without saying, of course, that any collegiate administration which uses the student government as a rubber stamp for official decisions or which gives responsibility without commensurate authority and thus makes the student group into a whipping-boy for administrative mistakes is being undeniably dishonest.

How much power and administrative authority should a student governmental group be permitted to exercise? How far can it be trusted? This, to be sure, may depend a good deal upon the character of the institution and its administration. Almost every kind and degree of variation on this point can be found in the two-year colleges of America. In some the faculty or administration may openly retain the power of approval or veto over every action of the student government. In such institutions the students may suggest policy but have no authority to carry it into effect. In others the students may be given complete, final authority over certain phases of the program. For instance, there are student councils that sit as courts of honor to try the cases of students who have been accused of cheating in class. Frequently such courts have the right of dismissing a guilty student from the campus.

One example of a very powerful type of student government exists at Mitchell College in Connecticut. Here the student organization controls its own funds, which are deposited for safekeeping in the college treasury but which the administration may not touch without the consent of the students. Through its general organization the student body, operating under a comprehensive constitution, also controls all other activity groups on the campus. No club may be formed without applying for and receiving a charter from the parent organization. Once chartered, any club may request and secure funds from the student body treasury if it can submit a satisfactory budget. The total budget for activities (including athletics) is carefully administered by the student officers. Those who favor this liberal type of administrative control over student activities argue that the best way of teaching and encouraging democratic attitudes and procedures is by permitting students actually to apply democratic principles in their campus life. They object to administrators and faculty who discuss democracy in the classroom and auditorium but enforce autocratic authority in practice. On the other hand, many educators believe that junior college students must not be considered as fully mature adults and that therefore they cannot be trusted with very much real authority. In general, it may be said that junior colleges which allocate fairly extensive powers to a well-organized student government seem unlikely to modify this policy in the direction of tighter control by the college authorities.

Student Government as General Education. A survey conducted among students in the California junior colleges a few years ago revealed that the students themselves consider "exercising the privileges and responsibilities of democratic citizenship" to be the first main goal of general education.[3] This belief is no doubt shared by many American educators. The possibilities of using a broad program of student participation in junior college government for this purpose appear highly promising. Unquestionably more and more institutions have been inclined to grant their students greater freedom and authority with respect to their campus organizations. This would seem to be one of the best methods used at this educational level to aid in the development of capable leaders in civic affairs— not to mention intelligent followers.

Although the maturity of junior college young people is considered by many well-informed persons to be sufficient for the exercise of sound judgment in relation to the conduct of student activities, the fact that individuals remain in the college no more than two years admittedly suggests the need for close faculty contact with the student government and the other organizations. Turnover of officers and members being rather frequent by the very

[3] B. Lamar Johnson, *General Education in Action,* American Council on Education, 1952, p. 30.

nature of the situation, there may be occasional gaps in the continuity of a student organization which will cause trouble unless carefully watched.

The fault lies not so much with students themselves as it does with the relatively short period of time in which they must learn to conduct student business. When one group of young leaders graduates, a new group may not yet be ready to assume its predecessor's responsibility. In one junior college of the author's acquaintance, the student association had full authority for supervision of admissions to the college's athletic contests. This entailed selling and collecting tickets at the gate and similar duties. Because of rapid changes in personnel, an alarming degree of mismanagement soon occurred, with the unfortunate result that the administration found itself compelled to take drastic action. The entire function has been removed from the students' hands and has been assumed instead by college authorities. With proper supervision, however, other institutions have worked out satisfactory methods of delegating such responsibilities to student organizations with almost no undesirable consequences.

Two teachers in a junior college have described an interesting plan of student-faculty organization at Phoenix College in Arizona.[4] Here the institution tried to devise an arrangement which would provide practice in democratic living and at the same time secure adequate supervision of all activities. The faculty and administration had to ask themselves, "What can be accomplished in two years to teach the students to think and act democratically? Is two years too short a time?"

The central governing group at Phoenix is an Advisory Committee composed of elected representatives of the student body, other students chosen by these same representatives, elected members of the faculty, and a few of the administrative staff. This committee serves as both a senate and a supreme court. It allocates all student

[4] Robert J. Hannelly and Walter Seifert, "Why Are We Here?" *Junior College Journal*, XX (January, 1950), 259–265.

funds. It judges major disputes on the campus. In addition to the Advisory Committee there are other groups with special functions. Among the most active of these are a student executive board and separate associations of men and women students. This plan seems an excellent example of the attempt, now so common among the two-year colleges, to integrate effectively the activity program into the total college program.

Reasons for Ineffective Student Government. Not all forms of student government are an unqualified success. The apathy of students toward any activity which is not primarily entertainment has been given frequently as the principal reason for failure. To be sure, in some institutions the administration deliberately discourages any sharing of responsibility with students, on the theory that the authority of the faculty and administration might be challenged.

Even when encouragement is given by the administration and a very liberal type of student organization is formed, however, there are instances in which the program becomes ineffective unless help is received from the faculty. The following reasons have been given as the most important in contributing to such failures: (1) the tradition that men are the natural leaders and that women should not hold high positions in the student government; (2) habits formed in homes in which the thinking of students has been done for them; (3) mental laziness; (4) the student's fear of standing on his own feet; (5) lack of coöperation on the part of the faculty; (6) lack of sufficient interest and a feeling of responsibility on the part of students; (7) lack of understanding by both administration and students as to the rights and powers of each; and (8) the tendency of some student governments to serve only a part of the student body rather than the whole.[5]

Whether these are the only important obstacles to a successful student government organization may be questioned, but certainly

---

[5] Some of these are mentioned in Barbara Gill, "Fostering Leadership in Junior-College Students," *Junior College Journal*, XVII (December, 1946), 148–151.

they constitute some of the more common sources of difficulty in making such an organization work for the good of students.

OTHER CLUBS AND ORGANIZATIONS

With the possible exception of the student government, which may have a unique place and more than ordinary importance in the two-year college, the other organizations and clubs very much resemble those found in the typical four-year institution. In the 1920's the matter of establishing an honorary scholastic fraternity similar to Phi Beta Kappa was widely discussed at national as well as local junior college meetings. A group known as Phi Theta Kappa had been established at Hardin Junior College in Missouri about 1910, and chapters of this organization had spread into other two-year institutions. In 1929 Phi Theta Kappa received the official endorsement of the American Association of Junior Colleges. All honorary scholarship societies then existing in the member colleges were urged to apply for charters from the national headquarters of this fraternity. Requirements for membership in Phi Theta Kappa are much like those for Phi Beta Kappa. Admission is based upon both scholarship and character. The student must have at least a B average in his academic subjects, and the total membership in any local chapter may not exceed 10 percent of its institution's regular enrollment. In 1956 the organization was reported to have 150 local chapters.

The junior college national organization, however, also voted to recognize officially other scholarship societies with standards "on a level equivalent to those of Phi Theta Kappa." This was found necessary because of certain state laws, like those of Kansas, which prohibit in the public schools any fraternity or sorority with Greek letters in its name. These laws, in turn, were the result of evils which had developed in the secret societies of the public high schools; but the laws applied equally to the junior colleges under public control. Thus, several other honorary scholarship societies are fairly common among junior colleges, especially those in the subject matter fields of art, science, forensics, dramatics, business, agriculture, social studies, and journalism.

Social fraternities, while not found ordinarily in the community college and not everywhere among the dormitory institutions, still are rather numerous on junior college campuses—again in imitation of the senior college pattern. The usefulness of such organizations may be seriously questioned. Some states, as we have already noted, forbid their establishment in any secondary school (which, as in California, may include the junior college), and many two-year institutions individually discourage this type of student group. Community-serving institutions have quite naturally taken a stand (unofficially, for the most part) against all secret societies as undemocratic and discriminatory. Such groups represent a danger to the effectiveness of community service. There seems little doubt, nevertheless, that a number of secret organizations are still in existence on junior college campuses without the knowledge or consent of the administration and faculty. On the whole, fraternities and sororities appear to be on the wane.

Religious clubs, e.g., the Baptist Student Union, Lutheran Students Association, Hillel Club, Wesley Foundation, Canterbury Club, Newman Club, and the like, flourish in many junior colleges. They are probably more likely to function with real effectiveness in the dormitory institutions, where college becomes "a home away from home." These residence colleges feel a responsibility to encourage the participation of their young people in campus religious activities. The community colleges do not as frequently sponsor such groups; since local churches, of which the students are already members, maintain such organizations off the campus.

Occasionally religious clubs can become divisive influences in a junior college when they extend their activities beyond their proper sphere. The author has observed junior colleges in which the candidates for student body offices were nominated regularly by the various religious groups in competition with one another. The same sort of thing, of course, can happen with aggressive sororities and fraternities or with student political organizations like the Young

Democrats and the Young Republicans. Organizations which have a tendency to divide the student body have little beneficial effect on any campus.

Extent of Participation. Two-year colleges appear to have a larger proportion of their students engaged in extracurricular activities than do the four-year institutions. This may be the result in part, however, of the smaller average size of the junior colleges. A growing enrollment, while increasing the number and variety of clubs, often reduces the actual percentage of the student body participating as officers or members.

In junior college activities the great proportion of membership may be found in athletic teams and clubs. The next most popular activity is the student government. Then follow such activities as publications, musical groups, dramatic and social clubs, and the special interest organizations. While the size of the institution makes a considerable difference in the degree of student participation, some junior colleges of every size report very little interest in the extracurricular program. A few seem to feel that students are overparticipating.

Those institutions reporting lack of participation explain the situation in various ways. In some cases the students live in a widely scattered area and are prevented by transportation problems from attending meetings at other than regular college hours. Many junior college students work during their spare hours. Surveys in some of the California junior colleges have revealed that as many as half the student body felt themselves unable to engage in outside activities because they were "too busy." To remedy the situation, many institutions now set aside an hour or two per week in the regular schedule for cocurricular activities.

The chief barrier to this portion of the college program, nevertheless, probably lies in the attitude of the faculty. Sometimes faculty sponsorship of nonclass activities is merely an added chore for an overworked teacher. New instructors are considered fair game by the older members of the faculty and staff as persons on whom to dump their extraclass duties and responsibilities. It is clear that all teachers in a junior college ought to take part in the supervision of clubs and other organizations and that such assignments must be recognized as part of the teaching schedule. A teacher with a full program of classes and the sponsorship of two or three activities in addition obviously canot be expected to do a satisfactory job. What is taught by a teacher in the course of club activities may often prove as important as what is taught in class. Students who theorize about human relations in their courses may be totally unable to apply their theories in practice; many clubs demonstrate the prevalence of snobbery, self-seeking, and discrimination based upon race, creed, socio-economic status, and the like. But they also can become, through the guidance of advisers, practical laboratories for the development of saner, more harmonious human relationships.

While the cocurricular activities of a college ought not to overshadow the academic program, there seems little question that the two-year college has an excellent opportunity to strengthen the development of character and leadership by sponsoring and properly supervising such activities. The educational value of these programs is apparent.

JUNIOR COLLEGE ATHLETICS

The most glamorous and exciting, and at the same time the most potentially dangerous, area of student extracurricular participation is the athletic program. Here, as elsewhere, the two-year college has tended religiously to follow the lead of the four-year college. The place of athletics in the junior college movement is probably still undetermined, but rapid strides have been made within the past two decades. Growing interest in junior college teams, with important intersectional contests, may be observed.

Efforts toward organizing a national association for junior college athletics began as early as 1937, when a meeting was held in Fresno, California, to launch the idea. The National Junior College Athletic Association officially took shape on May 14, 1938. Charter members included the institutions at Bakersfield, Chaffey, Compton, Fullerton, Glendale, Los Angeles, Pasadena, Riverside, Sacramento, San Bernardino, San Mateo, Santa Monica, and Visalia—all in California. The earliest activities of the group were in track and field events. A "national" track meet was held under its auspices at Sacramento in 1939. The second such meet, the following year, drew teams from Arizona and Colorado as well as California.

The 1941 meeting of the association, in Denver, had several college representatives from the east and south as well as from the west coast. The war, however, interrupted the activities of the association, and no further athletic meets were sponsored from 1942 until 1946. A track meet in Phoenix marked the revival of national junior college contests, and in 1947 plans were laid at Compton for a nationwide basketball tournament. Later several other sports were added to the association's program, including football, boxing, golf, gymnastics, tennis, and swimming. National champions in each sport are now being named annually. The country has been divided into 16 regions, each of which has its own tournaments to designate the teams which enter the national competition.[6]

The association adopted and now administers a set of guiding principles for conducting junior college athletics. This was first officially adopted in 1953 at the Hutchinson meeting. There is also available to member institutions the N.J.C.A.A. Intercollegiate Athletic Group Insurance plan to cover the expenses of athletic injuries.

In the early 1950's President Reed K. Swenson of Weber College in Utah conducted a survey of intercollegiate athletics among the junior colleges of the United States. Among other discoveries he learned that (1) there was little uniformity among the institutions as to what they were attempting to achieve educationally and otherwise through their athletic programs; (2) most often the objective stressed was individual achievement in team play and sportsmanship, mental and social development, organic or physical growth, and recreational skill; (3) in very few instances did institutions use

---

[6] For much of the information about the National Junior College Athletic Association, the author wishes to thank President Reed K. Swenson, president of Weber College in Utah, the association's chairman.

athletics to promote the welfare of the student group as a whole, of the faculty, of the academic program, or of the community; and (4) the accomplishment of worth-while objectives in intercollegiate athletic programs was partially prevented by questionable practices in obtaining athletes, lack of adequate finances, lack of proper facilities, inadequate leadership, lack of equitable competition within a reasonable distance, poor attitudes and habits of athletes, and incompatible philosophies and standards of schools and the public.[7] The National Junior College Athletic Association was organized at least in part for the purpose of correcting some of these difficulties. At the same time, there seems little reason to question that an important factor in the movement has been the desire to obtain publicity and support for junior colleges.

The two-year college, while attempting to secure educational benefits from competitive sports, has nevertheless rapidly adopted the athletic pattern of the four-year colleges and university. This is a pattern which, unfortunately, has produced numerous unsavory incidents and scandals and which has aroused almost constant criticism from educators and the public. In football, the junior colleges have established their own series of postseason "bowl" games. During 1955 no less than six games of this nature were played. They were at Everett, Washington (Evergreen Bowl); Lancaster, California (Alfalfa Bowl); San Bernardino, California (Orange Bowl); Bakersfield, California (Potato Bowl); Gulfport, Mississippi (Hospitality Bowl); and Pasadena, California (Junior Rose Bowl). In both football and basketball, All-American junior college players are being selected. In other words, nearly every step taken in the growth of junior college athletics has been an effort to duplicate the situation so familiar in our older institutions of learning.

A few voices have been raised in a vain struggle to stem the tide. Many junior college educators, on the other hand, have been in favor of encouraging intercollegiate athletics but have felt that the two-year institutions are in a better position than their seniors to control

---

[7] Reed K. Swenson, "Status of JUCO Athletic Program," *N.J.C.A.A. Bulletin* (mimeograph report), June, 1952.

its evils. Ralph Prator placed his finger on an important factor in the picture when he declared that the moral character of the athletic program depends largely upon the moral integrity of the junior college administrator. He warned:

> To permit the athletic program simply to be an appendage of the curricular plan for the junior college is both unrealistic and dangerous. Athletics as such have come to stay in junior college education, and all of the high ideals desired and the concomitant evils which sometimes appear are with us whether we like them or not. A basic principle which is evident is that there is no substitute for moral integrity on the part of the administrator of the junior college. As soon as the objectives of the junior college have been identified by the administrator, he has the unavoidable responsibility of bringing his athletic program in line with those objectives.[8]

The excesses of the athletic program, rather than participation in sports, bring the evils which American higher education has experienced, Prator believes. Like many others, he is aware of the moral weakening which comes from the pressure to win games and to lose sight of legitimate educational objectives of such a program.

DIFFICULTIES IN JUNIOR COLLEGE ATHLETICS

The two-year institutions have tried to forestall some of the customary evils that attend the development of athletic programs in many American colleges and conferences by adopting a rather detailed set of principles for the guidance of members of the American Association of Junior Colleges.[9] Whether this code of conduct for the institutions will prevent some of the abuses prevalent among senior colleges remains to be seen. Other difficulties, however, face the junior colleges as an inherent result of their special position in American education.

The junior or community college is to some extent in an "in-between" position, its teams being too young for competition with

[8] Ralph Prator, "Administering Junior College Athletics," *Junior College Journal*, XXIV (January, 1954), 283.

[9] See Appendix I for the official statement of guiding principles for junior college athletics adopted in 1953.

senior colleges but too old for competition with high schools. For this reason the teams frequently have had to schedule games with various noncollege teams, such as local clubs or military camps. This would appear to be a rather undesirable situation from the educational point of view. To secure the highest benefit educationally, junior college players presumably should restrict their competition to teams representing other academic institutions with players in a similar age range. The spread of two-year colleges throughout all parts of the country will, of course, eventually eliminate this difficulty.

A particular problem of scheduling is experienced by the four-year junior college (grades ten through fourteen). In fact, the lack of suitable opponents has been cited as one of the chief reasons for the gradual disappearance of this type of institution. A quarter of a century ago Eells pointed out this disadvantage of the four-year junior college. He presented the picture in some detail:

> With what schools can the four-year junior college have such athletic contests—with two-year junior colleges, or with four-year high schools? Neither type of school, quite properly, feels that competition with the four-year junior college is fair. The only alternative is for the four-year institution to maintain "upper division" teams, who play with other junior colleges, and "lower division" teams, who play with high schools . . . .
>
> The ready answer of the six-four-four advocates, of course, is that this condition is but temporary, a mere transitional annoyance which is only incidental, and that it will disappear as soon as sufficient four-year junior colleges are established to organize separate athletic conferences of their own. This is perfectly true, if and when a majority or a large number of schools adopt this form of organization. The practical administrator, however, facing facts and not theories, may well pause to wonder just how long it is likely to take to achieve such a result, when over twenty years of arguments and efforts have resulted in the organization of less than a dozen such institutions in widely scattered parts of the country. With hundreds of two-year junior colleges and thousands of senior high schools more or less definitely committed to their type of organization, the transition is not likely to be rapid.[10]

[10] Walter Crosby Eells, *The Junior College*, Houghton Mifflin, 1931, pp. 709–710.

Eells' prediction has been confirmed by subsequent events. The growth of the four-year junior college not only has not been rapid (though at one time there were nearly 40 of them), but the movement in the direction of this kind of institution seems to have reversed itself. Thus the problem of scheduling athletic games for institutions of the 6–4–4 plan is one of decreasing importance.

More serious is the matter of a small enrollment in many of the two-year colleges. An institution with a limited number of men enrolled necessarily experiences a considerable amount of difficulty in fielding teams of adequate size. Some smaller colleges try to deemphasize the sports program for this reason, but various pressure groups of students, alumni, and the local community are likely to oppose this policy. A college without an active athletic program seems to many persons a very weak institution, if not something of an anomaly in American education. Consequently, much administrative effort may be exerted even in a small college to enter as many teams as possible into intercollegiate competition.

The sport in which the largest quantity of manpower seems to be needed is, of course, football. Yet football is also the sport most commonly associated in the public mind with a collegiate athletic program. Thus administrators frequently feel that, if any sport is to be eliminated from the program, it should not be football. One solution proposed for this problem is a modified form of the game played with six men on each team. Six-man football has been played among some junior colleges for several years with satisfactory results, though some reluctance to enter this field of competition still exists. Francis J. Mueller describes persuasively some of the advantages of this sport for small institutions:

> Football, among all the usual collegiate sports, entails the largest squads, the most expensive equipment, and the highest officiating costs, and demands as well, the best of physical conditioning. When to this is added high student turnover, typical of most junior colleges, where the most a coach can hope for is two seasons of participation per player, it becomes really a wonder that these institutions manage to field a team at all . . . .

Basically, six-man football is a wide-open, fast-moving game, in which the emphasis has been transferred from power play to passing and running . . . .

Seemingly this six-man sport should be particularly suitable to the football needs of the junior college . . . . It is a rugged contact sport, demanding team play and sound physical conditioning; it has spectator appeal, requires less manpower, less expense, less time in learning plays, and places particular emphasis on those fundamental aspects of football which players like best to perform.

No team sport, however, is really worth its while without competition. This means that the adoption of six-man football by one junior college is just so much wasted effort unless other institutions of like standing take up the sport . . . .

[This is] advanced suggestively as a remedy to a situation which could, in time, lead to the complete abolishment of [eleven-man] football from many a junior college athletic program. Those persons interested in the future of junior college athletics might profitably investigate further the game of six-man football.[11]

While this may be an excellent solution for the smaller colleges, it is not one likely to be used by the larger institutions. As two-year colleges grow steadily in enrollment, one may expect to find more and more regular football (with eleven-man teams) being played.

Some authorities on physical education have suggested the substitution of intramural athletics for intercollegiate competition, especially in the smaller colleges. Greater educational values would be gained, it is argued. Sexson and Harbeson go as far as to predict that intramural contests will eventually do away with all other forms of athletics. They point out that

intercollegiate participation must necessarily be limited to a small group of competitors. Such exhibitions are great spirit makers, but many educators have come to question their educational contribution, especially in comparison with an extensive program of intramural activities . . . .

In the New American College [i.e., the four-year junior college] intramural athletics will gradually replace the intercollegiate.

In the intramural program, virtually the entire student population par-

---

[11] Francis J. Mueller, "Six Man Football," *Junior College Journal,* XXI (February, 1951), 361–363.

ticipates. Whatever values it has to contribute will be received by large numbers and the program becomes genuinely educational. In intercollegiate exhibitions, on the other hand, for every one person participating in the contest, there are a thousand in the grandstand yelling themselves hoarse to no purpose.

Intramural athletics seem not susceptible to the evils and abuses that sometimes characterize the intercollegiate.[12]

If intercollegiate competition is on the wane in the two-year college, however, the signs have not yet appeared. In 1953 about 83 percent of the public junior colleges in the United States were sponsoring intercollegiate athletics in some form, while only 59 percent had programs of intramural competition.[13] Intramural sports appear more popular in the private institutions, which are smaller on the average and in 65 percent of which there are intramural programs. These figures do not indicate any strong trend away from intercollegiate athletics, however, and other evidence tends to confirm the fact that the two-year college has entered the field of national athletics on a grand scale.

Another difficulty affecting the junior college athlete has been the question of his eligibility upon transfer to a senior institution. In some conferences the transfer student is not permitted to compete on an athletic team for a semester or even a year after admission. The reason for this rule is obvious. It prevents the raiding of one college's athletes by another. But the transfer student from the junior college would seem to belong in an altogether different category. If he transfers after two years in the junior college, he will be forced by such a rule to wait until his senior year before participating as a member of an intercollegiate team. For this reason some conferences allow a transfer student to compete in sports during his first year in the senior institution, but in many cases his total number of years in varsity competition must be limited to no more than three.

On the other hand, there can be no question that some four-year

[12] John A. Sexson and John W. Harbeson, *The New American College*, Harper & Brothers, 1946, pp. 288–300.
[13] Charles W. McLain, "The Present Status of the Junior College in the United States," unpublished doctoral field study, Colorado State College of Education, 1953, pp. 159–160.

colleges are now using certain two-year institutions as "minor league farms." A freshman in a large university who is academically ineligible or who is not quite ready for the team sometimes may be "sent back" to a selected junior college for training and seasoning. Such arrangements undoubtedly smack of professionalism. At the same time, athletic ability may very well be of importance to a student who is attempting to transfer from a two-year college to a university. The junior college thus probably has a definite responsibility to keep its athletic program on a high and effective level. Eells discovered some years ago that the junior college transfer student actually had greater opportunities than the nontransfer student in the four-year college to participate on competitive athletics.[14] Whether this is true today we do not know, but experience as an athlete in the junior college presents no handicap in transferring.

THE MORAL PROBLEM OF ATHLETICS

The greatest question with respect to junior college athletics is, of course, the same one faced by nearly all institutions of higher learning in America—the moral problem. To a certain extent the athletic programs of our large colleges and universities have tended to become openly or secretly professionalized. Members of the American Association of Junior Colleges frankly recognized this problem when they drew up their code of principles to guide the direction of athletic programs. Commissioners have been appointed in various conferences to serve as policemen for the administration of the rules, on the theory that some institutions will try to evade them. That such elaborate safeguards must be provided is one of the saddest commentaries that could be made upon the conduct of intercollegiate athletics.

The two-year colleges, like their seniors, very emphatically insist that the athletic program should be first of all educational. Just what can the student be expected to learn from the present plan of athletic competition? Some of the individual benefits claimed for athletics include physical fitness, development of good sportsmanship, training in recreational skills, character training, personality

[14] Eells, *The Junior College, op. cit.*, p. 633.

development, knowledge of health rules, loyalty to the group, and several others. Everyone will agree that these are worth-while objectives. Unfortunately, the plain truth seems to be that, in a considerable number of collegiate institutions, any of these will be ruthlessly subordinated to the main goal—to win games.

One remedy proposed by the junior college leaders has been that of keeping athletic programs firmly in the hands of the administration. To be sure, the men who most enthusiastically recommend such a remedy are the administrators themselves. Almost exactly the opposite approach would seem to be indicated. If the athletic program is really intended to be educational, it should clearly be in the hands of the faculty. By this method it may be integrated into the curriculum as a whole. If the administration retains control, the program almost invariably is run as something separate and apart from the curriculum. On the other hand, if the administration has full responsibility for athletics, it should also bear the blame for transgressions of the conference rules. Too often the athletic coach loses his job when some scandal "breaks" at the institution, while the president (presumably at the head of the program) sits in judgment and immune to attack. A president should be willing to support his principles and practices to the extent of risking his position for them.

What would happen if the faculty were to take charge of athletics? Since this procedure has been tried so seldom, it is difficult to know. It seems reasonable to suppose, however, that the present evils of the system would see the light of day and ultimately be eliminated. One or two persons in a faculty might be willing to break rules and utter falsehoods for the sake of winning teams, but it would be a poor faculty indeed which would not take a strong and vigorous stand for honesty and frankness in the administration of the athletic policy. Furthermore, educational objectives might once again receive something more than lip service.

There is no intention here to condemn junior college athletics categorically. Much that is fine and educationally sound has been produced by conscientious administration of the programs. Yet the faculty and administration alike recognize dangers and excesses which have crept in, largely as the result of aping the older colleges. These abuses ought to be corrected. The education of students in dishonesty and immorality cannot be justified. The two-year colleges, alarmed at the open scandals produced at various large universities by almost open professionalism, as well as by some evidence of a movement in the same direction among certain junior colleges, have adopted a carefully considered statement of principles and have taken steps to put these principles into effect. It is admitted by all, nevertheless, that these principles never can be fully enforced without good will on the part of the individual institutions and the people in them.

Charges have been made that junior colleges, like their senior institutions, have been "buying" athletes, that is, paying athletes to attend college primarily to play on teams. Other criticisms have included the charge that far too much money is being spent on sports to the detriment of other portions of the academic program; that sports-minded administrators have played up athletics for publicity and thus overstressed its importance; that competition has not been of an equal nature among institutions of different sizes; that small colleges have suffered much too large a proportion of injuries per player because of the tendency to seek opponents with far bigger squads of players; that the costs of intersectional competition outweigh the advantages to be derived; that players miss a great many days of classwork or carry heavier schedules than should be carried; and that gate receipts determine which of the sports will receive the largest amount of attention from the college authorities.

If one balances these real or fancied evils against the possible benefits of the athletic program, no doubt most administrators and a fairly substantial number of the faculty would be in favor of continuing athletics in some form or other. Certainly, however, more safeguards will have to be provided than are now set up to prevent the junior college athletic programs from following the same route downward as the large university programs. Junior college people recognize the danger and are taking steps to meet it. One hopeful sign has been the increasing emphasis upon sports which the student can play throughout later life. "When you're through with college, you're through with intercollegiate athletics," is a common saying. But the skills learned in golf, tennis, badminton, swimming, hunting and fishing, and several other sports carry over into more mature years. Since these "minor" sports are somewhat less strenuous than football, basketball, and the like, more students can be encouraged to take part; and they need not be restricted to a small group of highly skilled specialists.

There has also been a rising interest among the two-year colleges in athletic programs for women. In the past, women students very often have not been provided even with minimum facilities for physical education activities in some institutions. During recent years, however, educators have come to believe that, although the nature of the program should be somewhat different for women, there is an equal amount of educational value in competitive sports for women students as for men students. No movement leading to intercollegiate competition of women's teams on a large scale is, of course, likely to occur.

Every sign points to the conclusion that athletics on the two-year college campus will continue to increase in importance. If proper safeguards are created, and particularly if educational values and the welfare of the student are stressed, this may be regarded as a highly favorable development. Grave dangers, however, face the junior college movement at this point, and wise educational states-manship will be required if they are to be avoided.

IX

Teachers and Administrators

WHAT qualifications and professional training should the teachers and administrators in American two-year colleges have? This is a matter which has occupied the thinking of many educators for at least the past quarter of a century.

In some states no special certification of teachers in the public junior colleges is required. In others, such as California, there are carefully considered requirements which make it impossible for a junior college teacher to be hired without special training for his work.

In 1952 the research office of the American Association of Junior Colleges undertook to study the teachers of two-year colleges in an effort to learn what the characteristics of successful teachers in this field really are. The method selected for the study was a logical but unusual one. A letter and questionnaire were mailed in March of that year to the president of each junior college asking that he nominate his best teacher or, if he could not decide on one, his two or three best teachers. The object was to compile a list of teachers in junior colleges everywhere in the country who would, in the opinion of the institutional presidents, comprise the very highest quality and the most desirable type of junior college teacher. After this group of "good" teachers had been nominated, another group of teachers was picked at random from the junior college catalogue. The second, or control, group was presumed to constitute an "average" faculty, including both "good" and "poor" individual teachers. It was hoped that, by comparing the two groups, it would be possible to identify those characteristics which definitely mark the successful teacher in this type of institution. Unfortunately, after several years of study, during the course of which every teacher on the list was requested to supply detailed information about his training and experience, no conclusive differences between the two groups could be found. Thus we are left with the unsatisfying fact that we do not really know exactly what the necessary characteristics of a successful junior college teacher are. We have only opinion to guide us toward a judgment in this matter.

GOOD AND POOR TEACHERS

Certainly, however, there are good and poor junior college teachers. Not all teachers prove successful in this kind of institution. Some characteristics which many educators believe make for success in this field are: (1) a well-adjusted personality; (2) interest in teaching rather than in research; (3) a good cultural background; (4) interest in the subject matter taught; (5) adequate professional training; (6) good habits of citizenship, including active participation in community activities; and (7) a mature professional attitude (loyalty to the institution, interest in professional activities, and sound professional ethics).

Most of these qualities ought to be present in any teacher. Yet not everyone who has done effective teaching in a university or in an elementary school is necessarily a success on the junior college level. Most teachers in junior colleges today have entered them after training for high school teaching or after some experience in the high school. A smaller number come from four-year colleges and universities. Only a few actually have prepared themselves for teaching in the junior college exclusively. For high school teachers, a position in the two-year college may seem like a step upward; for university teachers, it occasionally seems like a step downward. Neither conception is true. Junior college teaching is not on a higher plane than high school teaching; nor is it on a lower plane than university teaching. It is, however, different from either.

In the first place, the student is more likely to be near maturity than is the high school student; he is able to do more work, is more skeptical in his attitude, and usually is more curious intellectually.[1] The student ordinarily desires to be treated as an adult but often may behave as an adolescent. He suffers from confusions relating to his choice of life work and life partner.

The high school provides fairly strict supervision in the classroom and in extraclass activities, whereas in college the student stands very much on his own feet. In the two-year institution, lying between the secondary school and the university, the student must be allowed freedom to develop his resourcefulness and independence; but at the same time guidance must be readily available for him. The student at this stage is likely to be more intensely motivated by his vocational aims than is the younger person. Thus he looks for the practical elements in his classwork. He has either chosen his life work or is under pressure to do so very soon. The junior college teacher must adapt his teaching techniques to this situation.

In the high school the teacher often has frequent and close contacts with parents of the students. In the university the teacher often hold himself aloof from the students' families and from the community. In the junior college, on the other hand, community contacts rank high in importance. The teacher must be familiar with conditions in the community and very often place students in local jobs. Thus he follows a pattern of procedure unlike that of either the typical teacher in high school or the professor in a university. Jesse Bogue states, "If the interests, needs, aspirations, problems, and purposes of the people are to be understood and education related vitally to them, teachers must have, in addition to all other qualities and experiences, close contact with the people of the community—all

[1] Ralph R. Fields and Arthur H. Pike, "Community College Problems," *Teachers College Record*, LI (May, 1950), 528–536.

sorts and conditions of people. They cannot get this experience from books, no matter how vicarious it may be." [2]

William R. Wood stresses the fact that the teacher's duties in a community-serving institution can result in a very strenuous way of living.[3] A large portion of the teacher's time every day must be given over to conferring with individual students regarding their personal problems—occupational, social, psychological, and philosophical; assisting groups of students to realize a full return from their experiences in classroom, laboratory, workshop, and library; interpreting data from tests and personal records; and directing student participation in college and community recreational activities and services. Instead of spending 12 to 15 hours a week in the classroom and having the remainder of his time for preparation, research, marking of papers, and committee work, he must be on duty on the campus and accessible to students for six or more hours per day. He may also spend an evening or two each week as a member of some adult group in the community.

"The old town versus gown tradition is gone for good," Wood believes. "Committees and conferences, in school and out, with students, staff members, parents, and other citizens from the community multiply like rabbits. If you have a lazy imagination, don't try teaching in the community college." [4] The average teacher in this kind of institution will find himself called upon to perform on the local radio program, write an article for the local paper, give a talk to the Rotary Club or the Chamber of Commerce, serve on committees of the League of Women Voters or the Council of Social Agencies, lend a hand with Red Cross and Community Chest fund-raising drives, teach a Sunday School class or sing in a church choir, and join in public discussions of current issues on the invitation of the Parent-Teachers Association or the Civic Planning Commission.

The successful teacher in the two-year college, then, probably

[2] Jesse P. Bogue, *The Community College*, McGraw-Hill, 1950, p. 320.
[3] William R. Wood, "Professional Personnel for Community Colleges," *Junior College Journal*, XX (May, 1950), 513–522.
[4] *Ibid.*, p. 517.

must be a particular kind of person—one who enjoys the stimulation that his job conveys and who is willing to accept the obligations that it places upon him. A sympathetic attitude toward students of the junior college age group may very well be the most important personal characteristic necessary for success. It is this characteristic which 194 junior college administrators marked as especially important in a study of the effective and ineffective teacher in the junior college made by John F. Mead at the Colorado State College in 1940.[5]

Mead sent questionnaires to the 325 presidents of junior colleges listed in the directory of the American Association of Junior Colleges in 1939. He asked these administrators to list the qualifications which they looked for among the teachers whom they hired. He asked them also to indicate which qualifications they considered of greatest value for successful teaching in their institutions. "A sympathetic attitude toward students" was ranked first by 58.73 percent of those replying. The list of ten "most valuable" characteristics, as revealed by Mead's study, follows:

1. Sympathetic attitude toward students
2. Ability to stimulate intellectual curiosity among students
3. Wide range of general education
4. Character which exerts a wholesome influence on students
5. Careful habits in planning class work
6. Ability to adjust instruction to students' needs
7. Broad and accurate knowledge of subject matter
8. Loyalty to colleagues, department, and college
9. Broad social sympathies
10. Ability to organize and present subject matter clearly

Among other conclusions derived from the study, Mead learned that inspirational power, originality in teaching, efficiency in teaching methods, social culture, and high general scholarship were the qualifications most difficult to find among applicants for teaching positions in the junior college.

[5] John F. Mead, *The Effective and Ineffective Junior College Teacher,* unpublished doctoral study, Colorado State College, 1940.

Weaknesses of Junior College Teachers

In what ways can the preparation and selection of teachers for junior colleges be improved? This is a question which has troubled educators since the 1930's. While undoubtedly a large number of the present instructors in two-year institutions are proving highly satisfactory, the notion persists that methods of selecting and training those who will enter this field in the future can be benefited by revision. Administrators frequently complain of the weaknesses of teachers.

To determine exactly what the present weaknesses are, David B. Pugh and Roy E. Morgan sent questionnaires to a group of leading educators in American junior colleges in 1942. Recipients of the questionnaire were asked to name the weaknesses they had observed among teachers in junior colleges with which they were associated. Replies came from 105 individuals in 72 different institutions. Fifty important weaknesses were mentioned—a rather shocking total. Only those mentioned most commonly are given below. The poorer teachers were those who

1. spent long hours in research and become so soured by lack of contact with other individuals that health and mental attitude are not good.
2. have impaired health due to severe grind of graduate work.
3. are frequently warped scholars instead of teachers.
4. come from the graduate schools and tend to be crushed under the weight of pedantry.
5. are graduates from schools of education and tend to be intellectually arid.
6. are social misfits on the one hand or intellectual snobs on the other.
7. are from graduate schools which have emphasized scholasticism at the expense of personality.
8. are subject-matter conscious, with the result that they teach subject matter only instead of students.
9. are too inclined to emphasize what they know rather than what the students need.

10. are illiterate except in their own field.
11. are immature emotionally.[6]

From these comments one may see that the preparation of junior college teachers in subject matter is hardly criticized, except in the case of those who have graduated from colleges of education. What is lacking among these teachers, instead, is concern for their students and certain desirable personality factors.

One might conclude from a study of the kind made by Pugh and Morgan that the institutions in which junior college teachers receive their training could probably provide a better kind of training than that now given. The graduate schools might offer courses in *how* to teach, and the schools of education might give a program of greater depth in a more varied subject matter. Some attention obviously might well be given also to the kind of person who is admitted to training as a teacher.

WHAT KIND OF TRAINING IS BEST?

Some agreement needs to be reached with regard to the kind of training which will prove most useful to teachers in the two-year college. An attempt to arrive at some conclusions on this matter was made by a Committee on Teacher Preparation of the American Association of Junior Colleges in 1948 and 1949. The study was directed by Leonard V. Koos, long one of the leaders in the junior college movement. Teachers from 50 public two-year institutions in the Midwest supplied information for the study.

Among other findings, the committee reported that over half these teachers were giving instruction in two or more subject matter fields, though only 6 percent of the teachers of special subjects (such as commerce, home economics, and music) were teaching anything outside their own areas. More than half of the total group indicated that their teaching was being done on both the high school and the junior college level. In small junior colleges, as one might expect, a multiplicity of teaching assignments (that is, teaching in more

[6] David B. Pugh and Roy E. Morgan, "Faculty Needs and Requirements," *Junior College Journal*, XIII (May, 1943), 427–435.

than one subject field) was more common than in the larger institutions. Incidentally, most of the junior colleges from which replies were received had small enrollments.

Koos and his coworkers in the study concluded from the facts which were gathered that, in the light of the actual circumstances revealed, the teachers in two-year colleges ought to be prepared to teach in two or more related subject areas. Instead of specializing in one subject only (such as English, history, or physics), the student preparing for teaching in the junior college might well broaden his field of specialization to a whole division of subject matter, such as the humanities, the social studies, the physical sciences, or the biological sciences. Furthermore, such teachers probably ought to be prepared to teach high school courses as well. In addition to preparation in the subject matter to be taught, the Koos report suggests that every teacher on this level should have a knowledge of (1) the philosophy and place of the junior college in American education; (2) the organization and administration of junior colleges; (3) the junior college curriculum; (4) the psychology of late adolescence and postadolescence; (5) student personnel problems in the junior college; and (6) methods of teaching junior college students. In addition, he should be given a chance to do practice teaching in a two-year college before assuming full-time teaching responsibilities.[7]

Francis H. Dolan, a school superintendent and junior college director in Illinois, made a similar study at about the same time as Koos, using slightly different methods. He recommended that "junior college teachers be given the same education courses commonly required of candidates for secondary school teaching, with the addition of audio-visual education, plus . . . special junior college courses." The special courses Dolan proposed are the following:

1. *The Junior College.* History, development, functions, and philosophy of the junior college, organization and administration, with a section on adult education.

[7] Leonard V. Koos, "Preparation for Community-College Teaching," *Journal of Higher Education*, XXI (June, 1950), 309–317.

2. *Psychology of Adolescence.* Particular emphasis on the psychology of post-adolescent years, understanding of human growth and development and of the problems of the junior college age group.

3. *The Junior College Curriculum.* Techniques of curriculum construction and evaluation procedures.

4. *Guidance and Counseling.* Guidance adjusted to the junior college age group; a study of the individual student and his problems.[8]

H. L. Smith, dean of a junior college in Missouri, in 1949 informally polled a group of other administrators with whom he was associated. He sought to determine what kind of training these deans considered most useful for new teachers in their institutions. This group agreed upon the necessity of three courses which all junior college teachers ought to have taken. These were: (1) an undergraduate course in psychology; (2) an undergraduate or (preferably) a graduate course in the techniques of teaching; and (3) a course on the junior college describing its place in the educational system, with information on professional ethics, administrative problems, and principles of curriculum-construction.[9] It will be seen that the deans as a group tend to require far less in the way of specific professional preparation than might be expected.

The present writer, on the basis of teaching and administrative experience dating back to 1938, has come to the conclusion that every teacher in the two-year college ought to have, in addition to a broad general education and excellent preparation in the subject matter which he will teach, a minimum of three professional courses. These are intended to help him understand what the junior college is, to make his teaching methods more effective, and to provide a better understanding of what this type of institution does and how it accomplishes its purposes. The recommended courses are the following:

1. *The Junior and Community College.* The history, functions,

---

[8] Francis H. Dolan, *The Preparation of Junior College Teachers,* unpublished doctoral study, Colorado State College, 1950.

[9] H. L. Smith, "Better Education of College Teachers—The Junior College," *North Central Association Quarterly,* XXIII (April, 1949), 391–396.

present status, and problems of the junior college and the community college.

2. *Junior College Teaching.* A study of the psychology of young adults, the applications of psychology in teaching, the basic principles and functions of counseling and student personnel work, measurement, and junior college teaching as a profession.

3. *The Junior College Curriculum.* Techniques of junior college curriculum-construction, with special emphasis on general education, vocational education, curriculum surveys, and the relationship of curricular offerings to the needs of the community.

If a candidate for a teaching position in the junior college has mastered the subject matter contained in these three courses, he should be able, if he is basically fitted for the profession of teaching, to make a successful adjustment to the requirements of the two-year institution. Most junior college teachers in the past have been greatly handicapped by their lack of knowledge of these fundamentals.

REQUIREMENTS FOR CERTIFICATION

Although it is an accepted principle that teachers in American public schools must qualify for their positions through the process of state certification, some confusion may be noted as to whether this principle should apply to teachers in the public junior and community colleges. Few states now have adequate standards and procedures for certifying junior college teachers. The result has been that very few of these teachers have secured special preparation for this type of work. Where standards for preparation have been established, they correspond very closely to the requirements for high school teaching.

Actually, about three-fourths of the states have no state requirements at all for the certification of teachers in two-year colleges. In the other fourth, the principal requirement is a master of arts degree, though a few states have higher standards. California and Illinois seem to lead the nation in insisting that junior college teachers be well-qualified for their jobs. In both these states the two-year college has been firmly established for some time as a regular part of the educational system.

In California, besides qualifying for secondary school teaching in general, the junior college instructor must have studied the aims, scope, and desirable outcomes of the junior college and have had four semester hours of directed teaching experience on this level. In Illinois, among the 20 semester hours of education required for certification, there must be some work dealing with the junior college and other work dealing with psychology and guidance. In most other states the requirements, if set down at all, are sufficiently vague to be of little consequence. In Colorado, for example, a junior college teacher may be certified if the institution hiring him recommends him to the state department of education. Some tightening of standards for certification, however, is now taking place.

When Koos investigated the preparation of teachers in two-year institutions during 1940 and 1941, he found that most of them had been trained as high school teachers.[10] He decided that such a background can prove highly valuable to these teachers, but he indicated also that special course work in the problems of junior college education would have been desirable. He found, on the other hand, that junior college teachers in general appear to have had somewhat more training than high school teachers. Comparing a typical group of 1,424 teachers in the two-year institutions with 1,006 teachers in public high schools, he noted 63.6 percent of the former held master's degrees, as contrasted with only 43.6 percent of the latter. Also, 6.3 percent of the junior college group had the doctoral degree; whereas only .06 percent of the high school people had this much training.[11] The master's degree has become, in fact, the accepted standard of preparation for junior college teachers in many sections of the country.

[10] Leonard V. Koos, "Junior College Teachers: Preparation in Education," *Junior College Journal,* XVIII (February, 1948), 332–344.

[11] Leonard V. Koos, "Junior College Teachers: Degrees and Graduate Residence," *Junior College Journal,* XVIII (October, 1947), 77–89.

TRAINING INSTITUTIONS

When the committee on teacher preparation of the American Association of Junior Colleges attempted in the 1940's to learn where special courses for two-year college teachers were being offered, only 34 institutions could be found which even pretended to supply training in this field.[12] In the vast majority of cases, a student wishing to become a teacher in a junior college could prepare himself either in the courses usually offered for high school teaching or in a broad program of general education. Those institutions giving courses aimed particularly at the preparation of teachers for junior colleges offered them, for the most part, in programs on the graduate level leading to the master's degree.

Not only has there been a scarcity of programs designed for the proper preparation of the two-year college teacher, but such programs as exist are vastly different from each other. Very little uniformity has been developed even today. Perhaps it should be emphasized, however, that a beginning of special preparation for teaching on this educational level has at least been made, and it seems likely that considerable development will take place in the future.

Among the institutions which had established carefully organized programs in this field by 1948–1949 were Stanford University, the University of Southern California, the University of Chicago, Michigan State University, the University of Michigan, Teachers College of Columbia University, Syracuse University, Pennsylvania State University, and the University of Texas.[13] In five of these the student received the opportunity of doing practice teaching in junior colleges. In a few instances, however, the program included only one course directly pertaining to the two-year institution. At least 30 colleges and universities were offering summer courses in junior

[12] Leonard V. Koos, "Programs of Junior-College Teacher Preparation," *Junior College Journal*, XIX (February, 1949), 333–346.
[13] "Where to Go for Junior-College Preparation," *Junior College Journal*, XVIII (April, 1948), 444–445.

college work during 1948 and 1949, and additional summer programs have been started since that time.

As an example of the kind of organized course of study available to students hoping to enter junior college teaching, we may cite the program of Stanford University. This is intended as preparation for the state junior college credential, which is required of teachers in the public junior colleges of California.

The program at Stanford is on the graduate level and leads to the master of arts degree. The student must complete work in a satisfactory teaching major and also in a teaching minor, besides which he must successfully complete three special courses. The three courses include one dealing with the aims and scope of the junior college, one in methods of instruction, and one in practice teaching. In addition, other methods courses are taken.

Michigan State University may be mentioned as an example of a Midwestern institution offering a program in this field. The Michigan State program is aimed at preparation for the Michigan junior college permanent certificate, although it purports to prepare administrators as well as teachers. This certificate requires a master's degree or other acceptable degree based upon at least five years of college or university work at an accredited institution. Besides a major on the graduate level in the subject to be taught in the junior college, the applicant for such a certificate must also have completed 15 or more semester hours in professional courses in education, including the following or their equivalents: principles of teaching, psychology of education, and history or philosophy of education. Courses in methods and in directed teaching are recommended though not required.

At Teachers College of Columbia University, the programs for training administrators and for training teachers are separated. Columbia offers a diploma in educational administration with specialization in administration of junior colleges. It also offers a course of study for teachers in the "community college, junior college, or technical institute." Students expecting to become teachers or administrators on this level plan their programs in consultation with faculty advisers. Thus individual backgrounds are considered, and not every student studies the same subjects. Among the courses available in recent years were the following: purposes and policies of higher education, introduction to American higher education, human relations and the college program, overview of college administration, administration of higher educational institutions, the community college, seminar in curriculum problems in community colleges, seminar in administration of community colleges, and the like.

The University of Texas offers courses of study on the graduate level intended to prepare students for teaching in many types of educational institution, including the junior college. Among the courses particularly planned for the latter are junior college curriculum, seminar in junior college curriculum, community services of the junior college, problems in junior-college administration, and the junior college.

These four programs—one from the West, one from the Midwest, one from the East, and one from the South—indicate in general the type of preparation which is now being offered candidates for the junior college teaching field. While they resemble one another in certain respects, they are considerably different in other respects.

It must be confessed that, in most American university departments of education or in the teachers colleges, very little work is now being offered for the specific preparation of junior college personnel. The typical pattern seems to be one which prepares the student for high school teaching and adds a course or two having something to do with the two-year college. As the numbers of those teaching in this kind of institution increase and as the state requirements for certification are raised, no doubt greater efforts will be made to insure that junior college teachers are prepared as effectively as possible for their jobs. Until this transpires, the two-year colleges will be forced by the present lack of specially trained instructors to do much of the training in their in-service programs.

Educators in the two-year colleges appear agreed that the kind of training usually given high school teachers or university professors will not suffice for teachers in this type of institution. Since it serves a different, though complementary, purpose in American education, its teachers must be of a different kind and prepared in a different way from those of other parts of our system. Exactly what kind of training will eventually be decided upon as most useful is not now apparent, but some of its elements probably will be: (1) a master's degree in the teaching field; (2) a broad foundation of general education; and (3) a substantial background of professional courses dealing specifically with the two-year college (possibly including a course on the junior college and its functions, one on educational psychology, one on the curriculum, and courses in methods and in practice teaching).

WORKING CONDITIONS FOR THE TEACHER

Teaching in the two-year college is more likely to resemble teaching in the high school than teaching in the university, though this depends a little upon the particular two-year college in which one is located.

The basic difference between university work and work in the junior college lies in the emphasis which the latter places upon teaching in contrast to research. Whereas a university professor may devote from eight to twelve hours per week to actual classroom duties and the rest of his time to productive scholarship (with a few hours given to conferences, committee work, and similar activities), the teacher in the junior college ordinarily devotes at least 15 hours to his classes each week. Often it is even more. The other working hours are spent in preparation for class, in conferences, in committee activities, and in contact with various groups in the community. The university professor may be said to spend half his working time in teaching and its related duties and the other half in research. The junior college instructor does little research, if any, but keeps busy during the entire week with actual teaching and related activities, consisting mainly of direct work with students, their parents, and their present and future employers.

This is not to say that the junior college teacher works harder or longer than the university professor. On the contrary, both are likely to be found on the job from 40 to 60 hours per week. The difference lies not in the amount of work done but in the nature of it. Perhaps the typical teacher in a two-year college divides his time roughly as follows: 15 hours in the classroom, 15 hours in lesson preparation, and 15 hours in conferences, community meetings, and similar activities. As can be seen, this makes a total of some 45 hours per week. The two-year college can hardly be considered, then, a place for a lazy person.

At the same time, the junior college instructor enjoys many of the privileges of people on a college faculty. Supervision does not have the same importance in the junior college as it seems to have in the high school. The teacher generally is regarded as an expert on his special subject and has greater freedom in presenting it to his students. Like the university professor, he may have the right of choosing the textbooks he will use or of eliminating textbooks entirely from his classes. Since he deals with older students, the teacher in this type of institution has to face fewer problems of discipline than does the high school teacher. He can deal with students pretty largely as adults. To many teachers this fact has a great appeal.

While most junior colleges do not establish academic ranks for their teachers (*i.e.*, instructor, assistant professor, associate professor, and professor) as nearly all four-year colleges and universities do, the result of having only one rank (ordinarily, that of instructor) seems to be a firmer unity and *esprit de corps* among the faculty. Harold H. Punke discovered in 1954 that only about 10 or 11 percent of the two-year institutions maintain the traditional system of academic ranking.[14] Wherever the matter of establishing such ranks has been put up to the faculty, there seems to have been strong opposition to the idea—or at least this has been the case in recent years.

On the other hand, many of the two-year colleges are still unable to protect the security of their instructors with a policy relating to

[14] Harold H. Punke, "Ranking, Tenure, and Sex of Junior-College Faculties," *School Review*, LXII (November, 1954), 480–487.

tenure. In the typical American college or university, a professor, after a probationary period of three to seven years, ordinarily receives what is described as a permanent or indefinite appointment. That is, he cannot be discharged except for gross incompetence, moral turpitude, or inability of the college to pay his salary (the latter only in the case of a demonstrable and unforeseen financial exigency). Many high schools also are able to provide tenure plans. This tends to make teaching more secure economically and to protect teachers against political pressures and the whims of administrators. Punke has shown that in 1954 over 46 percent of the junior colleges in the United States had no tenure policy at all. In 58 percent of the public institutions, however, and in 45.1 percent of the private, permanent tenure until the prescribed age of retirement was granted after three years of satisfactory service on the faculty.[15]

Among the complaints which junior college instructors express regarding their work, those set forth by Timothy P. Donovan seem typical. Donovan points out that, because of heavy extracurricular and community duties which he is expected to perform, the typical instructor in this kind of institution often does not have enough time to prepare his classwork in a thorough and scholarly manner. Thus his teaching may prove less effective than it might be under other conditions. Furthermore, says Donovan, the junior college teacher occupies a position, in the student's eyes, halfway between that of a university professor and that of a high school teacher. This appears to result in some confusion, and the instructor loses his feeling of "belonging" to some definite part of the educational system. Besides, Donovan believes, the teacher in the two-year college finds it extremely difficult to serve equally well the student who plans to transfer later to a four-year college or university and the student who will terminate his educational program at the end of two years. These groups of students have different and sometimes conflicting needs, and thus an instructor must be constantly adapting his presentation of the subject matter to student groups which are basically dissimilar in their needs and objectives. Donovan strongly recom-

[15] *Idem.*

mends that additional efforts be made to pattern the conditions of teaching in junior colleges more closely after those which exist in the universities. This, he thinks, will give teachers in two-year colleges greater dignity, authority, and self-confidence.[16]

Other special problems confront the instructor in community-serving institutions. T. G. Hawkins insists that such a teacher, besides having an obligation to know a good deal about the history, philosophy, functions, and even administration of junior colleges, must act constantly as a public-relations officer for his college. Thus he must know both his institution and the community well. He should be able to communicate effectively both with young people and with adults. He must participate actively in extracurricular programs. He should know his teaching field well without being a narrow specialist. He must understand the mental, physical, and institutional development of young people in junior colleges in order to make certain that every one of his students, whether adolescent or adult, secures what he needs and desires from his course work.[17] This, one must admit, is a rather large order for any teacher.

In spite of the present lack of adequate programs for training the two-year college teacher, in spite of the special difficulties which face him, and in spite of the various weaknesses which have been pointed out in the present faculties of junior colleges, there can be little question that the instructors in these institutions today are better trained and more fully aware of their particular opportunities and functions than were their predecessors of a generation ago. C. C. Colvert has shown that, if one considers quantity of training alone, the level of preparation for these teachers has risen considerably since 1918. The number possessing master's degrees, for example, has increased from 39 percent among the public junior colleges and 27 percent among the private institutions in 1918 to 68.5

[16] Timothy P. Donovan, "Problems of the Instructor in the Junior College," *Junior College Journal*, XXII (May, 1952), 494–497.

[17] T. G. Hawkins, "The Junior College Teacher—Some Unique Characteristics," *Bulletin of the National Association of Secondary-School Principals*, XXXVIII (October, 1954), 149–152.

percent and 62.9 percent, respectively, in 1955.[18] While these figures do not necessarily indicate a higher quality as well as increased quantity of training, they at least suggest that a better qualified group of instructors is now entering the junior college teaching field.

THE QUESTION OF SALARIES

How do the financial rewards of teaching in the two-year college compare with those in other educational institutions? Unfortunately, so much variation exists among the individual institutions that accurate general statements about salaries are very hard to make. While some two-year colleges, particularly the larger ones, pay comparatively high salaries to their teachers, many of the smaller institutions pay very little. Much depends upon size, and even more upon the type of support which the college receives. Public junior colleges tend on the average (though not invariably) to pay higher salaries than do those under private control. Perhaps it would be fair to state that salaries paid by the two-year institutions of a given area are likely to compare favorably with pay received in the high schools and four-year colleges of that area. In other words, the remuneration of a junior college instructor is not noticeably lower or higher than that of teachers in related institutions.

Colvert completed a study of junior college salaries for the Administrative Problems Committee of the American Association of Junior Colleges in 1953. The study undertook to determine the status of salaries in 1952–1953 and to compare the picture in that year with information derived from previous studies.[19] Data provided by 259 junior colleges throughout the United States pointed to several interesting conclusions. In the first place, it was found that the average salaries of teachers in the publicly supported junior col-

[18] C. C. Colvert, "Professional Development of Junior College Instructors," *Junior College Journal*, XXV (April, 1955), 474–478.

[19] Comparisons were made with data from the following studies: Henry G. Badger and Walter C. Eells, "Junior College Salaries in 1941–42," *Junior College Journal*, XV (April, 1945), 346–358; Sebastion V. Martorana and Leonard V. Koos, "Junior College Teacher Salaries in 1947–48," *Junior College Journal*, XIX (December, 1948), 185–194.

leges reporting were about $1,000 higher than the averages among the private junior colleges. This appeared to be true in all parts of the country, so far as the figures could be accepted as representative. Some variation was noted, however, with respect to salaries paid in different sections. Less variation occurred among the private institutions than among those under public control.

The academic degrees held by members of the faculty were found to have considerable bearing upon the amount of salary earned. In general, those with higher degrees earned larger salaries. On the other hand, certain instructors without academic degrees in the public institutions actually earned more than did those with master's degrees. This can probably be explained by the fact that it is necessary to recruit instructors of many industrial subjects directly from industry rather than from the ranks of trained teachers. The difficulty of obtaining well-qualified persons for such positions would account for the relatively higher salaries paid them.

Like salaries in other educational institutions, the salaries of teachers in two-year colleges have been rising steadily since 1941. They have not risen, of course, as fast as the cost of living, though they now show some signs of catching up. Among the public institutions the median salary for teachers increased by $1,161 from 1941–1942 to 1947–1948, and by $1,154 from 1947–1948 to 1952–1953. Among the private institutions, the increase has been slightly smaller. The median salary rose about $1,044 between 1941–1942 and 1947–1948, but only about $421 between 1947–1948 and 1952–1953.

The actual annual salary of teachers with master's degrees for approximately nine months of teaching in junior colleges of the United States reached an average figure of $4,171 in 1952–1953, and the average for all junior college teachers regardless of degrees was a little higher ($4,337). Public institutions, however, averaged $4,710, while private institutions average only $3,052. The western area (that is, the Pacific Coast region, especially California) tended to pay the highest average salaries. Teachers in the highest paid classification of the public two-year colleges there were receiving a median salary of $9,112, well above that of any other region. The lowest average salaries were found in the South and in New England. The median instructional salary for all institutions reporting from the South was $3,236, while in New England institutions (all privately controlled) it was $3,437. Salaries of teachers in all types of two-year institutions throughout the United States have risen, according to the figures at hand, from a median of $2,095 in 1941–1942 and $3,316 in 1947–1948 to $4,337 in 1952–1953—an increase of over 100 percent in a little more than one decade. A similar increase has taken place in the salaries of administrative officers, which are, of course, higher than those of teachers but which cover, as a rule, 12 months of active duty (not counting annual vacations.)[20]

A recent study of 1955–1956 teachers' salaries made by the Research Division of the National Education Association shows a further increase over 1952–1953. According to this report, public school classroom teachers in 1955–1956 earned an average salary of $4,000 for nine months of teaching; junior college teachers earned an average of $5,127; and four-year college and university professors of all ranks, an average of $5,243.[21]

While salaries of junior college personnel have been improving, steps have also been taken to add so-called "fringe" benefits in more and more of the institutions. Retirement plans have been instituted in the majority of those under public control; some institutions have entered the federal Social Security plan. Group insurance, especially hospital and medical insurance, has been made available. Definite salary schedules, based upon such factors as academic training, teaching experience, related experience, and professional growth, have become commonplace. On the whole, however, two-year colleges, and particularly those under private control, still have a long way to go in the direction of providing financial security to

[20] C. C. Colvert and M. L. Litton, *Junior College Teacher Salaries, 1952–53,* mimeograph report of the Research Office, American Association of Junior Colleges, Austin, Texas, March 10, 1953.
[21] *Salaries Paid and Salary Practices in Universities, Colleges, and Junior Colleges, 1955–56,* research bulletin of the National Education Association, October, 1956.

their teachers. They have not as yet reached the favorable position of many public high schools and the established four-year colleges and universities.

Although teachers in the two-year institutions do not enter this field primarily for its financial attractiveness, but mainly to be of service educationally, there seems little doubt that improvements in salaries and other benefits will help to keep the best instructors in the junior colleges rather than allowing them to be lured away by industry or other educational institutions. Failure to keep pace with the current trend toward increasing salaries and other measures of security will place the two-year colleges in an unfavorable position in the matter of securing and retaining first-rate instructors. While many teachers in this field will remain in spite of personal sacrifice and the attraction of other offers, each institution owes its faculty the right to a reasonably comfortable existence. No junior college—and this is true of all other elements of the educational system as well—can be any better than the quality of its faculty.

X

Legal Status and Accreditation

WHAT is the legal status of the American two-year college? Should the institution be regarded as a regular, accepted part of our public educational system, or is it something which cannot legally exist without special enactment of local or state legislation?

As far as privately supported junior colleges are concerned, of course, their legal basis ordinarily may be found in legislative charters. Every such institution applies (or should apply) to the legislature of its own state for a charter that establishes it as a legal entity. The charter, in effect, constitutes a kind of contract under which the trustees of the college agree to conduct an educational program of a specified kind for the common good and in return receive official recognition as a corporate body and, usually, permission to grant academic degrees or titles, to buy and sell property, to sue and be sued, and the like.[1] A charter sometimes may be revoked if the institution fails to maintain its part of the agreement—for example, if it engages in dishonest business practices or makes major changes in the nature of its work without securing prior legislative approval. The charter once given cannot, however, be revoked or altered arbitrarily by the legislature. This principle of American law was made clear in the famous Dartmouth College Case of 1819, one of the landmarks in American educational history. A private,

[1] See Appendix II for a typical junior college charter.

nonprofit junior college may be required in some states to register with the Secretary of State or similar officer as an eleemosynary corporation in order to secure exemption from taxation.

TWO-YEAR COLLEGES IN THE PUBLIC SCHOOL SYSTEM

Probably no special act of a state legislature is really necessary to guarantee the legality of a junior college or community college established as an extension of the public school system. American high schools have legally offered work on the level of the thirteenth and fourteenth grades as far back as the 1880's without being seriously challenged, ordinarily designating such programs as postgraduate education. In order, however, to avoid any questions of legality and also to forestall effective opposition to the extension of low-cost or free education to older students, the founders of the tax-supported junior and community colleges have considered it highly desirable to obtain legislative sanction in advance. The easiest and probably the best method of securing this is through what has been called "enabling" legislation.

The first example of such an enabling act for public junior colleges was that passed by the legislature of California in 1907. The act provided no state support but merely recognized the right of school districts to organize institutions of this type for their local students. Following the California law, enabling legislation of a similar type has been enacted in 25 other states as of 1956, as well as in the Territory of Alaska. Such laws, incidentally, have successfully passed the test of constitutionality in several states, including California, Illinois, Kansas, Kentucky, Louisiana, and Mississippi.[2]

A recent example of this kind of legislation is the Massachusetts law adopted in 1948. This grew directly out of previous provisions, made following World War II, for special two-year college programs offered in various communities for war veterans. The 1948 law gave towns and cities of the state authorization to establish public junior

[2] Charles W. Simms, *The Present Legal Status of the Public Junior College,* George Peabody College for Teachers, 1948, pp. 6–13.

colleges within their own local school systems. It also gave the state department of education the power to set up wherever necessary state controlled community colleges. It should be remembered, however, that the state of Massachusetts has a large number of extremely good four-year and two-year colleges under independent control serving nearly every part of the state. Under these conditions, publicly supported institutions have not been widely demanded, and, as the result, only two have actually been established, both of them quite small. Future developments under the new law remain to be seen, though many educators believe that the spread of public two-year colleges even in a state well served by private institutions is only a matter of time.

In 12 states which do not as yet have enabling legislation of the general type mentioned above, public junior colleges exist either by virtue of special laws pertaining to individual institutions or without any legislative sanction whatsoever. There seems to be no reason for questioning the legality of the public two-year colleges even in those areas in which the legislature has never taken steps to sanction them. In some other states public two-year insitutions have been established as branches of state universities or colleges. Thus they receive their support from public funds but are not locally controlled. An example of the latter type of institution is Nevada Southern (officially, Southern Regional Division, University of Nevada), which was opened at Las Vegas in 1955 as a junior college branch of the state university after a 1951 law providing for extension of work in some high schools beyond the twelfth grade was declared unconstitutional. This law, by the way, was voided by the state's district attorney rather than by the courts and is the sole example, apparently, of a negative decision on the validity of such a statute.

Laws Affecting District Organization

In addition to the general enabling legislation for two-year colleges and the special acts establishing particular junior or community colleges, the principal kinds of legislation passed since 1915 have been: (1) those relating to the formation of junior college districts and (2) those relating to state support for the two-year institutions. There also have been laws affecting junior colleges in other ways— those, for example, which have been passed recently in Florida, Illinois, Michigan, and Nebraska to describe exactly what the junior or community college is under the laws of each of these states. In some places—Texas, for instance—there are definite legislative requirements with respect to the subject matter offered in the public junior college curriculum. Elsewhere—in Florida since 1955—there may be a plan established by the legislature for state-wide supervision of all institutions of this type through a central body of control.

When public junior colleges first appeared, most people thought of them as constituting an extension of the high school program. Thus the logical method of setting up such an institution seemed to be through the local high school district. Many junior colleges came into existence in this way, being controlled by the same board which controlled the local high school and often being housed in the high school building. But some high school districts that wanted junior colleges were too small to support the additional tax burden, so that the next step in the development of districts consisted in the consolidation of two or more districts or, in some cases, counties, to form an entirely new district for the junior college. In some of the relatively early California legislation on the junior college, as well as in recent laws of such states as Florida, Michigan, and Nebraska, the formation of these union districts has been specifically legalized.

At the present time, a majority of the junior or community colleges of the public type are operating under the control of local (single rather than consolidated) high school districts. In other words, the same board which administers the local high school also controls the junior college. Martorana reports that "approximately 70 per cent of the local and district public junior colleges were operating under a common board with the high school" in 1952.[3]

---

[3] S. V. Martorana, "The Legal Status of American Public Junior Colleges," in Jesse P. Bogue (ed.), *American Junior Colleges,* American Council on Education, 1956, p. 21.

In the consolidated or union districts, however, and in those junior college districts which are separately organized (even though lying within the same geographical boundaries as the high school district), the two-year college has its own board of control. Frequently, as in Colorado, the junior college may be operated by a county district, and there are instances of the joining together of two or more counties as "joint county" districts. Other variations of these two distinct patterns of control occur, but the differences cannot be regarded as of great importance. In general, we may satisfactorily divide junior college district organization into two main types. These are: (1) districts which place control over the institution in the hands of the same board which operates the local high school and (2) districts which place control (whether within a single high school district or including more than one) in the hands of a board exclusively concerned with junior college education.

Other public two-year colleges may be directly controlled by designated central agencies of the states, whether the state board of education, the state university, or a special board. This appears to be the pattern now developing in Florida. Wherever junior colleges exist as branches of state universities, as in Louisiana, Nevada, Pennsylvania, and Wisconsin, control is out of the hands of local boards.

STATE FINANCIAL AID

It seems almost an axiom that public two-year colleges develop rapidly and strongly in the states which provide adequate financial assistance through a state-wide plan of regular support, but slowly and with difficulty in the states which leave the whole burden of support from tax funds in the hands of local taxpayers. Part of the recognized strength of the excellent system of junior colleges in California derives from the fact that these institutions have been well-supported by the state. As the result of such aid from the state, junior colleges throughout California are able to offer programs for which no tuition at all is charged the student.

The same conclusion can be drawn from the experiences of other states, though in varying degrees. In Colorado, for example, the growth of enrollment in two-year colleges (under county boards) has come about in large measure because of the state's willingness to support the institutions as members of Colorado's public educational system. Because the amount of state support is not very large, however, the students in Colorado junior colleges must pay certain tuition charges. The states which have enabling laws for junior or community colleges but limited provisions for state support have discovered, in general, that the public two-year institutions have developed slowly because of inadequate financial backing.

Thirteen states (Arizona, California, Colorado, Florida, Idaho, Illinois, Iowa, Michigan, Mississipi, Missouri, New York, Texas, and Washington) now offer substantial state aid for the operation and maintenance of their junior colleges. In South Carolina, on the other hand, the statutes of the state specifically forbid such direct help to the institutions. That the amount of money received from state sources remains at present insufficient for maintaining satisfactory programs appears to be indicated by the fact that most public junior colleges are continuing to charge tuition fees to their students. This clearly differentiates junior college education from other levels of the public educational system. That situation, of course, is not found in California, where the institutions have been enabled to prosper without any income from student tuition fees (the state, in fact, prohibiting the collection of any fees from students in the public schools) and where free public education through the fourteenth grade is a reality. In the state of New York, where some state funds are distributed to the junior colleges, the total cost of supporting a two-year college program is equally divided (in theory, at least) among the state, the local community, and the students, each one of these groups being expected to pay about one-third of the total amount required.

The majority of American citizens appear to favor the idea that every student going beyond the twelfth grade ought to contribute substantially to the cost of his further education, but a growing minority has been urging the extension of our nation-wide system of free (or nearly free) public education into the thirteenth and fourteenth grades or even into the university years. Whether this plan ever will be generally adopted is, for the moment, not easy to predict.

LEGAL RESTRICTIONS ON TWO-YEAR COLLEGES

When a state sanctions or finances a system of two-year colleges within its borders, it usually considers it necessary to place reasonable legislative restrictions upon the conditions of establishment and the functions of the institutions. For instance, it has been customary (though with a few exceptions) to permit the establishment of two-year colleges only in those communities which are not too sparsely settled to provide a sufficiently large minimum enrollment. In Iowa, South Dakota, and South Carolina, the junior college district must contain a population of at least 5,000 persons, a rather small number for the purpose, in the opinion of many educators; in Florida the district must have a population of not less than 50,000. Perhaps a minimum population of approximately 15,000 would be adequate for junior college districts in most of the states. Often the enrollment in the local high schools is used as a measuring stick. In such cases it is ordinarily considered wise to restrict the establishment of two-year colleges to communities in which the high school enrollment numbers at least 1,000 students. Obviously a junior college with an insufficient number of students—under 200—cannot offer a satisfactory program.

Possibly of even greater significance than population for the success of a junior college is the ability of a district to give it the necessary financial backing. Thirteen states (Arizona, California, Colorado, Idaho, Minnesota, Mississippi, Montana, Nebraska, Oklahoma, Oregon, South Carolina, Texas, and Wyoming) require that the assessed valuation of the taxable property in any junior college district must meet a certain minimum figure: from $3,000,000 in Montana to $20,000,000 in Colorado and Wyoming. The figure may depend somewhat upon the proportion of the total support which the local district will be called upon to provide. The greater the percentage of state support, the lower the minimum valuation of the district may be. As a rule of thumb, a figure somewhere around $10,000,000 may be considered adequate in most states.

While the state laws as a rule do not concern themselves with such matters as admission requirements, eight states (California, Kansas, Michigan, Mississippi, Montana, Nebraska, South Carolina, and Washington) have legislation stating the general standards for admission. In most instances, the single standard may merely be graduation from the twelfth grade or the equivalent, with some provision for special and adult students. Academic standards are left, on the whole, under the supervision of the state board of education or of some special agency of central control—if specifically mentioned at all in the statutes. For the most part, pressure for maintaining academic programs of suitable quality has come from regional and other accrediting agencies.[4]

ACCREDITATION OF TWO-YEAR COLLEGES

Although agencies for approving the programs of educational institutions of all types have not proved an unmixed blessing, their principal effect among the two-year colleges has been to encourage the development of better facilities and curriculums. Accrediting agencies traditionally have concerned themselves with the *quality* of educational opportunities offered students. Thus an officially accredited institution may be regarded as one in which adequate academic standards are being maintained. So far as the institution itself is concerned, accreditation gives it a kind of respectability which it can hardly achieve by any other method. Since junior colleges remain essentially a new phenomenon on the American educational scene, such evidence of respectability seems to be necessary for their acceptance by the public. Furthermore, students are protected from inadequate and poorly staffed programs if they avoid the institutions which fail to meet regional standards.

[4] Some helpful ideas for instituting new legislation may be found in *Suggested Procedures and Techniques for Initiating and Developing Legislation for a State Plan for Community Colleges,* published by the American Association of Junior Colleges, 1950.

Accreditation may be given by state boards or departments of education, by state universities and colleges, by private or voluntary state associations, and by groups representing various professions (engineering, music, nursing, and the like). By all odds the most highly respected accrediting groups, however, are the six regional associations.[5] These arose originally to devise a fair method of accrediting academies and high schools and of improving relations between the secondary schools and the colleges. Organized on a completely voluntary basis, the regional associations established not only rules for evaluating high school college-preparatory programs but also academic standards to be maintained by their own collegiate members. When more nonmember colleges applied for membership in these associations, the applicants were subjected to careful inspection and their qualifications voted upon before they were accepted. Thus a formal process of evaluation developed by which the work of an institution could be examined and, to a degree, measured. Nobody believes that membership in one of the regional associations is in itself a guarantee of excellence. Yet no other indicator appears to reveal so clearly the sincerity of an institution in its attempts to maintain minimum standards of quality in its program.

Regional Associations and Junior Colleges. Perhaps the greatest weakness of the regional accrediting agency—one which applies to other agencies as well, of course—is its tendency to perpetuate a single, traditional standard of higher education. When junior colleges began to arrive on the American scene, they had difficulty at first in securing accreditation because they were unlike the traditional four-year colleges. In some regions they were not accepted into the accrediting associations unless they exactly duplicated the universities' freshman and sophomore years. This actually remained the case in New England until well into the 1950's. Recently, however, the regional groups have shown more willingness than before

[5] The New England Association of Colleges and Secondary Schools, Middle States Association of Colleges and Secondary Schools, North Central Association of Colleges and Secondary Schools, Southern Association of Colleges and Secondary Schools, Northwest Association of Secondary and Higher Schools, and Western College Association.

to recognize the need for considerable variety among our educational institutions.

Currently the approved procedure among the regional associations is to evaluate the effectiveness of any educational institution in the light of the purposes which it is intended to serve. This opens the door to colleges of many kinds, including the two-year institution. Harry E. Jenkins reports that, although only 172 junior colleges had been able to secure regional accreditation by 1948, by 1952 at least 303 were accredited regionally.[6]

Accreditation by state universities began before World War I in such states as Wisconsin, Missouri, and Texas in order to provide a workable system of transferring credit from junior colleges to the universities. This accrediting service for a time encouraged the growth of stronger junior college programs, though its usefulness at present may be questioned. Accreditation by a state university might have facilitated the transfer of junior college graduates when regional accreditation was not available, but it has now ceased to be of much advantage and, in fact, may even be a hindrance to the development of good community-serving programs.

In some states there are accrediting services operated by the state department of education or by some other special public agency. Generally speaking, the standards enforced by these groups are neither as high nor as scrupulously applied as are those administered through the regional associations. New York State and Connecticut are among the few states in which this type of accreditation has proved effective, and Florida seems to be working in this direction.

Other private agencies, including religious denominations, have established accrediting bodies with varying degrees of effectiveness. In occasional instances, to be sure, these actually serve no beneficial purpose and merely set certain educational institutions apart from others. A few represent attempts to achieve respectability for border-

---

[6] Harry E. Jenkins, "The Accreditation of Junior Colleges," Bogue, *op. cit.,* p. 32.

line colleges which cannot meet the standards of the regular accrediting groups.

Accrediting Procedures. Through long experience a well-planned
and standardized system has been worked out for the inspection
and accreditation of every type of educational institution. Two-year
colleges are judged by most regional accrediting associations on the
basis of: (1) worthiness of purpose, (2) competence of the faculty,
(3) adequacy of the curriculum, (4) quality of the instruction
offered, (5) library facilities, (6) provisions for personnel services
to students, (7) administrative efficiency, (8) financial stability, and
(9) the adequacy of the physical plant. The North Central Association of Colleges and Secondary Schools describes the reasons for
the accreditation procedure as follows:

1. To describe the characteristics of institutions worthy of public recognition as institutions of higher education.
2. To guide prospective students in the choice of an institution of higher
   education that will meet their needs.
3. To serve individual institutions as a guide in interinstitutional relationships, such as the transfer of students, the conduct of intercollegiate student activities, the placement of college graduates, and
   the selection of college faculties.
4. To assist secondary schools in the selection of teachers and in advising
   students as to a choice of institutions, and to promote in any other
   ways the coordination of secondary and higher education.
5. To stimulate through its accrediting practices the improvement of
   higher education in the territory of the North Central Association.[7]

Ordinarily, the first step in the procedure of accreditation consists
in having the institution in question gather information with respect
to each of the criteria upon which its work is to be judged. The
accrediting agency customarily supplies printed blanks or questionnaires for such information. In one sense, the collection of detailed
and extensive data for the use of the accrediting body entails a kind
of self-study by the institution itself. This enables the college to

[7] From the Statement of Policy Relative to the Accrediting of Institutions of
Higher Education.

learn how nearly it measures up to the required standards for institutions of its type.

Once the factual information about its program and facilities has been furnished by the applicant, the accrediting body, as a rule, sends an inspection committee of representative educators to visit the campus. This committee seeks to make certain whether the data supplied are correct and complete and also to form a general impression of the college which it later submits to the officers and members of the accrediting agency. A conscientious inspection committee will carefully verify the statements which have been submitted by the institution by a direct perusal of records and by talking with faculty, students, board members, and others. The committee will also try to learn of any changes which are contemplated in the present program and of efforts being made to solve any major problems. Such a committee must particularly seek to avoid being misled, innocently or deliberately, by affable administrators interested in justifying everything the institution is doing.

Some educators appear to labor under the delusion that accreditation depends almost entirely upon the good impression which can be made upon the inspection committee. This is assuredly not the case. In actuality, the worth of an institution's program and the adequacy of its facilities can almost always be determined from the data contained in the questionnaire forms. The committee serves mainly to verify these data.

An institution may be refused accreditation for various reasons. It may have too small a library or one which is not being used effectively. The faculty may be overburdened or underpaid. The financial resources of the college may be too uncertain to guarantee stability. One junior college was denied accreditation because of the disparity between faculty salaries (average, $2,400 per year) and the president's salary ($20,000 per year). Refusal to accredit usually is intended as a protection for students and the general public, on the theory that a poor educational institution is taking money for an inferior product.

If a two-year college applies for but fails to receive the official approval of a regional accrediting agency, it will in most cases be told at what points its program is proving inadequate. This gives the institution valuable aid in the improvement of its work and facilities. Once the major inadequacies have been corrected and an attitude of sincerity demonstrated, it may apply for accreditation again with good prospects of success. Thus accrediting procedures ought to be regarded not as an evil but as a means of improvement.

Both legal restrictions and the supervision of accrediting bodies help to prevent the establishment of weak and ineffective junior colleges or of institutions which prey upon the gullibility of students. While the number of accrediting bodies has multiplied perhaps too rapidly for the good of the institutions (which, after all, must ultimately foot the bill), some organized method of control over the quality of education would seem to be desirable, especially at a time in our educational history when much of the emphasis has been upon quantity.

XI

Buildings and Record-Keeping

JUNIOR and community colleges have been housed in almost every type of building imaginable. Some are found sharing space with local high schools; others are making use of converted private mansions; a number have moved into former public elementary schools (sometimes previously abandoned because of obsolescence); and only a minority at present are occupying facilities constructed especially for the two-year college program.

Ideally, of course, a junior college, like any other educational institution, ought to have its own campus and buildings; but this may not always prove economically possible, particularly during the first few years of an institution's existence. Nevertheless, wherever it can be done, *separate* facilities for this type of institution should be provided. Junior colleges that share facilities with high schools may often be severely handicapped. For one thing, their students resent the fact that they still seem to be attending high school rather than college. Student interests and activities are beginning at this point to be decidedly different from those of the high school group, and the common use of a building or other facilities tends to force them into associations which they would normally avoid. Furthermore, the library of a typical public high school, not to mention laboratories and other special apparatus, will not usually serve to meet the more advanced needs of an effective junior college curriculum. This kind

220

of inadequacy, especially in a school library, constitutes probably the strongest argument against placing high school and junior college people together in the same building. For both practical and psychological reasons, though such an arrangement may seem economical, it is clearly not a good one. At best, it can be only a temporary expedient.

While many private junior colleges now occupy former estates of wealthy families, adaptations of this type must be considered of a temporary nature also. Buildings which have been designed as family dwellings obviously cannot be converted easily into efficient school buildings. Fire hazards frequently make the use of such buildings on a permanent basis extremely questionable. Some junior colleges, such as Pine Manor Junior College in Massachusetts, have been able, however, to adapt family dwellings to classroom use with skill and imagination. This can best be done when the individual units are fairly small. Very large buildings constructed chiefly of wood ought never to be used for junior college purposes unless extreme precautions are taken for the safety and comfort of students.

Former elementary schools have been converted successfully into collegiate buildings, but the expense of such rebuilding is usually rather high. Most elementary schools built before World War I were not efficient classroom buildings to begin with. Conversion of such obsolete and basically unsatisfactory buildings for the use of junior colleges can be surprisingly complicated and expensive.

SEPARATE BUILDINGS AND CAMPUS

In the long run, buildings and campus designed specifically for the special requirements of a two-year college will prove the most satisfactory, if not also the cheapest, solution of the institution's housing problems. Cecil Hardesty has estimated that junior colleges with enrollments of at least 400 students will find it economically desirable to maintain separate campus facilities, though he believes that smaller institutions may still find it necessary to share classrooms with the high school.[1] He learned by means of a questionnaire addressed to administrators throughout California that the vast majority of those consulted preferred separate housing for junior colleges. They based this preference upon three principal advantages of complete separation: (1) the enforcement of a single standard of discipline among all students rather than of different standards for the high school and college groups; (2) distinctly better student morale; and (3) the possibility of a unified extracurricular program.[2] Administrators also said they found it easier to maintain what they called "a college atmosphere" in the junior college with a separate campus than in the junior college housed in a high school building.[3]

What factors must be considered when planning the facilities of a modern junior or community college? In general, they should include at least the following:

1. The site (adequate in size and properly located).
2. The classrooms.
3. The library (including audio-visual aids).
4. Laboratories for instruction in science.
5. Shops for industrial training.
6. Gymnasiums and playing fields.
7. The auditorium or theater.
8. A food-serving unit (cafeteria or dining room).
9. Administrative offices.
10. Heating plant and maintenance area.
11. Dormitories, if needed.

Plans made in relation to these factors obviously will depend upon the local situation. In most communities the above elements (except for the first item which relates to the site only) can all be built satisfactorily into a single building. On the other hand, some institutions may prefer to construct several smaller buildings instead, but this plan tends to be less economical in several respects. As a

[1] Cecil Donald Hardesty, *Problems and Practices in Housing the Junior-College Program in California,* University of Southern California Press, 1934, p. 101.
[2] *Ibid.,* pp. 92–95.
[3] *Ibid.,* p. 95.

rule of thumb, one may assume that an enrollment of 250 full-time students will require a minimum of 100,000 square feet of floor space, while an enrollment of 1,000 students will require at least 400,000 square feet. Much depends upon the type of program to be offered. Costs will vary somewhat according to the locality and the kind of construction which is desired. In 1948 the average cost of buildings and equipment for all purposes in American junior colleges averaged approximately $2,000 per pupil.[4]

THE SITE

Among those who have studied the matter in detail, there seems to be substantial agreement that the site on which a modern two-year college is located should contain at least 30 acres of land. While many an institution is operating at present on a campus of considerably smaller size, 30 acres cannot be regarded as a particularly spacious area for a college of this kind.[5] The site must be large enough not only to allow for expansion in the future but also to provide sufficient space for athletics, parking area, and the activities connected with such courses of study as agriculture, aviation, and similar programs of the typical community-serving institution. Ideally, the site should be conveniently accessible through good roads or streets and by public conveyance, though a central location is no longer as important a matter as it once was. When the site is being acquired, the board clearly would be wise to secure more land than will be immediately needed.

CLASSROOMS

The number of classrooms built, as well as the size and character of each one, will vary somewhat with the precise nature of the subjects taught. Well-lighted and well-ventilated classrooms, of course, are essential. While most of the classrooms probably should accom-

[4] Benjamin Willis Jones, *Cost of Buildings and Equipment of Junior Colleges in the United States*, American Association of Junior Colleges, 1950.

[5] Hardesty, *op. cit.*, pp. 103–111; and Allan S. Hurlburt, *Community College Study*, State Superintendent of Public Instruction, Raleigh, North Carolina, 1952.

modate no more than about 30 students, a number of larger class-rooms will also prove desirable. As far as research has been able to determine, some subjects can be taught effectively even with a class of 75 to 100 students.

LIBRARY

The library should not only contain a supply of books and periodicals carefully selected by a well-trained librarian, but it should have study space and reading tables for not less than 10 percent (preferably 20 percent) of the total student body. Recordings, films, slides, maps, and other instructional materials are frequently a part of the library collection. As to the number and kinds of books which ought to be provided, this depends largely upon the scope and nature of the curriculum. Help in determining which books to purchase can be secured from the American Library Association and other sources.[6] Often the size of the collection is far less important than its usefulness in relation to the courses offered.

LABORATORIES

Needless to say, modern courses in the sciences cannot be well-taught without the application of theory in laboratory experiences. Provisions ought to be made for adequately equipped laboratories for at least the basic sciences, including biology, chemistry, and physics. Laboratories may also be required for such courses as homemaking, psychology, fine arts, journalism, communication, drafting, and business subjects.

SHOPS

It is obvious that various courses which impart vocational training (agriculture, electricity, building trades, machine operation, radio and television, and the like) require adequately equipped shops for demonstration and practice. These must be planned in relation to the courses and the number of students enrolled in each.

---

[6] See, for example, Foster E. Mohrhardt, *A List of Books for Junior College Libraries,* American Library Association, 1937.

GYMNASIUMS AND PLAYING FIELDS

The program in health and recreation (sometimes called physical education) for students in junior colleges is widely regarded as not only important but absolutely necessary. No junior college, then, can perform its duties without special facilities for this phase of its educational activities. At least one full-size gymnasium (that is, large enough to enclose a basketball court) must be provided. Other facilities, including various playing fields, tennis courts, possibly a swimming pool, and so on, will add variety and richness to the program.

AUDITORIUM AND LITTLE THEATER

A large room with a stage in which the entire student body can gather at one time for lectures, discussions, and entertainment is universally considered essential to a satisfactory junior college program of education. For practical purposes, an auditorium with a seating capacity of about 1,200 seems best for a junior college of any size. Such an auditorium should be made available for community as well as faculty and student functions. If possible, the college may also build a smaller theater (seating perhaps 300 persons) for activities which attract a smaller audience.

FOOD-SERVING UNIT

For the health of students, as well as because insufficient or unattractive food service can lower student morale more quickly than almost anything else on the campus, attention must be given to providing suitable space for the preparation and serving of appetizing meals. In most institutions, a clean cafeteria large enough to seat about half the student body (if not more) will suffice. The junior college with dormitories may maintain one or more dining rooms, usually close to the students' living quarters. While such dining rooms ought not to be too large and noisy (about 75 students in one room is a convenient number), a kitchen that prepares food for less than 150 persons per meal seems to be an uneconomical unit. It is usually a good idea to have the meals for two or more dining rooms prepared in a single kitchen.

ADMINISTRATIVE OFFICES

Besides classrooms, there must be in the main building or in the main area of a classroom building a sufficient number of offices located as conveniently as possible for administrative officials, guidance personnel, and student organizations. Fireproof storage space for permanent records is, of course, an understood necessity.

MAINTENANCE AREA

The heating plant and the workshops needed for proper maintenance and repair of the buildings and grounds are of major importance for the efficient operation of the whole college plant. Arrangements here, however, will differ somewhat in different localities.

DORMITORIES

Many institutions have found that the ideal dormitory is one which houses about 75 to 80 students. Larger dormitories appear to be more like hotels than like friendly homes for the students. As a rule, men's dormitories are built in one part of the campus, women's dormitories in another. Students ought to be assigned to joint occupancy of rooms, most of the rooms accommodating two or three students but no more. There should be simple but firmly constructed furniture and comfortable areas for study. Each dormitory ought to have a homelike apartment for house parents. Even in a dormitory for men, the presence of a mature woman can be of considerable help in maintaining discipline and in saving the house and furnishings from unnecessary damage.

In designing the campus and buildings, the best guide is always conservative good taste. Colleges no longer build elaborate Greek temples or medieval castles as classroom buildings, but are concerned instead with comfort, health standards, good lighting and ventilation, convenience and accessibility, simplicity rather than complexity of design, and economy in construction. Buildings and grounds are designed for use rather than merely for show. The general plan should be based upon the functions to be performed by the facilities provided.

RECORD-KEEPING IN THE TWO-YEAR COLLEGE

As mentioned earlier, every college ought to possess a large, fire-proof storage vault for its important records. There are some documents of such importance that their loss would be disastrous, and chief among these are the official administrative and financial records of the institution and the academic records of students. Every college has a direct responsibility for protecting those documents dealing with student achievement and progress. These can be vitally significant for the student in his further educational career or in his vocation. Safeguarding of academic records actually is implied in the written or oral contract under which the institution enrolls the student, and failure to supply an accurate and complete account of a student's academic work in the college may even be regarded as fraud.

Financial records are of nearly equal importance. They indicate how money has been collected and how it has been spent. Every educational administration has a responsibility toward the public and the students as well as toward its own board of trustees. The financial records must not only be kept in a safe place, but the figures must be audited annually (or oftener) in order to discover errors and secure a true picture of the business transactions of each year. An institution which does not clearly understand the nature of its financial position at any given moment or which cannot find and check the complete record of every financial transaction is likely to put itself into difficult straits within a very brief time.

Financial Records

Many attempts have been made within recent years to improve the financial accounting methods used by colleges and universities and to achieve a degree of uniformity in the systems of record-keeping employed in the various institutions throughout the country. State agencies consistently require annual financial reports from the public institutions, and regional accrediting agencies may ask for such reports from their members or from applicants for membership. The United States Office of Education has tried for several years to compile financial statistics for all the higher institutions, both public and private, and for this purpose has developed a record form which adapts itself to almost any satisfactory system of financial accounting now being used.

Any system used for financial record-keeping in a junior or community college obviously ought to provide convenient classifications under which all transactions may be recorded. Classifications, generally speaking, should be simple enough so that the president, the business manager, and the trustees can determine quickly and accurately the real financial status of the institution at the end of each month. While there may be some differences among the various institutions with respect to exact budgetary and accounting classifications chosen, most institutional accounting systems resemble one another to a considerable extent. Sources of income as well as kinds of expenditure are very nearly alike for all two-year colleges. Thus, except for slight variations in program or for special requirements imposed by local or state governments, these institutions might very readily agree upon a standard system of financial accounting. Such a plan has been proposed on several occasions. A more or less uniform system is outlined in a junior college accounting manual which ought to be studied carefully by any two-year institution that seeks to improve its methods of financial record-keeping.[7]

Budgets commonly represent estimates of income and expenses, usually for a year or more in advance. A budget may be prepared by the president or by the president and business manager together, usually after consultation with department heads, the most common procedure in preparing it being to begin with an estimate of the

[7] Henry Glenn Badger, *Junior College Accounting Manual*, American Council on Education, 1945.

coming year's enrollment and from this estimate arriving at the amount of expected income. Necessary expenditures will depend upon anticipated changes in the faculty, the condition of the college plant, the need for new programs or projects, the number of students to be served, and numerous other factors. Outlays for capital purposes, such as new buildings and permanent equipment, ordinarily have no place in the operating budget but are handled separately. Once the annual budget has been submitted to the trustees and approved by them, it becomes the obligation of the president to see that no expenditures are made which have not been allowed for in the budget. In case of unexpected events which grossly alter the financial situation of the institution, the budget can always be revised upward or downward in consultation with the trustees.

It should be borne in mind that the trustees, not the president, must bear ultimate responsibility for the financial stability of any college. The president, however, answers to the trustees for the actual conduct of the financial transactions. In a sense, he acts as the trusted agent of the board in supervising the collection and the dispersal of the institution's funds within the limits agreed upon in the approved annual budget. He has no right to exceed such authority as may be specifically allocated to him by the board, either in financial or other matters.

Because a college is not a commercial institution and therefore not expected to register a profit, its financial transactions cannot be judged in exactly the same way as the transactions of a business corporation. The college provides a public service rather than a product. Its financial records need not be the usual profit-and-loss statements of the well-run factory or department store. It should not be required to end its fiscal year with a financial surplus, though some cash balance is always desirable for current operations. The principal financial problem of the educational institution, other than the recurring question of securing its basic financial support, is not so much that of excessive expenditures as that of waste. The quality of an American college may actually be judged with considerable accuracy by determining the amount of its *effective* expenditure per student. This means the amount spent for the actual education of the student, eliminating from consideration all expenditures for other purposes, such as publicity.[8] Accurate financial records can greatly assist in deciding upon the true effectiveness of educational expenses and in the elimination of wasteful enterprises of the institution.

ACADEMIC RECORDS

The two-year college must be ready at all times to provide an accurate and complete statement of the academic record of every present and former student. The usual form in which a record of this type is reported to other agencies is the official transcript. The student may need copies of his transcript for an employer or for a four-year college or university to which he wishes to transfer.

Transcripts, unfortunately, take many forms. They may be rather simple typewritten or even handwritten statements issued by one of the administrators, or they may be extremely detailed and carefully prepared printed forms. Frequently copies are reproduced by the photostatic process. Because transcripts exist in diverse forms, they are sometimes difficult to read and understand. Registrars and admissions officers of colleges and universities have long complained about the lack of standardization and completeness in the transcripts of high schools and junior colleges in particular. They have also noted the relative ease with which copies may be forged by dishonest persons.

After several years of discussion and study of problems relating to transcripts and record-keeping, in 1946 the American Association of Collegiate Registrars and Admissions Officers (at that time known as the American Association of Collegiate Registrars) issued a report on what the organization believed a satisfactory transcript should contain. These recommendations were supplemented in 1949 and somewhat revised in 1952.

Adequate and intelligently prepared academic transcripts, the A.A.C.R.A.O. declares, are a major responsibility and a matter of

[8] For further information, see John Dale Russell, *Efficiency in College Management*, Indiana University Press, 1931.

good faith on the part of college and university officials, as well as a primary obligation and fulfillment of trust on the part of an educational institution toward its students. The system of maintaining academic records, this organization states, ought to include at least the following items as a minimum: (1) a permanent and carefully planned record form which will meet the needs of students and of other institutions; (2) a storage file offering protection for all permanent and original records; and (3) full understanding and appreciation by the institutional staff of the important aims and purposes of the record-keeping system.[9]

The transcript is defined as "a complete and unabridged academic record without deletions or omissions prepared for the purpose of communicating information concerning a student from one institution or agency to another institution or agency."[10] The essential matters to be covered on a good transcript, as described by the A.A.C.R.A.O., are the following:

1. The student must be identified. The transcript should give the student's full name and address, the school from which he was admitted, the time of his graduation, dates of his attendance, his course of study, and his grades.
2. The institution must be identified. The official name and address of the college must be given.
3. Institutional policies must be explained. The transcript should show the length of the term, the customary load per term, a description of the grading system, identification and definition of the credit unit, and the number of hours of credit earned for graduation.
4. Items on the transcript must be properly arranged. The transcript should have a credit column clearly indicated, all course numbers, the descriptive title of each course, a clear designation of transfer credit, and some special identification for extension courses and others of a similar nature. The whole transcript must be legible and the wording understandable.
5. The student's terminal status must be described. There should be a statement of the student's formal graduation or other type of separa-

[9] *An Adequate Transcript Guide,* American Association of Collegiate Registrars and Admissions Officers, 1952.
[10] *Ibid.,* p. 4.

tion from the college, a description of his degree or academic status, a certificate of honorable dismissal, and the signature of the proper official or officials, plus the institutional seal.

Recently the A.A.C.R.A.O., because of recurring difficulties in the evaluation of transcripts received from various parts of the country, has proposed the establishment of a Transcript Appraisal Center. In an effort to improve transcripts and record-keeping in general, such a center would provide advice to the institutions regarding the adequacy of their transcript forms. The principle of such an appraisal center was approved by the executive committee of the A.A.C.R.A.O. in 1956.[11]

Two-year college officials, who sometimes experience trouble understanding and evaluating transcripts received from high schools, might well give considerable attention to their own procedures in keeping academic records and in preparing suitable transcripts. They can profit greatly from establishing contact with national organizations, such as the A.A.C.R.A.O., which have been studying these matters for many years.

[11] For helpful information in the preparation of this chapter the author is gratefully indebted to Roy E. Carson, Registrar of the Colorado State College. Mr. Carson served on the original Subcommittee on Adequacy of Transcripts and still is an active member of the committee.

XII

The Community College Survey

MUCH has already been said in this book about the community survey to determine the educational needs of youth as a preliminary measure in the establishment of a two-year community college or as a means of determining whether such a college is really needed. How may such a survey best be conducted? Can the people of the community make such a survey themselves, or should they hire outside experts to tell them how to proceed?

To answer such questions, the following outline of a typical community survey is given. Only the major steps in the process are described. In general, a community survey undertaken along these lines will provide the necessary information to serve as a basis for wise decisions with regard to need for and nature of a local community college. On the other hand, the outline should not be thought of as the description of an inflexible, unvaried method of procedure but merely as a general guide.

STEPS IN CONDUCTING A SURVEY

DEFINING THE GEOGRAPHICAL AREA

The geographical area to be served must first be defined. Ordinarily this will present no serious difficulties. The usual radius of the area from which a community college will attract its students is about 15 to 20 miles. As a rule, then, the total area which may be served by a community college is not likely to cover more than 1,000 to 1,250 square miles. It is important that, as the survey proceeds, the conditions and requirements of the entire area—not only the most heavily populated central portion of it—be considered.

ORGANIZING A COMMITTEE

A survey committee, large enough to represent public opinion in the entire area but small enough to form an effective working group (ideally, from 7 to 25 members), should be organized for the purpose of directing the survey. Such a committee might be called together by the superintendent of schools, by the school board, by some civic or service club, or by a voluntary group of individual citizens. It will prove helpful to have on the survey committee persons who reside in different parts of the area to be served and who have also had some first-hand contact with educational problems of the community. Officers of respected civic organizations, of religious groups, of social agencies, of labor unions, and of similar civic-minded bodies are likely to be interested in improving educational opportunties. If possible, a variety of occupational interests ought to be represented. The survey committee has the important responsibility of carrying on the study and then reporting its results to the general public.

FINANCING THE SURVEY

An arrangement should be agreed upon for financing the survey. Often this is accomplished through a direct appropriation made by the school board or the city council, but some other source of the necessary funds may be preferred. A large community may decide to purchase the services of outside educational experts. Properly planned, the survey need not be unduly expensive. The state department of education or the educational staff of a nearby university may be willing to contribute both advice and practical assistance without charge. It is essential, however, to decide well in advance what the community is willing to spend for an accurate survey.

ORGANIZING THE FACTS

The survey itself will center around the answers to several important questions. These can be answered fully only by gathering the facts directly relating to them in the particular community which is being studied. Gathering these facts requires time and workers. Although trained, paid workers no doubt will do a more thorough job, especially if well-supervised, volunteers often prove perfectly satisfactory. The work of each person engaged in the survey should be completely understood by the committee and should be carefully outlined in advance.

The chief questions for which accurate answers must be obtained in the survey are:

Is there a demonstrable need in the area for a community college? The most reliable data on this question will come from a study of the high school graduates in the community. How many of them have continued their education in colleges? How many of them would like to secure further education but are unable to do so? How many of them think they would enroll in a community college if one were established? What are the educational desires and plans of the present high school seniors? When information relating to these matters has been compiled, it may be possible to gain a fairly clear picture of the student body which the contemplated community college might serve.

Are there enough potential students in the area to justify setting up the proposed new institution to serve them? A community college with fewer than 200 full-time students is not likely to be very strong economically or educationally, though other factors may in certain cases outweigh these considerations. It should be remembered that a full enrollment cannot be expected the first year, and both the demonstrated effectiveness of the institution's program and future increases in population will attract more students. On the average, nevertheless, it is probably true that a high school enrollment in the immediate area amounting to at least 1,000 students is the minimum required to guarantee a sufficient enrollment for the community college.

Are other facilities already adequately supplying the need? If there is another good college in the neighborhood, perhaps it will prove willing to adapt its program to local requirements. If a university extension program is in operation, its contributions to educational opportunity for local students ought to be carefully assessed. There seems to be no purpose in duplicating educational facilities which already exist nearby.

Can the community afford to finance the proposed institution? Probably no community should agree to extend its public education into the thirteenth and fourteenth grades unless the assessed valuation of taxable property within the area amounts to at least $10,-000,000. Even this assumes a willingness on the part of the state to aid in financing a community college. If the entire cost of the new program is to be borne locally, presumably the assessed valuation ought to be nearer $25,000,000. On the other hand, the decision regarding the community's ability to pay the costs will depend partly on the current tax rate, other commitments already made, and the desire of the citizens to increase their tax load in order to improve their educational system. A complete study of all possible sources of revenue for the proposed new institution must be made. In some places private funds can be secured in the form of gifts or endowments for capital outlay (buildings and equipment) or operation.

What kind of curriculum should be planned? Since every community is unlike others in some of its aspects, a study of economic problems and characteristics of the community—especially the employment situation—is of paramount importance. Not only the expressed wishes of potential students but also the present and future needs of local employers of the institution's future graduates must be explored. Is the economy of the area primarily agricultural, mercantile, industrial, or a combination of these types? How many typists and stenographers enter new positions there each year? Is there a shortage of trained people in any vocational field in this area? What is the long-term prospect of economic development of the region? These and many similar questions must be answered by the survey in order to know what kind of curriculum will prove most useful to the students and the community.

POLLING PUBLIC OPINION

Both public and expert opinion with regard to the need for and the feasibility of a new community college ought to be surveyed. It is especially wise to ask the advice of the state department of education in this matter. The presidents of all colleges in the state may also be consulted. Within the community itself, recognized civic leaders may be invited to state their points of view, and the attitude of the ordinary citizen certainly must be taken into account. On the whole, it is not good policy to establish an educational institution, regardless of the worthiness of its aims, if public sentiment seems to be against it.

ESTABLISHING LEGALITY

Legal provisions of the state with respect to educational institutions must be studied carefully. Is there permissive or other legislation affecting community colleges? Are there legal bars to the establishment of such an institution? Does the state have minimum standards (and enforce them) as to quality of instruction or facilities, amount of local financial support required, special certification of teachers, and the like? Is there any provision for state or county aid? Legal restrictions of the state and of other governmental units may have a strong bearing upon the plans.

SECURING TEACHERS

Some thought must be given to the availability of qualified teachers. Usually such information can be found in the state department of education or in nearby universities. Can teachers of the local high schools be employed in the community college? In recent years the shortage of teachers in certain fields has made the staffing of two-year colleges more difficult than it was before World War II.

INVESTIGATING OTHER COMMUNITY COLLEGES

The experiences of other communities in setting up community colleges may cast important light on the problems to be faced. The survey committee, or at least a subcommittee of it, should visit one or two such communities to examine in detail the methods of organization and operation used in establishing and maintaining the college. This experience can be particularly valuable in discovering mistakes to be avoided.

CHOOSING THE LOCATION

The most appropriate location for a community college in the area must be found. The question of convenience to prospective students ought to be considered first. Needless to say, the location should be as central as possible with respect to the distribution of the student population; but the direction of future growth of the population should be determined, if possible. Can part of the present high school building be used temporarily? Is there sufficient space available in the location chosen to provide for later expansion and for athletic and similar activities? Probably the new institution should have a campus of not less than 30 acres. One or more separate building would be desirable.

PRESENTING SURVEY RESULTS TO THE PUBLIC

As the survey nears completion, the committee must present all pertinent facts, both favorable and unfavorable, to the public and also secure public response. If the college is to be successful, the citizens must have the opportunity of signifying their desire for it and their willingness to support it. The final decision as to whether the institution will actually be established is, of course, in the hands of the local voters.

ESTABLISHING A GOVERNING BOARD

Assuming that the survey has clearly demonstrated a real need for the community college, has found the means of adequately financing it, has determined at least in a general way the kind of curriculum it should offer, and has elicited a favorable reaction from the voters, the next step is actual organization. Advice on this portion of the work may be secured from the state department of education, the American Association of Junior Colleges in Washington, regional or state accrediting agencies, and several other sources. The essential step in organization, as far as the survey committee is concerned, entails the selection of a permanent governing board for the new institution. In most cases this may be the elected school board of the district, but in some instances the community may prefer to designate a special board of control.

Organizing Officially

Once the authority and responsibility for the new college have been properly established, the governing board may proceed with official organization, keeping in mind the following suggested principles:

1. The primary functions of a governing board are the determination of general policies for the institution, the protection of its property and financial status, and the selection of its chief executive. The board, of course, has other but less vital duties, including official approval of all contracts, the formal authorization of all degrees or certificates, and the like.

2. The chief executive (usually designated as president, dean, or director) should administer the educational and business affairs of the college within the limits of board policy. He should be the official and exclusive liaison between the board and the faculty. His principal job, for the good of the educational program, is that of obtaining and supervising good teachers.

3. The details of curriculum planning should be the responsibility of the administration and faculty, but the broad outlines of the program should be understood and approved by the board. The main concern here should be to meet the actual needs of the community.

4. Regular policies regarding faculty salary scale, a retirement plan, health protection for students and faculty, and similar matters

ought to receive consideration as early as possible. These details can be fully as vital to the success of the college as the development of an effective curriculum.

For further suggestions and information regarding the organization of a community college, the survey committee and later the board of control might wish to consult such a practical guide as *How to Organize and Operate a Junior College*, by Jesse P. Bogue. The experiences of six different communities in founding local junior colleges have been described by Elbert K. Fretwell, Jr., in *Founding Public Junior Colleges*. These and other books on the subject of junior and community colleges will be found listed in the bibliography at the end of this book.

XIII

Problems and Patterns of the Future

THE President's Commission on Higher Education has declared that approximately half the people of the United States have the ability to profit by some form of education beyond the high school. On the basis of this belief, the Commission recommended in its report following World War II a vast expansion of American two-year college facilities. If adequate opportunities are made available, the Commission has predicted, about half our young people will be enrolled in colleges within the foreseeable future. By 1960 as many as two and a half million young persons, under ideal conditions, might well be enrolled as college freshmen and sophomores. A considerable proportion of these, given the opportunity, would enroll in junior and community colleges.[1]

It should be noted, of course, that the Commission has not predicted what will happen but has only described an educational ideal which may not be realized for many decades to come. Its report constitutes not so much a description of the future as an outline of desirable goals for American higher education. If the "historical potential" of post-high-school enrollment is actually to be reached, a tremendous and unprecedented growth of our facilities for col-

[1] *Higher Education for American Democracy*, Harper & Brothers, 1948, I, 39–46.

legiate education will have to take place, and the present barriers to educational opportunity further broken down.

James A. Starrak and Raymond M. Hughes have presented an estimate of the number of junior and community colleges needed in the United States to serve all young people adequately and equally. If tuition-free, two-year institutions are located within the reach of all eligible students, they point out, it will mean that the present number of junior and community colleges in the United States must be more than doubled. Had this ideal been achieved in 1948, there would have been 1,346 two-year colleges enrolling 872,400 students.[2]

If we compare these estimates of what is needed with the actual number and capacity of two-year institutions, we can see at once that continued and rapid growth of the junior college movement is necessary. A glance at the current scene shows us, however, that such growth is at present occurring only sporadically. If the necessary educational facilities are to be provided in an orderly and economical manner, careful and immediate planning obviously is called for.

In looking toward the future development of junior and community colleges, while keeping in mind that their purpose must be to serve only the demonstrable needs of students, we can discern several guideposts that offer the means of maintaining proper direction for our efforts. The most important of these are: (1) state-wide planning, (2) state subsidies, (3) local autonomy, and (4) community surveys.

STATE-WIDE PLANNING

A committee that studied higher education in California not long ago had this to say about the junior college system of that state:

It has been more than 25 years since California adopted the policy of providing junior college education at public expense for all who wish it.

---

[2] James A. Starrak and Raymond M. Hughes, *The New Junior College,* Iowa State College Press, 1948, pp. 56–60.

The ideal toward which the State has been striving is the establishment of a network of institutions so located throughout the State as to be available to students who live at home. A similar ambition was voiced by the nation a half century ago in the development of publicly supported high schools. California has not yet accomplished the ideal with respect to junior college education. Although all youth may attend, the State still contains areas which do not have these institutions.[3]

Thus we see that, even in the part of the country in which the two-year colleges have made their most spectacular growth, further planning and extension of opportunity still seem to be needed.

No state in our nation, with the possible exception of Mississippi, now has a deliberately designed and fully coördinated system of community colleges. Until every state formulates and puts into effect such a plan, it is hard to see how the needs of all potential students can be met. While community colleges have been founded in many areas by reason of local awareness of needs, in a far greater number of instances the pressure of need has not become strong enough to result in constructive action. On the other hand, local pride occasionally has been responsible for starting an educational institution where one was not really needed. A state-wide plan seems to be the wisest method of avoiding duplication of effort and making sure that all qualified students are served.

THE STATE SURVEY

The state plan ordinarily begins with a state-wide survey to determine what educational services really are desirable and what services already are being performed. In conducting such a survey, it may be well to bring in educational experts from outside the state who presumably will preserve an objective point of view and whose self-interest will not be involved. In any case, the committee sponsoring the survey should be composed of capable men and women who are open-minded and who have no fixed, preconceived notions of the results desired.

[3] *A Report of a Survey of the Needs of California in Higher Education,* 1948, p. 4.

Such a committee will make a thorough investigation of the population trends within the state; the transportation facilities in different areas; agricultural, commercial, and industrial activities; the general organization of public secondary education; present opportunities for training beyond high school; the number of students interested in continuing their education beyond the twelfth grade; the types of training desired by post-high-school students; and the ability of the state to finance higher education.

In general, and as a rule-of-thumb, average community colleges ought not to be spaced farther than 25 to 50 miles from each other. In heavily populated sections of the state they should probably be somewhat nearer; in a few areas they probably cannot be adequately supported in the numbers implied by such a distribution. In any case, the question of where to locate the institutions must be answered by an examination of the data disclosed in the survey. States will vary, of course, not only as to population but also as to their financial and other characteristics. While not every state will meet the problem in exactly the same way, in each the methods adopted should be based upon the principle of making further educational opportunities available to all students within a convenient distance from their homes.[4]

STATE SUBSIDIES

The most successful development of junior and community colleges appears to have taken place in the states which have provided sufficient financial backing to guarantee the stability of the institutions.

Legislation for public junior colleges has begun usually, as it did in California, with purely permissive legislation—that is, with a law permitting the communities or school districts to extend public education beyond the twelfth grade. Legislation of this kind may, if nothing else, at least encourage the local districts to exercise their initiative in meeting educational needs. Other legislation, such as

[4] Leonard V. Koos, "Essentials in State-Wide Community College Planning," *School Review*, LVII (September, 1949), 341–352.

laws enabling districts to consolidate for the purpose of setting up union district junior colleges, may follow.

Sooner or later such beginnings are likely to produce actual state aid. Few communities appear able to support a really strong community college program without financial help from the state. Problems of equalization, of course, apply to this level of education just as they apply to the elementary and secondary schools. On the whole, it would seem to be true that an adequate state-wide system of public junior and community colleges requires a state subsidy in some form.

LOCAL DIRECTION AND CONTROL

Community colleges apparently serve most effectively when they have complete local autonomy. It has already been stated that only the community-minded institution is likely to discover and provide for the community's real needs. Institutions which are controlled either by the state department of education or a large university must have policies in conformity with those of the parent organization. Such policies in some instances may conflict with local requirements. Furthermore, junior college branches of universities often seem to be regarded as "feeders" for the upper years of work on the central campus. The curriculum in such cases must be aimed primarily at meeting the regulations with respect to transfer and cannot easily be adjusted to the needs of students who desire a well-rounded two-year program.

When a state-wide plan for the necessary junior and community colleges has been formulated and some provision for state financial support has been made, committees to organize the institutions themselves, if they are not already established, should be set up within each of the communities affected. Full control of the college's affairs must be retained within the community, although, as a safeguard for quality, it may be wise for the state to enforce minimum standards with regard to equipment and instruction. State financing, however, should not be made the excuse for state control.

In the long run, the locally controlled institution will serve the community most satisfactorily because of its particular sensitivity to the community's needs and problems.

COMMUNITY SURVEYS

One of the most promising developments during recent years, as we have already observed, has been the community survey, by means of which the college attempts to determine the special types of instruction which are desired and other factors essential to effective operation and service. While the techniques of the educational survey have not yet been perfected, considerable progress is now being made.

Every community-serving institution will find it useful to conduct frequent or continuing surveys of its area to discover the changing character of the community's life and needs. In addition—and the point requires emphasis—the information gained from surveys of this kind must actually be used in curriculum planning, public relations programs, and the utilization of local resources for training. The survey is useful only as it results in constructive changes of the program, a matter which demands the constant and thoughtful attention of the administration and faculty. By becoming thoroughly familiar with its own constituency, the institution is not only able to do a better piece of work in its educational program but is also likely to command a much higher degree of respect and support within its community than would otherwise be possible.

PROBLEMS TO BE FACED

Several vital problems face the junior and community college movement in the United States today. Chief among these is the question of financing. The others include locations for new institutions, the types of curriculum suitable in the various communities, military conscription, adequate administration, and the ultimate place of the private junior college.

FINANCING

It now seems fairly clear that no satisfactory system of community colleges can be built up without state subsidies. Most school districts balk at the idea of adding the burden of an expensive two-year program to the already heavy tax load. Until state financial help is available, these districts will continue to ignore the educational needs or to hope that they will be met by some private agency. Except for those communities which are intensely interested in better education and relatively wealthy, there are few places in which local support alone can provide a really strong junior college program. The first step in financing these institutions, then, ought to be state aid in one form or another.

While it has been argued that any school in which the student pays a fee of any sort cannot be regarded as truly offering free public education, this principle may or may not apply to the public junior college. In California, junior colleges charge no tuition. In Colorado and other states there is a small tuition fee. The tremendous appeal of the California institutions has often been attributed to this policy of assessing no charges against the student. With so striking an example as that of California before them, the educators and laymen who have conducted the recent state surveys of higher education have rather overwhelmingly adopted the attitude that public education on the junior college level should be provided absolutely without cost to the student. It should be made, they seem to agree, as free as high school education.

Of course, private junior colleges collect a substantial part of their income from students and will probably continue to do so. In spite of endowments and occasional philanthropic gifts, the expense of providing instruction of a high quality forces the private institutions to rely upon student fees for at least a portion of the income necessary to remain in operation. As a matter of fact, in the typical private junior college, which, by and large, is an institution without extensive endowment funds, student fees account for well over 90 percent of annual income. Naturally, this factor limits enrollment somewhat. Even when scholarship funds are available, the college that must charge $200 to $500 for a year's tuition cannot hope to enroll more than a fraction of the deserving students whom it would be desirable to serve. The financial barrier to educational opportunity will not be broken down until the services of the community college are offered free or at a price within the reach of every student.

As far as the public junior college is concerned, local taxation must pay its fair share of the cost. The community should, as a minimum duty, accept the responsibility for providing the buildings and equipment necessary for a satisfactory program. While some states may be willing to subsidize building construction, the most feasible arrangement with respect to state aid seems to be that of having the state supply sufficient funds to guarantee a program of instruction capable of meeting reasonable standards as to quality, and of requiring the community to erect the essential buildings and to add enough support to raise the level of instruction as high as possible. Most communities of any size, granted the basic subsidy of the state, can afford to do this.

LOCATIONS FOR NEW INSTITUTIONS

The best locations for junior and community colleges ought to be determined in a general way by the state-wide survey. As a rule, no new institution should be established in a community if a college already in operation there proves willing to adopt the community-serving function. For example, an area which already has a state university, a college of education, or some similar institution—unless it is a heavily populated urban center, such as New York City or Chicago—probably does not need another college. The existing institution can very likely be persuaded to adapt a portion of its program to the community's needs. In some sections, however, there may be justifiable reasons for having more than one collegiate institution—for instance, when the city is large enough to support a number of educational centers in various locations or when the existing institution refuses to change its program in order to serve the specific needs of local students.

On the whole, as has already been stated, community colleges ought to be spaced not farther than 50 miles apart and not closer than within 15 to 25 miles of one another. There are, of course, many possible exceptions to this general rule. If two sizable centers of population are located only ten miles apart, it may be feasible as well as highly desirable to have two separate colleges to serve them.

The ideal area served by a community college is usually the trade area, that is, a city or town surrounded by a rural community. Such trade areas, in which the town is a shopping center for a widely dispersed population, may be found in every part of our nation. If the college is to be financially stable and efficient, the high school enrollment within this area should probably be somewhere near 1,000 students; and the normal assessed value of taxable property which can be used as the tax base for the support of the institution, at least $10,000,000. In unusual circumstances, there may be ample justification for establishing a community college in a more sparsely settled area, where both the high school enrollment and the assessed valuation of property are low, but it should be kept in mind that such an institution cannot hope to provide a varied or extensive program.

The chief problem in selecting the best locations is that of coordinating all types of educational offerings without excessive duplication of effort and at the same time taking all possible steps to meet the actual needs of students.

Types of Curriculum

It is always easier to pattern the curriculum of an educational institution after that of some well-known school or college than it is to develop a special curriculum suited to a particular community. Imitation has the advantages of custom and respectability, and teachers ordinarily are happiest when they can teach the subjects with which they are most familiar. A surprising number of young colleges decide upon their programs after studying the catalogs of other institutions.

When this procedure is followed by a community college, the

students risk the danger of being forced into programs which do not fully meet their needs. The community-serving institution, therefore, must exercise both ingenuity (in discovering what curriculum is really most useful to local students) and courage (in offering such work even when educational traditions of long standing may be violated).

This raises, of course, various irksome problems, such as those related to accreditation by the regional and other agencies and to the acceptance of transfer credits by other colleges. A few of the established agencies which accredit institutions of higher learning seem stubbornly to resist the recognition of new programs which do not exactly fit into customary patterns. For a long time, in some sections of the country, junior colleges could not be accredited unless they were merely copying in their programs the freshman and sophomore years of the standard liberal arts curriculum. While the situation has now eased somewhat, accrediting bodies as a group have tended naturally to be extremely conservative and resistant to new ideas, and this fact may even now prevent some community colleges from adapting their programs entirely to local needs. The desire of many junior college graduates to continue their education in four-year institutions has raised a similar issue with respect to the transfer of credits, though the early difficulties have been largely allayed by the excellent records which these graduates have made after transfer.

There is no intention here to condemn all tradition in the field of education. Much of it has firm and continuing value and has proved important in maintaining generally high levels of educational accomplishment. Perhaps the stabilizing influence of established custom in education has actually been more beneficial to new institutions than its effect in resisting change has been harmful. At any rate, the essential point is that a strong tradition alone cannot be relied upon to give students of many different abilities, needs, backgrounds, and interests the varied educational experiences which will prove most acceptable and useful to them. Of much greater significance in curriculum planning for the community college is the painstaking study of the community itself, to the end that a curriculum will be designed which really meets local needs.

The program of one community college, then, may differ from that of another in the same way that the communities themselves differ. Some aspects of all the programs, of course, may be very much alike. Every institution of this type should probably devote a good share of its program to general education. The most striking differences presumably would occur among the various vocational courses of study and in the work offered as adult education.

Each community college has its own individual problem of determining the special needs of its constituents. Methods of meeting the problem will vary considerably but should not be hampered by the heavy hand of tradition. The community college must be willing to recognize the values of educational tradition, but only to the extent that it improves rather than detracts from the service rendered by the institution in meeting the community's real needs.

MILITARY CONSCRIPTION

While nobody can say with certainty what effect the military training of our young men will have upon higher education in America, it might well result in some profound changes. There is a strong likelihood, for example, that the armed forces may provide many forms of strictly vocational training of the kind now offered in the community colleges and technical schools. It has even been proposed that general college courses be included in the military training program. A large number of the men and women already in service are pursuing their education by correspondence and other means through the agency of the United States Armed Forces Institute (U.S.A.F.I.), now a permanent organization under civilian control.

Will educational opportunities provided in the course of, and incidental to, military training preclude the need for extension of our community college system? Frankly, there is at this point no way of giving a definite answer to the question. The matter itself, however, may have an important bearing upon the future of all higher education.

TRAINING EDUCATIONAL LEADERSHIP

As we have already seen, some attempts have been made in various ways to secure special training for teachers in junior and community colleges. Perhaps even more essential is the preparation of active and capable administrative and philosophical leaders in this area of our educational system.

By and large, understanding of this phase of American education is not as widespread as it should be. Most of the teachers and administrators now being prepared in our colleges and professional schools learn very little about the junior college during their period of training and become acquainted with it only through their later experience. Research in the field also has failed to keep up with actual developments.

As the result of these deficiencies, the movement is not as rich as it might be in active leadership. This implies no criticism of present leaders; it merely recognizes the need for greater efforts to train more new leaders for the future.

THE FUTURE OF INDEPENDENT JUNIOR COLLEGES

The greatest gains in the junior and community college movement within recent years have been made by the public institutions. At the same time, the privately controlled junior colleges have lost ground, and many of them have been forced into closing.

Many advantages are claimed for the independent institution, and most educators agree that private colleges constitute an important factor in higher education. The independent institution may, if it wishes, make religious instruction a major part of its curriculum, a privilege incompatible with the functions of public institutions. The private college—in theory, at least—seems better able to experiment with new ideas. Because of its dependence upon the financial support derived from tuition, it must be constantly alert to the changing needs of students and willing to adjust its program to new demands.

It ordinarily holds itself entirely free of political control, though this problem does not appear to be a serious one in most of our public educational institutions. Perhaps most significant of all, the private junior college may concentrate its efforts upon doing an outstanding piece of work in a single educational area and may select the students who will be most likely to profit from the type of curriculum offered.

In spite of these and other advantages, the trend in our educational system at present is more and more toward public support and control. The decreasing value of endowments and the rising costs of maintaining a satisfactory program have imposed a particularly weighty burden upon the small private institution. How shall we retain the acknowledged benefits of this kind of education and still supply to all our young people the equality of opportunity in which we believe?

One answer obviously lies in more philanthropic aid from individuals, corporations, and foundations. Religious bodies which desire to establish and operate educational institutions must be willing to provide sufficient monetary backing to develop strong and worthwhile programs. On the other hand, local or state-wide movements toward the establishment of community colleges must not ignore or seek to compete with serviceable private institutions. The policy of setting up a public facility where a private organization is already rendering good service would seem to be short-sighted, both educationally and economically.

Some independent institutions, it seems clear, ought to be taken over by public authorities, especially when there is the prospect of ultimate failure under private auspices. Others might well be given some form of public support without absolute control. One method of keeping the independent institution strong is the allocation of state scholarships to deserving students. Under such a plan the scholarship is awarded not to the college but to the student, and he has the right of selecting the institution, public or private, at which he prefers to pursue his studies.

The independent junior colleges of the United States admittedly have provided an educational service of considerable magnitude, and they may be justly proud of their achievements. They are faced now quite generally with serious financial problems. Most of those which are firmly established will probably maintain their places in our system, while others will fail unless public aid is granted. In view of the probable need for more facilities rather than fewer within the next few years, increased financial support for these institutions in one form or another seems amply justified.

DANGERS TO THE COMMUNITY COLLEGE MOVEMENT

Perhaps the chief dangers, other than those already implied or mentioned above, which the junior and community colleges of America face are: (1) the temptation to expand into traditional four-year institutions, (2) the "chamber of commerce" point of view, and (3) the influence of the universities upon the curriculum.

THE TEMPTATION TO EXPAND

A committee which in 1948 examined the needs of California with respect to higher education noted with alarm the tendency of some junior colleges to desire the expansion of their offerings into the junior and senior years of college. The committee's report carries the following statement:

Proposals have been made to expand certain junior colleges by adding to their present offering an upper division to include the third and fourth college years, to be supported by the State. The Survey Committee unanimously disapproves of this type of expansion of junior colleges. . . . It is the judgment of the Survey Committee that if junior colleges were to be expanded to four-year institutions they would inevitably follow the four-year pattern and neglect . . . their primary purposes. In short, we should have standard four-year colleges replacing junior colleges. . . .

In addition to this objection, however, which is educational in character, the Survey Committee feels very strongly that if two, three, five, or six junior colleges were thus expanded, it would at once set in motion a great stream of requests to the Legislature for similar action on the part of other junior colleges. As has been pointed out, a number of such requests have been made; one, indeed, came from a junior college containing fifty students, which boldly asked for expansion to a four-year institution.[5]

The chief incentive impelling junior colleges toward expansion into four-year institutions is obviously the desire for greater prestige and respectability. Rarely can such a move be justified by actual need. Unfortunately, the change is likely to result in a weaker academic program. Junior colleges now performing excellent service will, in most cases, do well to avoid the temptation of becoming mediocre four-year colleges. It is the special type of opportunity offered by the two-year institution, and not the traditional four-year program, whose extension appears most necessary at the present stage of our educational history.

Because of the tremendous appeal in academic circles of traditional patterns of organization, the temptation before the junior colleges to change into four-year colleges constitutes an ever present danger.

The "Chamber of Commerce" Point of View

In preparing the way for a new or proposed community college, the temptation to sell it to the community as a business proposition should ordinarily be resisted. While an institution of this kind may bring various economic benefits to local business and industry, there seems to be an unrealistic tendency to regard the establishment of a college in much the same terms as one would regard the establishment of a factory—as a means of providing employment and attracting money into the area.

Businessmen who support the establishment of a college entirely as a financial investment of the community are likely, upon close examination of the outcome, to be rather disappointed. A college is not, or should not be, an object of exploitation. It should be understood and accepted by the community merely for what it is, not for something which it cannot be.

[5] *A Report of a Survey of the Needs of California in Higher Education, op. cit.,* pp. 78–79.

The community college offers educational opportunities to those who can benefit from them, and this fact in itself should be sufficient to justify its existence. An appeal to the profit motive as the excuse for building a new college is usually not only misleading but in most instances wholly unnecessary. A factory brings financial returns to the community. A college brings educational opportunity and culture, both desirable elements in themselves; and the financial benefits, while they may actually result, are ordinarily very indirect.

THE INFLUENCE OF THE UNIVERSITIES

Although the junior and community college movement owes a large debt of gratitude on many counts to the influence of several universities, beginning with the University of Chicago, the fact remains that the universities as a group tend in some ways to hamper the efforts of the two-year institutions to adapt their courses of study to the real needs of students.

For many years there have been frequent complaints from the high schools about the interference in their work resulting from inflexible college entrance requirements. The junior and community colleges complain of a similar problem with respect to transfer of credit. In California, for instance, the junior college student who plans to enter the state university in his junior year must follow a course of study specified by the university.

Since this matter has been the subject of previous discussion (see p. 245), there is no necessity of going into further detail at this point. It will be sufficient to say that the influence of the universities in dictating the rules of transferring credit—and thus of determining the subjects to be studied—represents a possibly harmful restriction upon the program of the community college. When one considers that those junior college students who complete the approved courses do not appear markedly superior to other students in their preparation for additional college work, the need for any restriction of this kind may be questioned.

The danger, of course, lies in the possibility that junior and community colleges, instead of ascertaining and providing for the true needs of their students, will fall back upon mere tradition as their guide in curriculum-building.

TRENDS TOWARD FUTURE DEVELOPMENT

Three clear trends are apparent in the development of the junior and community college movement. One is the increasing emphasis upon public support and control. Another is the need for more two-year colleges in many areas not now adequately served. A third is the growing attention being given in higher education to purely local needs.

If present indications can be relied on, the time is not far off when every state interested in the welfare of its young people will have a coördinated system of community colleges. Not every state will follow the same pattern in developing such a system. Under-lying the whole movement, however, is the swelling pressure for the upward extension of free public education. Instead of stopping at the twelfth grade, public education seems likely to be extended generally into the fourteenth grade, or even higher. Nothing in today's configuration of events argues against our eventual adoption of this major change in our educational policy.

The conviction that more two-year institutions are needed is already widespread in the United States. The studies made by the President's Commission on Higher Education and by the various state commissions all point in this direction. The question has now become not so much whether enlarged facilities are needed but rather of where they shall be located and how they shall be financed. Educators and the American public have pretty much made up their minds that no young person in our nation shall be denied the right to as much education as he can profitably use. The further develop-ment of community colleges follows from this as a matter of course.

The one great new idea which has sprung into full flower in American education during the past few years is that of providing an educational program suited to local needs. Educators are sure that a single pattern of collegiate experience will not fit all students equally well. The community college is founded upon the belief that individual differences among our people require variations in the types of training offered.

Some still resist or deny this belief, arguing that education in our schools and colleges should be the same for all. Yet the merest glance at the variety of instruction currently available shows unmistakably which of these two divergent principles has proved more effective in practice, and which is demanded by our American students. If community colleges are successful and popular, the fact serves as an illustration of our continued respect for decisions arrived at through democratic means. On the whole, the American people choose and support the kind of education which they discover to be most beneficial to them.

Having established itself by virtue of its inherent merits as the most rapidly growing movement in American education and as the unique contribution of our system to the entire history of education, the junior and community college movement has now become a permanent characteristic of our national society. To many people, it still remains new and unfamiliar. In another generation, one may venture to predict, it will be as much a part of the accepted educational pattern for Americans as the kindergarten and the junior high school. The junior and community college, in all its various forms, occupies a firm place in our system simply because it effectively supplies a vitally needed educational service.

Selected Bibliography

Adams, Harlen Martin, *The Junior College Library Program*, Stanford, Calif., Stanford University Press, 1940.

Adams, Henry Albert, *Criteria for the Establishment of Public Junior Colleges in Kentucky*, Lexington, University of Kentucky, 1940.

Arbuckle, Dugald S., *Student Personnel Services in Higher Education*, New York, McGraw-Hill, 1953.

Armsby, Henry H., *Cooperative Education in the United States*, Washington, U.S. Government Printing Office, 1954.

Badger, Henry Glenn, *Junior College Accounting Manual*, Washington, American Council on Education, 1945.

Bethel, Lawrence L., Bogue, Jesse P., and Lindsay, Frank B., *Junior College Terminal Education in Your Community*, New York, McGraw-Hill, 1948.

Bogue, Jesse P. (ed.), *American Junior Colleges*, 4th ed., Washington, American Council on Education, 1956.

Bogue, Jesse P., *How to Organize and Operate a Junior College*, Washington, American Association of Junior Colleges, 1947.

Boucher, Chauncey Samuel, and Brumbaugh, A. J., *The Chicago College Plan*, Chicago, University of Chicago Press, 1940.

Brownell, Baker, *The College and the Community*, New York, Harper & Brothers, 1952.

Campbell, Doak S., *A Critical Study of the Stated Purposes of the Junior College*, Nashville, George Peabody College for Teachers, 1930.

Colvert, Clyde C., *The Public Junior College Curriculum*, University, La., Louisiana State University Press, 1939.

Colvert, Clyde C., and Bright, H. F., *Suggested Materials for In-Service Training Programs for Junior Colleges*, Washington, American Association of Junior Colleges, 1950.

Colvert, Clyde C., and Heyl, Arnold A., *Qualifications of Junior College Teachers, Administrators, and Board Members in the United States*, Washington, American Association of Junior Colleges, 1951.

Davis, Wayne, *How to Choose a Junior College*, New York, Harper & Brothers, 1939.

Deutsch, Monroe E., *et al.*, *A Report of a Survey of the Needs of California in Higher Education*, Sacramento, Calif., 1948.

Diekhoff, John S., *Democracy's College*, New York, Harper & Brothers, 1950.

Dixon, Henry Aldous, *The Organization and Development of Terminal Occupational Curricula in Selected Junior Colleges*, Ogden, Utah, Weber College, 1944.

Eells, Walter Crosby, *Associate's Degree and Graduation Practices in Junior Colleges*, Washington, American Association of Junior Colleges, 1942.

Eells, Walter Crosby, *Bibliography on Junior Colleges*, Washington, U.S. Government Printing Office, 1930.

Eells, Walter Crosby, *The Junior College*, Boston, Houghton Mifflin, 1931.

Eells, Walter Crosby, *Present Status of Junior College Terminal Education*, Washington, American Association of Junior Colleges, 1941.

Eells, Walter Crosby, *Why Junior College Terminal Education?* Washington, American Association of Junior Colleges, 1941.

Engleman, Lois E., and Eells, Walter Crosby, *The Literature of Junior College Terminal Education*, Washington, American Association of Junior Colleges, 1941.

Fowlkes, John Guy, and Ahrnsbrak, Henry C., *Junior College Needs in Wisconsin*, Madison, University of Wisconsin Press, 1947.

Fretwell, Elbert Kirtley, *Founding Public Junior Colleges: Local Initiative in Six Communities*, New York, Columbia University, 1954.

Gager, William Atkins, *Terminal Business Mathematics in the Junior College*, Nashville, George Peabody College for Teachers, 1940.

Gray, William S. (ed.), *The Junior College Curriculum*, Vol. I of *Proceedings of the Institute for Administrative Officers of Higher Institutions*, Chicago, University of Chicago Press, 1929.

Greenleaf, Walter J., *Junior Colleges*, Washington, U.S. Government Printing Office, 1936.

Griffith, Coleman R., and Blackstone, Hortense, *The Junior College in Illinois*, Urbana, University of Illinois Press, 1945.

Hardesty, Cecil Donald, *Problems and Practices in Housing the Junior-College Program in California*, Los Angeles, University of Southern California Press, 1934.

Henry, Nelson B. (ed.), *The Public Junior College*, 55th yearbook of the National Society for the Study of Education, Chicago, University of Chicago Press, 1956.

Hester, Edna A., *Books for Junior Colleges*, Chicago, American Library Association, 1931.

Higher Education in Maryland, Washington, American Council on Education, 1947.

Hurlburt, Allan S., *Community College Study*, Raleigh, N. C.: State Superintendent of Public Instruction, 1952.

Johnson, B. Lamar, *General Education in Action: A Report of the California Study of General Education in the Junior College*, Washington, American Council on Education, 1952.

Jones, Benjamin Willis, *Costs of Buildings and Equipment of Junior Colleges in the United States*, Washington, American Association of Junior Colleges, 1950.

Joyal, Arnold Edward, *Factors Relating to the Establishment and Maintenance of Junior Colleges, with Special Reference to California*, Berkeley, University of California Press, 1932.

Junior College Directory, Washington, American Association of Junior Colleges, published annually.

Kidd, Kenneth Paul, *Objectives of Mathematical Training in the Public Junior College*, Nashville, George Peabody College for Teachers, 1948.

Koos, Leonard V., *The Junior College*, 2 vols., Minneapolis, University of Minnesota Press, 1924.

Koos, Leonard V., *The Junior College Movement*, Boston, Ginn, 1925.

Koos, Leonard V., and Grayson N. Kefauver, *Guidance in Secondary Schools*. New York, Macmillan Company, 1932.

Love, Malcolm A., *The Iowa Public Junior College: Its Academic, Social, and Vocational Effectiveness*, Iowa City, State University of Iowa Press, 1938.

Martin, A. B., *Per Student Cost of Administration, Instruction, and Operation and Maintenance of Public Junior Colleges*, Washington, American Association of Junior Colleges, 1949.

McDowell, F. M., *The Junior College*, Washington, U.S. Government Printing Office, 1919.

Minnesota Commission on Higher Education, *Higher Education in Minnesota*, Minneapolis, University of Minnesota Press, 1950.

Mohrhardt, Foster E., *A List of Books for Junior College Libraries*, Chicago, American Library Association, 1937.

Morris, John T., *Considerations in Establishing a Junior College*, New York, Columbia University, 1929.

President's Commission on Higher Education, *Higher Education for*

American Democracy, 6 vols. in 1, New York, Harper & Brothers, 1948.

Proctor, William Martin (ed.), *The Junior College: Its Organization and Administration*, Stanford Calif., Stanford University Press, 1927.

Russell, John Dale, *Efficiency in College Management*, Bloomington, Indiana University Press, 1931.

Sammartino, Peter, and Tompkins, Ellsworth, *Community College in Action*, Rutherford, N. J., Fairleigh Dickinson College Press, 1950.

Saylor, Galen, *et al.*, *Junior College Studies: Legislation, Finance, and Development of Public Junior Colleges*, Lincoln, University of Nebraska, 1949.

Seashore, Carl E., *The Junior College Movement*, New York, Holt, 1940.

Sexson, John A., and Harbeson, John W., *The New American College*, New York, Harper & Brothers, 1946.

Simms, Charles Wesley, *The Present Legal Status of the Public Junior College*, Nashville, George Peabody College for Teachers, 1948.

Starrak, James A., and Hughes, Raymond M., *The Community College in the United States*, Ames, Iowa State College Press, 1954.

Starrak, James A., and Hughes, Raymond M., *The New Junior College*, Ames: Iowa State College Press, 1948.

Stoddard, George Dinsmore, *Tertiary Education*, Cambridge, Harvard University Press, 1944.

Stone, Ermine, *The Junior College Library*, Chicago, American Library Association, 1932.

Tead, Ordway, *Equalizing Educational Opportunities beyond the Secondary School*, Cambridge, Harvard University Press, 1947.

Ward, Phebe, *Terminal Education in the Junior College*, New York, Harper & Brothers, 1947.

Wattenbarger, James L., *A State Plan for Public Junior College, with Special Reference to Florida,* Gainesville, University of Florida Press, 1953.

Wellemeyer, J. E., and Walker Earl, *The Public Junior College in Kansas*, Kansas Association of Public Junior Colleges, 1937.

Whitney, Frederick Lamson, *The Junior College in America*, Greeley, Colorado State Teachers College, 1928.

Woellner, Robert C., and M. Aurilla Wood, *Requirements for Certification of Teachers, Counselors, Librarians, Administrators, for Elementary Schools, Secondary Schools, Junior Colleges*, Chicago, University of Chicago Press, published annually.

Appendixes

I. Guiding Principles for Junior College Athletics[1]

THE widespread interest in athletics in America is evidence of the wholesome influence which this phase of the educational program can bring to our communities. As much as any other activity in education, athletics emphasize personal qualities which have come to be regarded as part and parcel of the democratic way of life: a high degree of initiative, moral and physical courage, and respect for the principles of good physical and mental health. Athletics permit a release of activity which is in keeping with normal development of any young person. Competitive sports should be fostered and encouraged as an integral part of the educational process. At the same time, administrators should be mindful of the responsibilities which they have for the proper direction of junior college athletics.

This report is divided into three parts. Part I is a statement of policy for the organizing of junior college athletic conferences. Part II is a statement of policy for the junior college administrator in dealing with his athletic problems. Part III is a code of sportsmanship for spectators.

[1] Officially adopted in 1953 by the American Association of Junior Colleges and the National Junior College Athletic Association.

Part I

Statement of Policy for Organizing Athletic Conferences

1. There should be a well-organized, functioning junior college conference available to each junior college participating in intercollegiate athletics.

2. In case a junior college is so located geographically that it cannot hold membership in a conference of other junior colleges of comparable size and athletic ability, such junior college should attach itself for eligibility purposes to a near-by conference.

3. Each junior college conference should have printed a handbook stating its purpose, membership, officers, rules, and regulations.

4. In case of inter-conference competition, each college represented should conform to the eligibility rules of the conference in which it holds membership.

5. Each junior college conference should have an executive (or other designated) committee with final authority to act for the conference in which it holds membership.

6. Each junior college conference should have a designated commissioner or executive secretary to receive and check eligibility forms, receive protests, investigate infractions of the rules, and otherwise act for the conference and executive committee. The rulings of such commissioner shall be final—subject to appeal to the executive committee or the entire conference.

7. Each member junior college should pay such annual dues to the conference as may be needed to defray necessary expenses of the central office.

Part II

Statement of Policy for Administrator in Dealing with His Athletic Problems

The athletic program of the junior college is a meaningful part of the total offerings of the institution. Like all other aspects of the educational process, the athletic activities are a reflection of the attitude of the head of the institution, the faculty and students who make up the institution, and the community which the institution serves. No amount of legislation can make of the athletic program a symbol of all that is fine in education. Without proper leadership in athletics, the competing teams of any institution can be of great concern not only to the institution represented by the team but to all neighboring institutions and to all communities in which such teams play. High ideals in athletics will be realized if proper educational leadership is evident throughout the total program of athletics in any given junior college.

Any statement of principle such as this is for the guidance of the administrator in periodically measuring the conduct and direction of his own athletic staff. He may expect of this staff the highest type of professional loyalty. No single instructional field touches more intimately the basic emotional drives of young people than does competitive athletics. No single subject matter teaching group is exposed to so many conflicting pressures as is the group teaching knowledges and skills of competing teams in sports. Therefore, as much if not more so, our teachers of athletic teams need to have an unflinching faith in the underlying principles of fine sportsmanship. Such principles are the primary, if not the sole, directional forces in our competitive games.

The teachers of sportsmanship are entitled to the unwavering support of the administrative staff of the college. "Loyalty down and up" must be a reality, not simply a theory, if the athletic staff is to make of competitive sports the wholesome experience which has long been claimed for this phase of the educational program.

Each director, principal, or president of a junior college should examine his own program of athletics carefully. He should measure it periodically against a statement of principles which should bring out the results desired in maintaining a sound and practical program. The following principles are recommended:

1. The program of athletics supported by any institution should be kept within the total facilities, the staff, the student body, and the financial resources of the institution.

   a. An overemphasis in athletics through providing facilities and staff out of line with facilities and staff provided for other phases of the educational program cannot be justified.

   b. The stated objectives of the college should make it clear that athletics must contribute to the mission of the college.

2. The participants in the athletic program should be *bona fide* students of the institutions they represent.

   a. If there be financial scholarships, grants-in-aid, or other inducements offered outstanding performers in athletics, they shall be controlled by the head of the institution or by a committee appointed by him which is responsible for granting such aid to all students. (Normally the number of men in athletics receiving such aid should have about the same ratio to the total recipients of aid as does the ratio of students in athletics to the total number of students enrolled.)

b. The schedule of courses carried by all members of athletic teams should be comparable to the schedule of courses carried by other full-time students of the institution. All students participating in athletics should be making normal progress toward their educational objectives or degrees.

c. The hours of class attendance expected of athletes in an institution should be in keeping with those expected of other members of the student body.

d. Since most junior colleges are community colleges, it is expected that representatives of the athletic teams should be drawn from the normal area or clientele served by the institution.

e. Academic scholarship attainments for participants in athletics should compare favorably with the scholarship attainment expected for participants in other activities of the college.

3. Members of the coaching staff should be *bona fide* members of the instructional staff of the college.

a. Instructors in athletics should have the same faculty status and tenure privileges as are granted to other members of the instructional staff.

b. Coaches' salaries should be in line with the salaries of other members of the instructional staff, keeping in mind duties and responsibilities assigned.

c. The faculty load index of the member of the staff instructing in athletics should compare favorably with those of other members of the college faculty.

d. The same professional qualifications should be evidenced in the members of the instructional staff assigned to athletics as is true of all other members of the college faculty.

4. The control of the athletic program should be in the hands of the administrative head of the college.

a. The athletic program is a part of the total offerings of the college and should be as carefully supervised by the head of the institution as is any other activity under his direction.

b. Policies in athletics should reflect directly the stated objectives of the institution.

c. Athletics should at all times be a matter of faculty concern, as would any other important aspect of the instructional program of the college.

d. Community agencies organized for the promotion of athletics are likely to lead to overemphasis and should be discouraged.

e. The seasons for all sports should be clearly defined, and all institutions should live up to the spirit as well as the letter of the law or regulation. The football season will normally begin the first week of September and end by the first week-end in December. Basketball season will normally begin about the middle of November and end about the middle of March. Baseball and track seasons should close on or before the end of the regular school year.

f. The athletic teams of any institution which engage in intercollegiate sports should compete with institutions that have comparable enrollments and purposes.

g. The athletic program should exist for a large number of students. Therefore, every effort should be made to encourage widespread participation by students in all forms of athletics.

Part III

Suggested Code of Sportsmanship for Spectators

This code is offered as a guide for junior colleges to use in promoting sportsmanship for students and other spectators. The purpose of such a code is to put the principle of the Golden Rule into operation on the athletic field.

1. I will treat members of visiting teams and their fans as guests and will extend to them every consideration which I would expect as a visiting fan.

2. I will applaud excellence in performance exhibited by either team during and after the contest.

3. I will consider the officials as the final authorities to make decisions and will accept their decisions without demonstration.

4. I will support the team and coach regardless of the winning record of the team.

5. I will take pride in promoting good sportsmanship among the spectators, players, and coaches.

II. The Charter of a Two-Year College

THE following charter is typical of those under which private junior colleges are established. It officially defines the authority of the governing board and provides for the recognition of the college as a nonprofit corporation. The charter is written as a bill which was presented to the General Assembly of Connecticut and enacted by that body into law. In essence, the charter constitutes a contract between the trustees and the people of the state.

AN ACT INCORPORATING MITCHELL COLLEGE [1]

Be it enacted by the Senate and House of Representatives in General Assembly convened:

Section 1. Winslow Ames, Russell Beckwith, Alfred M. Bingham, Waldo E. Clarke, Ruth R. Darmstadt, Joseph B. Downes, Alfreda Mitchell Gregor, Adah C. Hickey, Max Johl, Edna D. Knox, Ralph W. Matteson, Francis F. McGuire, Ernest Nibbs, Anita L. Simpson, Carl H. Wies, Clarence A. Wimpfheimer, and such other persons as they may associate with them and their successors are constituted a body politic and corporate forever, by the name of Mitchell College, and by that name to have perpetual succession with power to contract, to sue and be sued, plead and be impleaded, to have and use a common seal, and to hold and use any estate, real or personal, and the same to lease, sell, and convey. Said corporation shall be located in the town of New London or at such other place within the county of New London as may from time to time be fixed by the by-laws of the corporation, provided, whenever it is voted to

[1] Mitchell College, formerly New London Junior College, is located in New London, Connecticut.

change the location of the principal office, notice thereof shall be filed with the secretary of state.

Section 2. The exclusive purposes of said corporation shall be to establish, organize, maintain, and conduct an institution for higher education, and said corporation shall have all lawful powers necessary for the execution of such purposes, including the power to borrow money and to issue promissory notes or other evidences of indebtedness.

Section 3. The care, control, and disposition of the property and funds of said corporation and the general management of its affairs shall be vested in a board of trustees. Said corporation shall have power to adopt by-laws for the government of its affairs, which by-laws shall prescribe the number of trustees, their terms of office, and the manner of their election. By-laws may be adopted and repealed or amended by a two-thirds vote of all trustees at any meeting of the trustees duly held upon proper notice, provided the notice of such meeting shall set forth the terms of the action with regard to the by-laws to be taken at such meeting.

Section 4. Said corporation shall not operate for profit; nor shall any officer, member, or employee thereof receive any pecuniary profit from the operation thereof, except reasonable compensation for services in effecting one or more of such purposes or as a proper beneficiary of its strictly educational purposes.

Section 5. All property and assets received by said corporation shall be held in perpetuity under the terms thereof; but, in the event of the dissolution of said corporation, no officer, member, or employee thereof shall receive any profit from or share in any of the property, assets, or surplus of said corporation; and the trustees thereof shall give, grant, convey, and deliver any and all of said property, assets, or surplus of said corporation to some Connecticut corporation or association having purposes and powers similar to those of said corporation and the property of which is exempt from taxation; or the said trustees may, at their option, liquidate said corporation in accordance with law, provided the property of said corporation or the income therefrom shall be used only for educational purposes in Connecticut.

Section 6. Said corporation shall be organized by the action of the incorporators in adopting by-laws and electing a board of trustees, any of whom may be chosen from among the incorporators. Meetings of the incorporators for the purpose of organization may be called by Waldo E. Clarke, Ralph W. Matteson, and Anita L. Simpson by written notice mailed to all the incorporators, stating the time and place of meeting.

Section 7. Said college shall have power, in accordance with the by-laws and subject to such requirements and standards as may be prescribed by the state board of education, to confer such degrees and grant such diplomas as are customary in institutions of education.

Section 8. This act shall take effect from its passage.

Statement of Purpose: To incorporate Mitchell College and to grant said college power to confer degrees.

Index